L'AFRIQUE DE L'INNOVATION

Politiques nationales et partenariats panafricains

Les Afriques de demain

Collection dirigée par Driss Guerraoui et Alioune Sall

La collection « Les Afriques de demain » vise à promouvoir les publications axées sur l'analyse des transformations que connait l'Afrique pour en dégager les inflexions majeures et les ruptures fondamentales, identifier les facteurs et les acteurs du changement, et mettre en exergue la prospective des stratégies de développement pouvant permettre aux États et aux peuples du continent de lutter contre les nouvelles générations d'insécurité, de risques et de guerres.

Le champ d'action de la collection englobe les questions économiques, sociétales et géostratégiques, les sciences politiques, l'histoire et les problématiques de nature culturelle et civilisationnelle.

Déjà paru

Driss Guerraoui (dir.), *Marocains et Portugais. Regards croisés*, 2023.

Sous la direction de
Driss Guerraoui

L'AFRIQUE DE L'INNOVATION

Politiques nationales et partenariats panafricains

L'Harmattan

5-7, rue de l'Ecole-Polytechnique, 75005 Paris
http://www.editions-harmattan.fr
ISBN : 978-2-336-40537-7
EAN : 9782336405377

LISTE DES AUTEURS

M. Adoum Youssouf Ibrahim, Vice-Président du FAAIE, Président de l'Association Tchadienne d'Intelligence Economique, **Tchad**

M. Boulamine Mostapha, Économiste, expert IES, Président de l'Association Nigérienne d'Intelligence Economique – ANIE, Vice-président du FAAIE, **Niger**

Mme Baulant Camille, Professeure agrégée des universités à l'Université d'Angers-GRANEM, **France**

M. Devendranath Chamroo, Investment & Trade Consultant at CITC, **Ile Maurice**

M. Philippe Clerc, Président de l'Académie de l'Intelligence Economique, Président de l'Association Internationale Francophone d'Intelligence Economique, Senior Chief Economist à CCI France, Vice-Président du GFII, **France**

M. Mora Dandagui Sero, Expert en communication, Administrateur du Portail Coton-afrique.com, **Bénin**

Mme Mouna El Haddani, Enseignante-chercheuse, GRANEM-Université d'Angers, **France**

M. El Moustapha Sidi Mohamed, Vice-Président FAAIE, Président de l'Association Mauritanienne de l'Intelligence Economique, Mauritanie, **Mauritanie**

M. Omar Ezziyati, Directeur Veille Stratégique, Innovation et Influence, Bank of Africa, **Maroc**

M. Soufyane Frimousse, Maître de conférences, docteur et habilité à diriger des recherches en sciences de gestion, université de Corse, université de Montpellier 3, **France**

M. Driss Guerraoui, Président de l'Université Ouverte de Dakhla, et du Forum des Associations Africaines d'Intelligence Economique, **Maroc**

Mme Siham Harroussi, Vice-Présidente du FAAIE, Directrice Prospective, Relations Extérieures et Gouvernance, **France**

M. James Kizito-Mayanja, Market Intelligence and Information Manager, **Uganda**

Mme Shitaye Haile Lemma, Vice-Présidente du FAAIE, Experte en développement du commerce international. Ancienne fonctionnaire des Nations Unies, **Éthiopie**

Mme Khady Evelyne Denise Ndiaye, Directeur du Secteur Privé, UEMOA, Sénégal

M. Mohamed Ourdedine, Secrétaire Général de la Chambre de Commerce International ICC, **Maroc**

M. Mounir Rochdi, SG du FAAIE, Président de ThinkTankers. Expert international en Market et Competitive Intelligence, **Maroc**

Mme Caroline Sack Kendem, présidente Women Association For Technological Innovation, **Cameroun**

M. Imad Saleh, Professeur des universités en Sciences de l'information et de la communication, Paris 8, **Palestine**

Mme Marie Saade, Professeure des universités en Sciences de l'information et de la communication, Paris 8, **Palestine**

M. Paul Santilli, Strategic Competitive Intelligence for Professionals (SCIP), Organisation CEO and Board Chairman USA Hewlett Packard Enterprise (HPE) Head of Industry Intelligence & Strategy - Worldwide OEM Division, **Etats Unis**

Mme Nisha Sewdass, Professor, College of Economics and Management Sciences, **Afrique du Sud**

M. Mohamed Smani, Directeur de R-D, **Maroc**

M. Mostapha Taouji, spécialiste en entrepreneuriat et start-up, **Maroc**

M. Emilio Jovendo ZECA, Researcher, Center For Strategic and International Studies – CEEI-ISRI, **Mozambique**

AVANT-PROPOS

Le présent ouvrage s'appuie sur les actes de la 3ème Rencontre du Forum des Associations Africaines d'intelligence économique, organisée à Dakhla **sous le Haut Patronage de Sa Majesté le Roi Mohammed VI**, dans le cadre de l'Université Ouverte de Dakhla, par l'Association d'Études et de Recherches pour le Développement, les 5, 6 et 7 décembre 2022, sur le thème : « L'Afrique de l'innovation, politiques nationales et partenariats panafricains ».

Cette Rencontre, à laquelle ont contribué des Associations Africaines d'intelligence économique, des acteurs institutionnels et des experts africains et non africains travaillant sur l'Afrique a vu la remise du « Prix de l'Intelligence Economique en Afrique » dans sa deuxième édition et la signature de plusieurs conventions de partenariat entre le FAAIE et les nouvelles Associations Nationales d'intelligence économique institutionnalisant ainsi leur qualité de membres du dit Forum.

Elle a bénéficié de l'appui des Ministères des Affaires Etrangères, de la Coopération Africaine et des Marocains Résidents à l'Étranger, de l'Intérieur et de l'Industrie et du Commerce, de l'Agence Marocaine de Coopération Internationale, de la Caisse de Dépôt et de Gestion, de Bank of Africa, de la Wilaya et la Région de Dakhla-Oued Eddahab, du Conseil de la ville de Dakhla et du Conseil provincial de Oued Eddahab.

Qu'ils trouvent tous dans cette publication l'expression de nos sincères remerciements et de notre profonde gratitude.

Driss Guerraoui

INTRODUCTION GÉNÉRALE

Driss Guerraoui

La question de l'innovation est cruciale pour le présent et l'avenir de l'Afrique. Elle est au cœur de son développement actuel et futur. Certes, nous constatons une certaine dynamique produisant de réelles succes-stories dans de nombreux pays du continent, portées soit par des start-up soit par des champions nationaux, mais force est de constater que le continent est le dernier dans les classements internationaux pour tous les indicateurs liés directement ou indirectement à l'innovation.

En effet, en 2019 l'Afrique qui représente 17 % de la population mondiale ne dispose que 2,4 % des scientifiques et ne produit que 2,6 % des articles dans le monde[1]. Par ailleurs, elle compte seulement 79 scientifiques pour un million d'habitants. Selon l'UNESCO, le continent représente 1,3 % seulement des dépenses mondiales de R&D et 2,6 % des publications scientifiques recensées au plan mondial sont issues de la recherche africaine[2].

Au-delà des success-stories, somme toute relatives, réalisées par-ci par-là dans certains pays Africains, les problématiques et les expériences examinées dans le présent l'ouvrage par les membres du réseau du Forum des Associations Africaines d'Intelligence Economique, révèlent que ce dont les pays du continent ont besoin, ce sont de véritables écosystèmes nationaux et régionaux d'intégrés d'innovation.

Or, cette perspective nécessite à ce que ces écosystèmes soient armés, de façon concomitante, par quatre leviers essentiels.

---

1. Commission de l'Union Africaine, 2015, Agenda 2063 version populaire, Addis-Abeba, Éthiopie

2. UNESCO cité par l'hebdomadaire « Jeune Afrique », in « Afrique recherche chercheurs désespérément », 28 /10 /2015

Le premier de ces leviers est le levier économique. Car l'innovation est avant tout et surtout tirée le plus souvent par l'existence de systèmes productifs forts qui tout en investissant dans la recherche scientifique et technologique font des résultats de l'innovation un facteur de la compétitivité et de l'excellence de leurs entreprises et de leurs territoires, qui constituent des facteurs clés qui fondent leur attractivité. De ce fait, l'observation empirique et l'évaluation comparative des classements mondiaux en cette matière montrent qu'il y a, en effet, une relation de cause à effet entre le taux de croissance, la création de valeurs et le volume de ressources financières consacrée par les États, les entreprises et les territoires à la recherche et à l'innovation.

Le deuxième levier est le capital humain au sens où l'innovation est prédéterminée en amont par la capacité des Nations à mettre en place des politiques publiques appropriées d'éducation et de formation en mesure de permettre à l'école, à travers tous ses étages du fondamental au supérieur, de contribuer à produire des élites scientifiques et à former des compétences, dont le rôle est déterminant dans la création d'écosystèmes nationaux et territoriaux d'innovation. Dès lors, ce levier est lié aux nouvelles missions de l'école qui doivent correspondre aux mutations que connaissent les systèmes productifs nationaux et régionaux dans la Nouvelle Économie Mondiale. À ce niveau, l'analyse de ces mutations révèle que les nouvelles missions de l'école devraient s'inscrire dans quatre directions essentielles :

- Apprendre à apprendre, c'est-à-dire produire un savoir. Cette mission consiste à éduquer les enfants et les jeunes en leur offrant les outils qui leur permettent de comprendre l'environnement dans lequel ils évoluent ;
- Apprendre à entreprendre en permettant aux apprenants de s'approprier un savoir-faire qui débouche sur une professionnalisation les prépare à exercer un métier;
- Apprendre à être, c'est-à-dire former à la citoyenneté en essaimant dans la société à travers l'école le socle commun de valeurs partagées mentionnées précédemment ;
- Et enfin, apprendre à créer et à innover en privilégiant les programmes et la pédagogie qui favorisent la production du génie, de l'intelligence et de la veille stratégique.

Ce sont ses missions interdépendantes qui aident à charpenter et à bâtir des écosystèmes nationaux d'innovation solides et qui permettent aux économies et aux sociétés de disposer d'un capital humain qui les aide à mieux gérer la complexité économique et financière, la rareté des ressources, les fragilités des systèmes productifs, les vulnérabilités des systèmes écologiques et corrélativement à faire face aux nouvelles générations d'insécurité et de guerres.

Le troisième levier réside dans le capital culturel au sens où l'innovation est aussi portée par un socle commun de valeurs qui guident l'action de toutes les composantes de la collectivité nationale. En économie, et en relation avec la problématique de l'innovation, ces valeurs sont l'importance du travail, de l'effort, de la prise du risque et de l'initiative. L'intérêt de ces valeurs est qu'elles impulsent dans toute la société des pratiques quotidiennes qui homogénéisent les comportements des individus, des groupes et des institutions autour d'une rationalité systémique qui libère les énergies, favorise la créativité et donne un sens à l'action au sein de toutes les organisations qui structurent la vie en société, de la famille à l'entreprise.

Le quatrième levier, enfin, est celui de la gouvernance. En effet, la dynamique de l'innovation est fonction, également, de la qualité des institutions qui favorisent, encouragent, incitent et financent la recherche scientifique et technologique. Elle est de ce fait tributaire de la mise en place d'instances constitutionnelles de gouvernance et de régulation économique responsables et indépendantes, qui veillent à garantir le respect de la liberté d'entreprendre, la concurrence loyale et juste, l'égalité des chances entre les entreprises devant l'acte économique, la lutte contre toutes les formes de rentes, les monopoles, les passe-droits et la corruption. C'est cette gouvernance qui contribue à créer un climat des affaires favorable à la prise de risque en matière d'innovation, qui renforce la confiance des acteurs économiques, des scientifiques, des chercheurs et des inventeurs dans leur écosystème national d'innovation et qui offre par conséquent une visibilité économique et une lisibilité politique aux investisseurs potentiels nationaux et étrangers et les encouragent à mettre en place des programmes volontaristes de moyen et long termes consacrés à la recherche scientifique, technologique et à l'innovation.

Autant dire que la problématique de l'innovation est systémique, complexe et multidimensionnelle.

Certes, l'Afrique ne part pas de rien à ce niveau. En effet, conscients qu'aucun pays africain ne pourra à lui seul construire une politique nationale efficace à proprement parler en matière de souveraineté scientifique, technologique et d'innovation, les États du continent ont inauguré une dynamique d'alliance stratégique à l'échelle de l'Union Africaine. C'est ainsi que le Nouveau Partenariat pour le Développement de l'Afrique, ratifié en 2002, a fait de la science, la technologie et l'innovation un instrument essentiel de la réalisation du programme d'action de l'Union à l'horizon 2063. Dans cette perspective, un « Plan d'action consolidé pour la science, la technologie et l'innovation » a été adopté. Ce plan a été remplacé en 2014 par « La Stratégie pour la Science, la Technologie et l'Innovation pour l'Afrique 2024 ».Ce nouveau plan a proposé « un cadre de suivi, des mécanismes de financement et un fonds panafricain consacré à l'innovation scientifique et technologique. Son objectif est de réaliser les initiatives continentales décrites dans deux documents stratégiques, la position commune africaine sur le programme de développement post-2015 et l'Agenda 2063, qui identifient tous deux les sciences, la technologie et l'innovation comme sous-tendant la réalisation des aspirations africaines ».

Au-delà de ces déclarations d'intention, inscrites dans des documents officiels de la Commission de l'Union Africaine, beaucoup reste à faire sur le plan opérationnel. Aussi, l'enjeu panafricain majeur est de réfléchir collectivement comment passer de la volonté réelle affirmée et de la vision claire arrêtée à l'action. À ce niveau comme d'autres, l'Afrique fait face à deux défis importants :

- L'effectivité des politiques de promotion de la science, la technologie et l'innovation. Car tout se passe comme si les politiques ne sont imbibés de la maxime : « dire ce que l'on fait et faire ce que l'on dit » ;
- Et le rapport au temps, au sens d'identifier ce qui est nécessaire à faire à très court terme, ce qui est possible à moyen terme et ce qui est souhaitable à long terme, et ce en vue de réunir les conditions objectives de réalisation de raccourcis technologiques.

Dès lors, parce que le Monde ne va pas attendre l'Afrique et parce que le Monde Nouveau qui se profile à l'horizon connaît une impressionne dynamique de l'innovation, que les avancées rapides de l'intelligence artificielle sont en train de révolutionner, les États, les entreprises et les territoires de l'Union Africaine doivent susciter une réelle mobilisation générale de leurs savants, leurs chercheurs et leurs inventeurs en vue de mettre leur génie, leur intelligence et leur veille stratégique au service de l' Afrique de l'innovation.

Le présent ouvrage pose les termes de cette problématique (**Driss Guerraoui**), présente des stratégies nationales d'innovation menées par quelques pays du continent (**Nisha Sewdass, Emilio Jovendo Zeca, Shitaye Lemma, Mohammed Smani, Driss Guerraoui et Caroline Sack Kendem**), examine l'innovation en Afrique dans ses relations avec le développement économique **(El Moustapha Sidi Mohamed, Adoum Youssouf Ibrahim, Mounir Rochdi, Paul Santilli, Philippe Clerc**), met en perspective les approches qui débouchent sur une innovation durable et inclusive en Afrique par la formation, la création de start-up et l'action sociale et environnementale (**Khady Evelyne Denise Ndiaye, Soufyane Frimousse, Marie Saade, Imad Saleh, El Haddani Mouna , Baulant Camille, Mohamed Ourdedine, Omar Ezziyati, Mora Dandagui Sero, Mostafa Taouji, Devendranath Chamroo, et Boulamine Moustapha**), pour conclure sur les enseignements à tirer en termes de réalités à prendre en ligne de compte, de défis futurs à relever, de priorités à identifier, de partenariats panafricains à promouvoir et de pistes de transformations pouvant enclencher une dynamique de l'innovation portée par une coopération panafricaine audacieuse, volontariste et ouverte sur l'avenir **(Driss Guerraoui**).

I
STRATÉGIES NATIONALES D'INNOVATION EN AFRIQUE

AN OVERVIEW OF THE AFTERMATH OF COVID-19 ON AFRICAN ECONOMIES AND THEIR COMPETITIVENESS

Nisha Sewdass

Introduction and background

The sudden onset of the coronavirus had left countries around the world scrambling to cope in an attempt to control the pandemic from spreading. The global economy was not spared and the impact of the widespread of the virus had led to a massive global economic crisis, once again impacting companies. Some of these companies are still reeling from the last global economic meltdown of 2008. As countries went into lockdown all over the world, it is meant that the complete shutdown of companies and this had affected supply chains and production and operation capacities of all companies.

Companies had to look for new business models and innovative ways very speedily of doing business and this meant the adoption of technology as most companies relied on working from home in an attempt to continue operations and save their companies from complete collapse. In some way it has driven many companies that were limping their way to the adoption of the fourth industrial revolution into this and even the fifth Industrial Revolution. Companies who were already using technological innovations to conduct their businesses were in a better position to cope with the abnormal situation posed by COVID-19. These companies found it easy to continue operations and even in some cases to differentiate their operations because of the unique skills and capacities that their human resources possess e.g. Automobile companies were producing ventilators that were in shortage and clothing manufacturers were making masks for various sectors.

The pandemic has forced businesses to reinvent themselves and has also revealed gaps that exist in several areas. In addition, business analysts and economists have predicted that the current state of "business unusual" that most countries are operating under at this time is likely to make companies relook at their operations and practices post COVID-19. The global economic crisis has already caused several companies in different sectors such as the airline industry, tourism, finance and banking, manufacturing and retail and restaurants as well as several small business/entrepreneurs to go out of business and many more companies are expected to follow after the pandemic despite the measures taken by governments globally to assist these companies. This situation will leave gaps in several areas providing an opportunity for new and existing companies. However, to identify these opportunities, companies will need new business models and tools such as CI/EI and innovation to assist them to create a "new normal" in business.

Africa as a continent has been the last to be impacted by COVID-19 and has had a lead time to prepare and learn from the experience of those countries that were severely impacted by the sudden onset of the virus such as China and the UK. However, with its already challenging business environments and lack of resources, Africa has also been impacted by this pandemic.

Economies, enterprises, and workers across Africa were impacted by the COVID-19 pandemic which brought about unprecedented changes to the workplace. Some of these changes include disruptions to supply chains because of lockdowns that forced enterprises to close, the redesign and changes to workflows and operations, alterations in where and how people worked, changes in traditional norms and practices. However, despite these many changes, one finds that unexpected improvements in productivity or working conditions have emerged in some enterprises.

The impacts of the COVID-19 pandemic on "lives and livelihoods in Africa continued in 2021 and it has been estimated that about 30 million Africans were pushed into extreme poverty in 2021 and that about 22 million jobs were lost in African countries the same year. These outcomes are likely to continue in 2022 and 2023". (African Economic Outlook, 2022:2). In addition, Africa's low vaccination rates have delayed a faster economic recovery. It is estimated that only 15.3 percent of people in Africa were fully vaccinated by end-March 2022 against a target of at least 60 percent in most other global regions. This has been attributed to the supply- and demand-side impediments. Improving vaccination rates by tackling vaccine hesitancy and improving vaccine supply is key to reducing infections and mortality and to quickening the economic recovery (Economic Outlook,2022). It therefore becomes critical for African countries to speed up their current vaccination rollout to meet the global target of at least 60 percent .

Top ten workplace trends driven by the pandemic

The International Labour Organization (ILO) and the ILO Regional Office for Africa, in partnership with employer and business membership organisations (EBMOs) from across Africa conducted a survey covering fifteen countries in Africa from June to November 2021 covering 1,017 formal sector enterprises, most of whom are members of EBMOs. Collectively, they employ some 750,000 workers. The survey was complemented by 126 key informant interviews with top management and human resources professionals from the private sector. An additional five in-depth case studies with multinational enterprises that have operations in at least five African countries were conducted. While these various sources of information do not cover all parts of every economy in Africa, they provide deep and broad insights about how workplaces at urban, formal enterprises in Africa are changing in the aftermath of COVID-19 (ILO, 2022: v). The report of this ILO study identified changes in organisations and how enterprises from across Africa view and respond to them. An overview of the top ten workplace trends driven by the pandemic are summarised below and having knowledge of this will guide decision makers on the economic impacts and competitiveness of African enterprises.

Remote work has grown dramatically during the pandemic

From the responses of the nearly 750,000 people working for the more than 1,000 enterprises surveyed, nearly 36 percent worked remotely during the pandemic. It was also found that the higher-paying service sector enterprises/ formal sector had the greatest share of remote workers while remote work is more limited in lower-wage sectors such as hotels and restaurants, retail and wholesale trade, and manufacturing/ informal sector.

Figure 1 : Share of workers who work from home, by industry and average monthly earnings

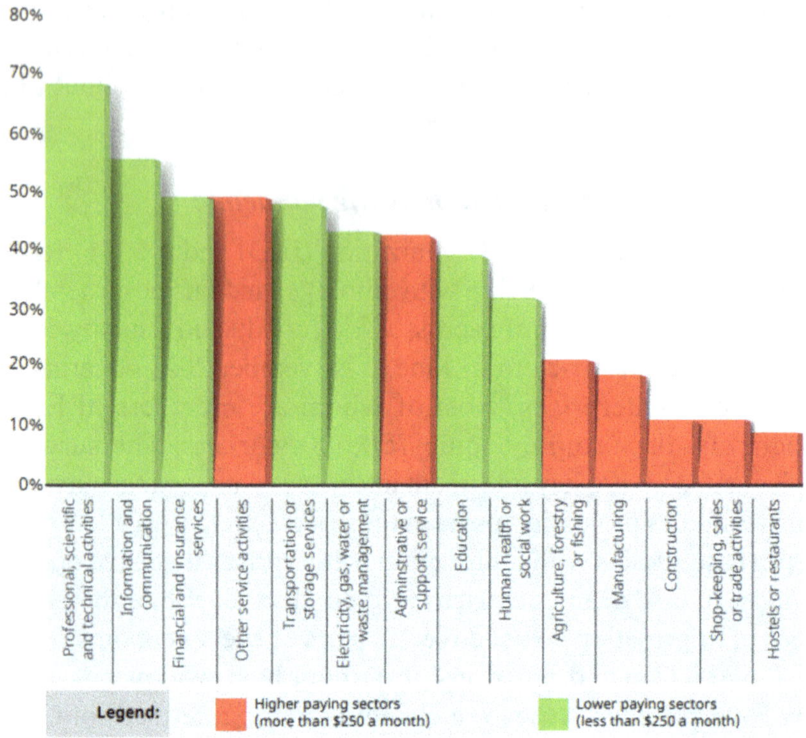

Source: ILO ACTEMP Survey of Enterprises in Africa, 2021:12

Most future workplaces in Africa will be in-person or hybrid, not fully remote

While remote work became an important mode of working during the pandemic, most enterprises in Africa still have an in-person component of their operations and plan for their post-COVID workplaces to be in-person or hybrid. Results indicate that 85 per cent of enterprises had some remote work during the pandemic, however, less than 6 percent were completely remote. After the pandemic only 4 percent said they planned to have a fully remote workplace.

Figure 2 : Future business model, by sector

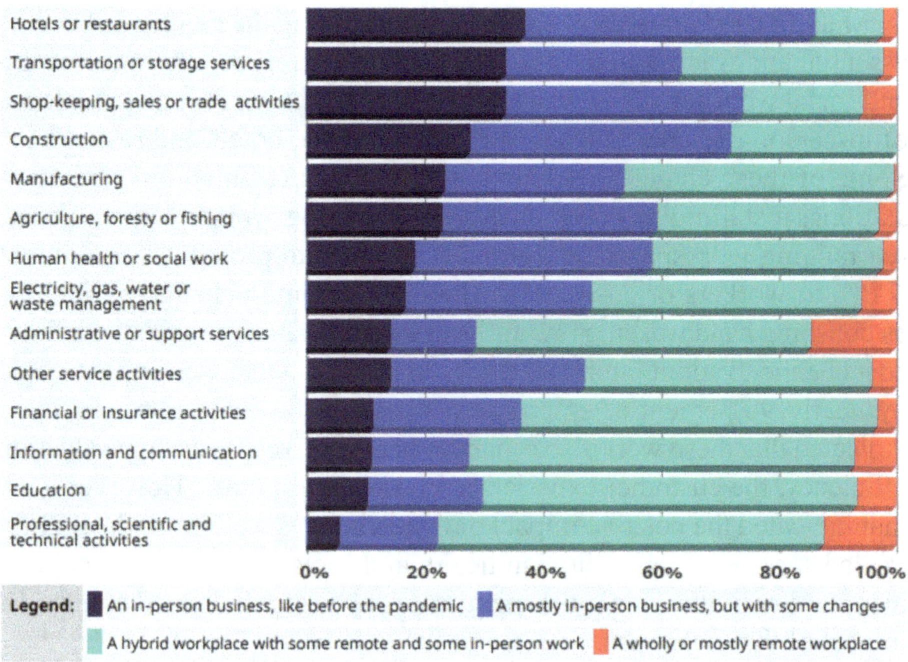

Source : ILO ACTEMP Survey of Enterprises in Africa, 2021

Remote work is changing how some enterprises hire employees

The COVID-19 pandemic has led to significant changes in the way that enterprises consider their future workforce. Some flexibility is noticed as they seek workers who are the best fit for their business. Three in ten enterprises in Africa have already changed their hiring criteria to include new groups of workers they had not previously considered, such as fully remote workers not living near the workplace. This trend was strong in administrative services (45%) and communication services (40%) and only 4 percent of African enterprises have planned to have a fully remote workplace. Workers can be located nationally or internationally and this leads to more competition for skills, talent and salaries as companies attempt to retain their staff and make negotiations difficult by offering better pay and benefits.

Health and safety measures were widely adopted and beneficial for workplaces

Making changes to physical workplaces during the pandemic became essential and was applied by several enterprises, especially in the health and social work sectors as well as those enterprises with a high prevalence of in-person presence, such as manufacturing or hotels and restaurants. Some of these changes included steps such as establishing sanitation stations, installing protective barriers, checking worker temperatures, rearranging workspaces, and providing personal protective equipment (PPE) to workers or customers. The most common change by far was establishing hand washing or sanitising stations. This was a relatively low-cost change to adopt but it had a very high impact and was implemented by nearly 90 percent of enterprises. Many of the enterprises surveyed indicated that these workplace changes had positive effects on production efficiency, the customer experience, and worker morale. However most that indicated the positive impact of these changes were from the higher-skilled services, such as human health and social work or financial and insurance activities while the manufacturing sector indicated a negative impact of these changes.

Flexibility & adaptability have helped enterprises navigate the pandemic

The results of the survey found that flexibility was one of the most used words that enterprises used to described changes to their working environments. Two thirds of enterprises reported that workforce flexibility had become more important during the pandemic. Not only did work environments become more flexible, but also the workers. The situation also necessitated the contracting out of some areas of work to external workers. Flexibility from workers allowed for several enterprises to increase shift work and or reduced working time to prevent redundancies. This was clearly noted amongst manufacturers, with over 40 percent increase their use of reduced hours contracts. Overall, about one in five enterprises indicated that they increased the use of contractors during the pandemic. The two most common reasons for this were the need for a more flexible workforce and the need for skills that were not part of the core business.

Figure 3 : Most important reason that an enterprise expanded its use of external workers

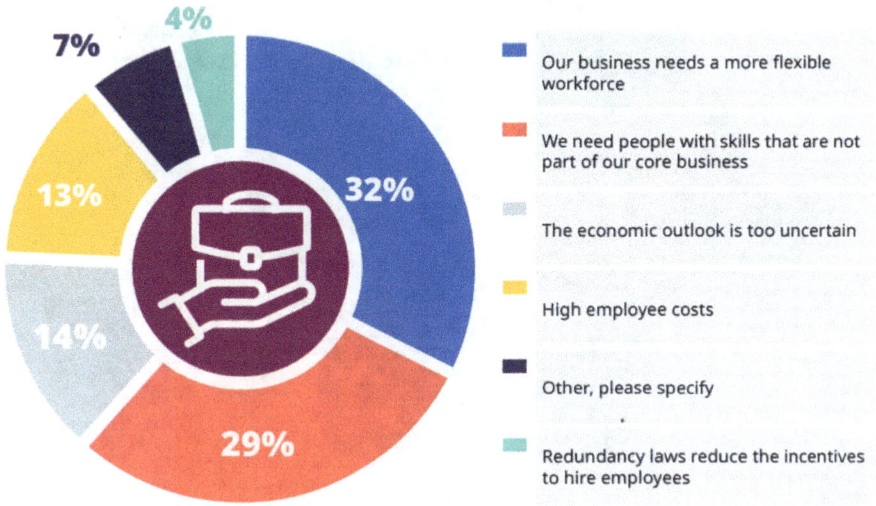

Source: ILO ACTEMP Survey of Enterprises in Africa, 2021 : 28

Digital, communication, creativity and innovation and teamwork and collaboration skills are now top priorities for enterprises

Four different types of skills were reported as being vital to the future success or the enterprises : digital skills, communications skills, creativity and innovation-related skills and teamwork and collaborative skills. More than 40 percent of enterprises cited each of these skills as a top three need in the future and workers with a range of complementary skills were highly favoured. Training, sharing knowledge and collaborating also changed in enterprises with technology playing an important role e.g. digital training courses were reported to have been adopted by over 50 per cent of enterprises that participated in the survey. However, most enterprises experienced continuous challenges with the cost of reskilling and upskilling staff, with two thirds noting that these costs should be borne either by enterprises and donors or public funding from the regular government budget.

Figure 4 : Top four skills set that are most important for the future success of your business

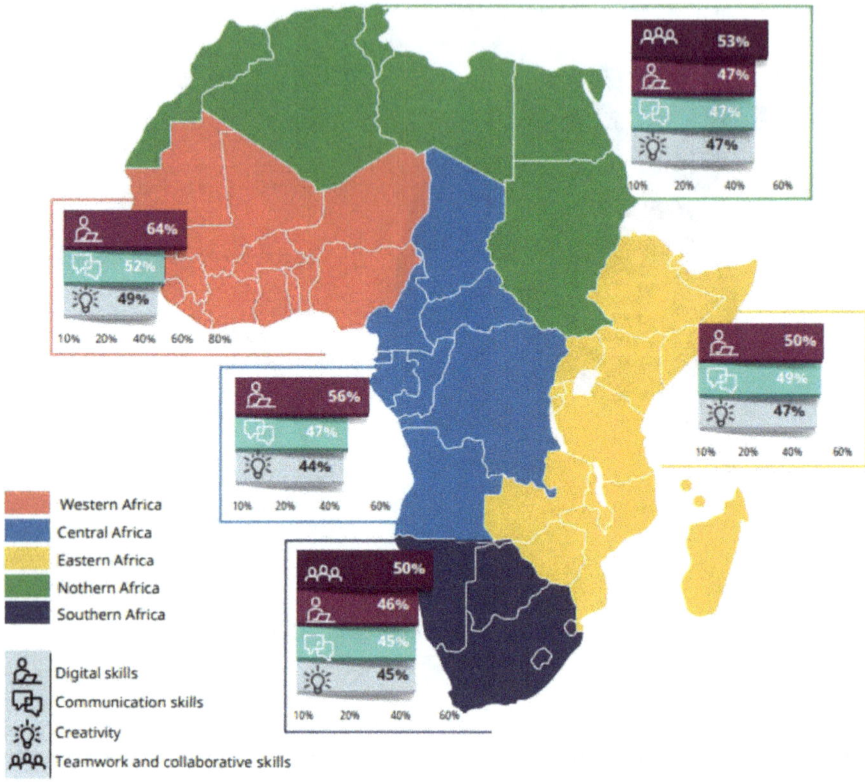

Source: ILO ACTEMP Survey of Enterprises in Africa, 2021:30

Productivity has improved or remained constant at most enterprises

Respondents from 46 percent of Africa's formal enterprises reported that COVID-related changes resulted in productivity gains, while another 39 percent said that production efficiency had remained the same. Most of the productivity gains were noted amongst service enterprises, while this was not the case amongst manufacturers, who may have found that it had worsened their efficiency. Most productivity gains were because of applying digital processes to replace analogue ones. Several enterprises also reorganised their physical workspaces which sometimes led to more productive ways to organise workspaces. Approximately four out of five enterprises reported that they changed how they measure productivity, with a similar share saying they had increased their focus on outputs as the key measure of productivity and less focus was paid on time spent on activities. Only 1 in 8 enterprises indicated that they focussed on measuring hours spent on an activity.

The pandemic has deepened gender inequality at work

Women in Africa experienced a disproportionate burden of home responsibilities and care work that they are generally associated with. This burden increased due to school closures which, in an extreme case like Uganda, stretched nearly two years. Women are generally responsible for caring for sick family members and well as others. It has been reported that across all of Africa, 70 percent of health workers, a vital but high-risk front-line occupation, are female. Hence one can easily see how the effects of the pandemic could contribute to women's jobs and livelihoods being more vulnerable. These realities mean that working from home often presents unique challenges for women. The pandemic has also contributed to an increase in other employment-related risks that have disproportionately affected women, such as the increase in gender-based domestic violence while working from home. This was reported as a global problem that was exacerbated by the pandemic and lockdowns.

Social dialogue has been reinvigorated during the pandemic

The COVID-19 pandemic brought about unprecedented change at rapid speed and scale. Although these changes were essential at the time and did pose several challenges, many enterprises in this survey reported that they contributed to an improvement in the relationship between enterprises and their workers. The majority of enterprises surveyed indicated that they had workplace dialogue during the pandemic, with the most common topic being workplace health and safety, discussed at 86 percent of workplaces. Trade unions and EBMOs taking on important roles representing their members and contributing to numerous bipartite and tripartite agreements across the continent. 37 percent of enterprises said that relations with workers had improved while only 14 percent said they had worsened. These were mainly enterprises with a significant in person component to their work, such as manufacturers or hotels and restaurants.

Labour laws have struggled to keep pace with rapid workplace changes

The COVID-19 pandemic has impacted several aspects of work and in some instances has led to new trends emerge as soon as possible as these changes had to be adopted due to the urgent necessity to keep the business operational. One example of these changes includes the mass shift to remote work which is also defining the future of work in some enterprises and becoming the new normal. However, the legal and regulatory frameworks in many countries have not kept up with the changing ways people work. Respondents of the survey outlined numerous issues that enterprises need to be addressed, for example workplace health and safety and governance of remote work. It was suggested that labour law modernisation is needed, to help reflect the fundamental changes to work that have come about during the pandemic. Several business leaders noted their opinion that the labour market regulations were behind the curve.

Conclusion

The pandemic has sent shock waves across the world of work, upsetting many long-standing norms and practices. Enterprises are questioning fundamental assumptions about their operations, such as whether they still need physical premises and how they measure what workers do. Workers are also rethinking key assumptions about work. This will drive long-term changes in the types of work being done, how work is performed, and what skills are required to do that work. This in turn will have severe impacts on the economic and competitive abilities of enterprises in Africa. The research done by ILO ACTEMP will be able to assist African enterprisers and their networks and policy-makers to address these complex and interrelated issues and perhaps consider innovative and new ways of doing business to enhance their economic competitiveness.

References

African Economic Outlook 2022. Supporting Climate Resilience and a Just Energy Transition in Africa. African Development Bank. Available online at: https://www.afdb.org/en/knowledge/publications/african-economic-outlook#:~:text=The%20theme%20of%20the%202022,of%20the%20 2022%20Annual%20Meetings. [Accessed 20 November 2022]

International Labour Office, Geneva "The Next Normal. The changing Workplace in Africa. Ten Trends from the COVID-19 Pandemic that are Shaping Workplaces in Africa" 2022. Available online at: https://www. ilo. org/wcmsp5/groups/public/---ed_dialogue/---act_emp/documents/ publication/ wcms_844770.pdf [Accessed 28 November 2022]

International Labour Organization. ILO ACTEMP Survey of Enterprises in Africa, 2021 The Next Normal: The Changing Workplace in Africa, March 2022.

ILO The Bureau for Employers' Activities (ACT/EMP)

International Labour Organization, "Employer and Business Member Organisation Guide to COVID-19," April 2022. Available online at: https:// www.ilo.org/wcmsp5/groups/public/---ed_dialogue/---act_emp/documents/ publication/wcms_844770.pdf. [Accessed 20 November 2022]

THE EXPERIENCE ON PUBLIC POLICY TO PROMOTE INNOVATION IN MOZAMBIQUE

Emilio J. Zeca

Introduction

Mozambique is a Lusophone country located in Southern Africa bordered by the Indian Ocean to the east, Tanzania to the north, Malawi and Zambia to the northwest, Zimbabwe to the west, and Eswatini and South Africa to the southwest. The sovereign State is separated from the Comoros, Mayotte, France and Madagascar by the Mozambique Channel to the east. The capital and largest city of Mozambique is Maputo. Mozambique became independent from Portugal on 25 June 1975. Between 1976 and 1996, Mozambique experienced a civil war between the Mozambican Government, led by FRELIMO – Mozambique Liberation Front and RENAMO – Mozambican National Resistance.

The civil war ended on 4 October 1992, with the Rome General Peace Accords, first brokered by the Christian Council of Mozambique – Council of Protestant Churches and then taken over by Community of Santo Egidio. Peace returned to Mozambique, under the supervision of the Peacekeeping Force of the United Nations – ONUMOZ. The new Constitution was enacted in 1990 and provided for a multi-party political system, market-based economy, and free elections. In 1994, held the first multi-party elections in Mozambique and after that, the country embarked on a liberal democratic regime (Vines, 1997 : 66-71, Cabrita, 2000 : 128-130 and Schwartz, 2010 : 34-38).

Mozambique's foreign policy has been guided by pragmatism, guided by the principle "make friends, avoid enemies and diversify partnerships". In this perspective, Mozambique is a member of the United Nations, the African Union, the Southern African Development Community

– SADC, the Community of Portuguese Language Countries – CPLP, the Non-Aligned Movement, the Organization of Islamic Cooperation, the Commonwealth and Francophonie.

Mozambique is endowed with rich and extensive natural resources such as mineral coal, natural gas, heavy sands, graphite, among others, notwithstanding the country's economy is based chiefly on agriculture, fishery and a growing industry of food and beverages, chemical manufacturing, aluminium and oil. The tourism sector is expanding. South Africa remains Mozambique's main trading partner, preserving a close relationship with Portugal with a perspective on other European markets. Since 2001, Mozambique's GDP growth has been thriving with an economic growth of around 7.0%. This situation of economic growth reduced with the emergence of terrorism and Islamic insurgency, in northern Mozambique, Cab Delgado, since October 2017, the situation of the COVID 19 Pandemic and the confirmation of Islamic State presence, since 2020, that support the Ansar al-Sunna[3],an Islamic militant insurgency group who swore allegiance to the Islamic State's Central Africa Province, abbreviated IS-CAP.

Nevertheless, the previous processes and experience observed in the 1970s and 1980s, the proper and systematised management of science, technology and innovation in Mozambique dates of the end of the 1990s and early 2000s. The Ministry of Science and Technology was created by Decree nº 13/2005, 4 February. The first Mozambican Science, Technology and Innovation Policy dates from 2003. From 2008 the Ministry of Science and Technology assumed the role of formulating Science and Technology Policy. In 2015, the Presidential Decree nº 1/2015, 16 January, created the Ministry of Science and Technology, Higher Education and Vocational Training. In recent years, the Government of Mozambique has undertaken a process of restructuring the national science, technology and innovation system, including its governance, institutions, funding mechanisms and deepening achievements in off-grid sustainable energy.

---

3. Also called by Al-Shabaab of Mozambique is an Islamist militant, insurgency, Sunni, Salafist and Jihadist group active in Cabo Delgado Province, Mozambique, since October 2017. Since 2019, Islamic State has formally claimed al-Shabaab as an affiliate under ISIS – Central Africa Province.

Science, Technology and Innovation in Mozambique

The issues related to science, technology and innovation entered Mozambique's government agenda in the late 1990s and early 2000s.

In the first decade of the 2000s, significant steps were taken towards the creation of a legal and institutional framework for science, technology and innovation in Mozambique. The creation of the Ministry of Science and Technology, by Decree nº 13/2005, 4 February, and the approval of the Science and Technologies Policy and the Strategy for its Implementation, by Resolution nº 23/2003, of July 22, consolidated all the strategic process for the development of science, technology and innovation in Mozambique.

The development process of science, technology and innovation, in Mozambique, was based on four principal pillars, namely, research focused on the production of knowledge; education aimed at building the foundations of scientific knowledge and critical learning of culture for technological innovation; innovation based on creative capacity, use and adaptation of local technologies; and creating a culture of innovation. The development of human resources, education, agriculture, health, energy, fisheries, marine sciences, construction, water and mineral resources were defined as strategic areas. In addition to these areas, the social sciences, human sciences and culture, gender equity, the fight against HIV/AIDS, environmental sustainability and ethnobotany were defined as cross-cutting areas.

Since the early 2000s, it emerged an interesting legal and institutional framework about science, technology and innovation sector in Mozambique, composed by more than 60 law, regulation and new institutions. Also, the Mozambican government signed more than 30 international agreements[4] on science and technology and innovation.

---

4. Memorandum of Understanding between the Government of the Republic of Mozambique and the Government of the Republic of Malawi on scientific, technological and innovation cooperation (2013); South Indian Ocean Fisheries Agreement – SIOFA (2012); Memorandum of Understanding between Mozambique and Botswana 2011; Cooperation Agreement between Mozambique and Cape Verde (2010); Cooperation agreement between Mozambique and Italy-P. Autonomous of Trento (2010); Cooperation agreement between Mozambique and Finland (2010); Memorandum of Understanding between Mozambique and Zimbabwe (2010); Memorandum of Understanding between Mozambique and Namibia (2009); Cooperation agreements between Mozambique and Japan (2009); Memorandum of Understanding between Mozambique and Zambia (2008); SADC Protocol on Science and Technology (2008); Memorandum of Understanding between MCT and the National Agency of Information Society of the Republic of South Korea (2008);

In 2021, in partnership with the United Nations Educational, Scientific and Cultural Organization – UNESCO and with the financial support of the Islamic Development Bank – IsDB, the Mozambican Ministry of Science, Technology and Higher Education conducted the "Mapping Research and Innovation in the Republic of Mozambique". This report presents the Science, Technology and Innovation – STI Country Profile of the Republic of Mozambique.

The concerns and issues raised in the interviews and workshop in this mapping coalesce as :

Funding at all levels; ensuring the appropriate science, technology and innovation policy mix; concern with coordination, information sharing and effective technology transfer; the need for evaluation throughout the innovation cycle ; innovation and research impact on the community and environment ; reconfiguration – ensuring fitness for purpose ; institutional

---

Agreement and Cooperation Protocol between Mozambique and China (2008); Memorandum of Understanding on Increasing Technological Cooperation between Mozambique and Germany (2007); Cooperation agreement between Mozambique and Angola (2007); Program of Work on Scientific and Technological Cooperation between Mozambique and Brazil (2007); Memorandum of Understanding between Mozambique and Tanzania (2007); Cooperation Agreement between Mozambique and South Africa (2006); Memorandum of Understanding between Mozambique and Malaysia in the area of STI (2006); Memorandum of Understanding between Mozambique and Argentina (2006); Memorandum between the Government of the Republic of Cuba and the Government of the Republic of Mozambique (2006); Memorandum of Understanding between Mozambique and Egypt (2006); Protocol of Interventions for Cooperation between the Government of the State of Ceará-Brazil and the Ministry of Science and Technology of Mozambique (2006); Memorandum of Understanding between Mozambique and Vietnam (2005); Agreement between the National Council for Scientific and Technological Development (CNPq) of Brazil and the Ministry of Science and Technology of Mozambique (2005); Memorandum of Understanding between the Government of the Republic of Mozambique and the Government of the Republic of South Africa (2005); Memorandum of Understanding between the Ministry of Higher Education, Science and Technology of Mozambique and Oracle Systems Limited of Dubai, United Arab Emirates (2004); Cooperation agreement between the Republic of Mozambique and the Republic of Portugal in the fields of higher education, science and technology (2004); Cooperation agreement between Mozambique and Sweden (2003); Educational cooperation between Mozambique and Brazil (2004); Memorandum of Understanding between Mozambique and India in the area of STI (2003); Memorandum of Understanding between the Ministry of Higher Education, Science and Technology of Mozambique and the Ministry of Science and Technology of the Federative Republic of Brazil on a hydrological and environmental monitoring (2002) and SADC Protocol on Education and Training of 1997 (UNESCO, 2021: 56-57).

differentiation; the need for use-oriented applied research and extension; anticipatory actions; disaster preparedness and response (prevent, detect, respond); water, health and food security are critical areas; awareness of the danger of the 'resource curse'; problems in entering commercial value chains; inadequate certified testing and quality control laboratories; the need for partnerships and learning from others; the need for a Talent Master Plan, with an emphasis on the oil and gas industry, and attention to the pipeline from primary through to tertiary level, technical and vocational education and training included; funding for postgraduate studies is inadequate; gender equity must be prioritised; an engineering cadre, sensitive to the social and environmental consequences of resource exploitation, must be built with haste; concerns with attracting and retaining talent; and the need for the introduction of coding skills across the education system (UNESCO, 2021:6-7).

Mozambique is presently a low-income country, but the large-scale exploitation of natural gas, mineral coal, graphite and other strategic resources put the country on the threshold of lower middle-income status. So, there is an important transition in the national productive matrix that will be consolidated in the near future. This transition must be managed with great care to ensure sustainable development in all spheres – humans, and the biosphere at large. According to the Mozambican Ministry of Science, Technology and Higher Education, Professor Daniel Daniel Nivagara the Government of the Republic of Mozambique considers the strengthening of the Science, Technology and Innovation sector as a priority, so that it contributes effectively to the increase of scientific knowledge and technological innovation, poverty mitigation and, promotion of growth and accelerated economic development in the country (Nivagara, 2021:5).

The Mozambique Science, Technology and Innovation Strategy, appreciated and approved by the Council of Ministers at the 15th Ordinary Session on 27 June 2006, is based on the view that "all Mozambicans have the right to access and equity in the availability of use of science, technology, innovation and information and communication technologies with a view to accelerating the process of creating wealth, eradicating poverty and, in this way, accelerate the improvement of your quality of life".

There are several instruments, mechanisms and criteria to measure the level of science, technology and innovation in the world. One of them is the

Global Innovation Index, an annual ranking of countries by their capacity for, and success in, innovation, published by the World Intellectual Property Organization – WIPO, since 2007. This index is computed by taking a simple average of the scores in two sub-indices, the Innovation Input Index and Innovation Output Index, which are composed of five and two pillars respectively. Each of these pillars describes an attribute of innovation, and comprise up to five indicators, and their score is calculated by the weighted average method. The index gives excessive significance attributed to factors that aren't integral to innovation, such as ease of paying taxes, "electricity output and ease of protecting minority investors.

According to OECD (2015 : 46), an innovation is the implementation of a new or significantly improved product, good or service, or process, a new marketing method, or a new organisational method in business practices, workplace organisation or external relations. The "Mapping Research and Innovation in the Republic of Mozambique", conducted by UNESCO, Ministry of Science, Technology and Higher Education of Mozambique and the Islamic Development Bank – IsDB found interesting data on science, technology and innovation in Mozambique.

In Mozambique, there are 56 higher education institutions – universities, high institutes and high schools – where 22 are institutions and 34 are private.

In the period between 2005 and 2018, the number of higher education graduates has risen 6.7 times over the period displayed. Over this time, the proportion of STEM graduates shows a median value of 11.0%. It is clear that there is an emphasis on engineering fields, in which there has been a very marked increase. On the other hand, UNESCO Institute for Statistics data shows that education, some 30%, is the dominant area of study. The higher education system is strongly focused on undergraduate studies. Eduardo Mondlane University (UEM), with an enrolment of 30.000 students, remains the leading higher education institution (HEI). UEM student enrolment has expanded rapidly, with the proportion of academic staff with doctoral degrees having risen from 17.0% in 2011 to 21.0% in 2016, and senior professors comprising some 6% of staff. UEM masters and doctoral programmes remain constrained, with the university having graduated 94 masters in 2018, and 2 doctorates. Across the system as a whole, as of 2016, 13% of all researchers possessed a doctoral degree. One fifth of these were women researchers. In 2018, some 2.967 Mozambican students were recorded as studying abroad, with 1.248 in North America/ Europe, 539 in sub-Saharan Africa – SSA and 425 in Latin America (UNESCO, 2021 : 23).

In Mozambique, the total research involved on Science, Technology and Innovation sector are around 6.281 Peoples. In the field of research, there are 8 public scientific research institutions; 27 research centers; 4 research laboratories; and 12 research units, which include archives, museums and agricultural stations. According to the statistical data available on the website of the Ministry of Science and Technology, Higher Education and Vocational Training, these research units are :

Public Scientific Research Institutions : Instituto de Investigação em Águas- IIA; Instituto Nacional de Meteorologia – INAM; Instituto de Investigação Agrária de Moçambique-IIAM; Instituto de Investigação Sócio Cultural –ARPAC; Instituto Oceanográfico de Moçambique; Instituto Nacional de Saúde-INS; Instituto de Pesquisa da História da Luta de Libertação Nacional-IPHLLN; Instituto Nacional de Desenvolvimento da Educação-INDE/MINEDH.

Research Centers : Centro de Investigação e Transferência de Tecnologias para o Desenvolvimento Comunitário-CITT; Centro de Investigação e Desenvolvimento em Etnobotânica- CIDE; Centro Nacional de Biotecnologia e Biociências-CNBB; Centro de Estudos Africanos – CEA; Centro de Análise de Políticas-CAP; Centro de Coordenação dos Assuntos do Género- CeCAGe; Centro de Biotecnologia-CB; Centro de Direitos Humanos- CDH; Centro de Estudos sobre o Direito da Integração Regional da SADC- CEDIR; Centro de Estudo Industriais Segurança e Ambiente (CEISA); Centro de Estudos em Engenharia-CEE; Centro de Estudos de Agricultura e Gestão de Recursos Naturais –Ceagre; Centro Regional de Excelência em Estudos de Engenharia e Tecnologia de Petróleo e Gás- CSOGET; Centro de Estudos Estratégicos e Internacionais –CEEI; Centro de Investigação Interdisciplinar e Extensão-UP; Centro de Formação Jurídica e Judiciária– CFJJ; Centro de Investigação em Saúde da Manhiça –CISM; Centro Regional de Desenvolvimento Sanitário – CRDS; Centro Zonal Sul; Centro de Investigação e Treino em Saúde de Chókwé; Centro Zonal Centro; Centro de Experimentação Florestal; Centro de Liderança e Pesquisa do Arroz; CIP (Centro Internacional da Batata Doce de polpa alaranjada; Centro de Pesquisa de Águas Marinhas e

Pescas- CEPAM; Centro Zonal Nordeste; Centro de Investigação Agraria de Mapupulo – Montepuez;

Research Laboratories : Laboratório de Engenharia de Moçambique – LEM; Laboratório de Biotecnologia; Laboratório de Sementes de Chókwe;

Laboratório Veterinário. **Research Units :** Arquivo Histórico de Moçambique- AHM; Museu de História Natural- MHN; Museu Nacional de Geologia – MNG; Museu das Pescas-MMAIP; Agência Nacional para o Controlo da Qualidade Ambiental-AQUA; Posto Agronómico de Nhacoongo; Estação Zootécnica de Angónia; Estação Agrária de Sussudenga; Estação Zootécnica de Angónia; Núcleo de Investigação Operacional de Pemba (NIOP); Posto Agronómico de Ntengo Umodzi – Angónia; Estação Agrária de Gúrué.

FIGURE : Gross Expenditure on R&D by Field of R&D in MZN Millions : 2014-2017

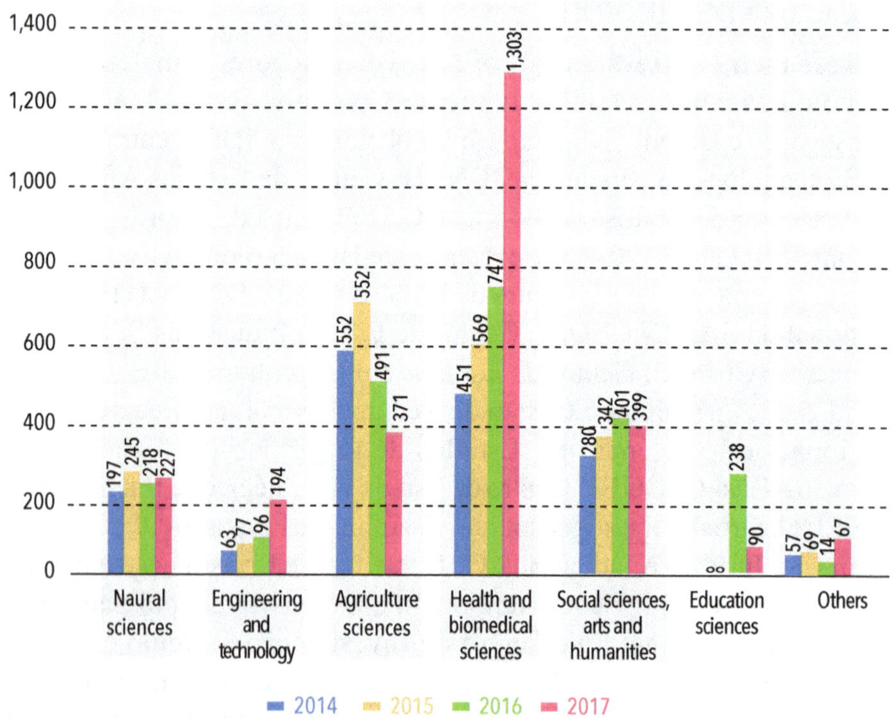

Source : MCTESTP (2018).

According to the chart, above, health and biomedical sciences, agricultural sciences and social sciences, arts and humanities are the areas that most concentrate on research and innovation and attract the largest number of researchers, in Mozambique. Between 2006 and 2014, most research focused

On public environmental occupational health, infectious diseases, tropical medicine, immunology, science technology, other topics, environmental sciences ecology and parasitology.

TABLE : Publications by Research Area in Mozambique : 2014-2018

Nº	Research and Publication Areas	Publications
01	Public Environmental Occupational Health	332
02	Infectious Diseases	314
03	Tropical Medicine	259
04	Immunology	150
05	Science Technology Other Topics	148
06	Environmental Sciences Ecology	126
07	Parasitology	117
08	General Internal Medicine	112
09	Agriculture	103
10	Cardiovascular System Cardiology	80
11	Microbiology	73
12	Health Care Sciences Services	71
13	Plant Sciences	57
14	Respiratory System	52
15	Engineering	48
16	Pharmacology Pharmacy	46
17	Business Economics	45
18	Geology	45
19	Paediatrics	45
20	Education Educational Research	44
21	Water Resources	43
22	Food Science Technology	41
23	Virology	40
24	Marine Freshwater Biology	32
25	Social Sciences Other Topics	30

Source : UNESCO (2021: 49).

The Mapping Research and Innovation in the Republic of Mozambique show a strong orientation toward the health sciences, with more than 1.500 publications. The second broad field of interest to Mozambican scientists lies in environmental sciences/ecology, agriculture and plant sciences.

Engineering and technology, not to mention the natural sciences, receive low attention. Taken as a whole, publications cluster very strongly in the health sciences, namely public environmental and occupational health, infectious diseases, tropical medicine and immunology, that together make up 50.0% of all publications (UNESCO, 2021: 43).

In the period between 2012 and 2018, in terms of science, technology and innovation, the Mozambican researchers produced several intellectual products. The Intellectual property rights comprise patents, trademarks, copyright, registered designs and plant breeders' rights, also known as plant cultivars. The table below presents the Mozambique Intellectual Property Right Awards, relating patents, trademarks, copyright, registered designs and plant breeders' rights.

TABLE : Mozambique Intellectual Property Right Awards : 2009-2018

Mozambique Intellectual Property Right Awards			
Year	**Patents**	**Trademark**	**Design**
2012	16	1403	18
2013	13	1190	28
2014	19	1690	22
2015	24	1565	30
2016	15	1792	30
2017	24	1492	30
2018	34	1254	5
Total	**145**	**10386**	**163**

Source : UNESCO (2021:49)

In the period under review, 2016 and 2014 were the years with the most patent registrations, with 1792 and 1690, respectively. In Mozambique, 78.6% of firms engaged in innovation activities, resulting in both successful and unsuccessful outcomes. Thus, 66.90% pursued organisational innovation; 38.8% pursued marketing innovations; 45.60% of firms introduced an innovation new to their market; and 27.70% of firms introduced an innovation new to themselves. The main reasons for carrying out innovation activities were for quality improvement (60.0%) and 'flexibility' (43.0%). The main barrier to innovation was the cost incurred (25.0%). In 2015, firms spent 1.12 billion revenue on innovation activities. Acquisition of machinery and software was MZN 40 million.

TABLE : Type of Innovation by Sector in Mozambique

Economic activity	Firms with innovation activities (%)	Firms with product and process innovation (%)	Firms with produc innovation (%)	Firms with process innovation (%)	Firms with organizational innovation (%)
Water supply ; sewerage, waste management and remediation activities	66,7	33,3	33,3	66,7	66,7
Financial and insurance activities	90,5	66,7	66,7	76,2	76,2
Real estate activities	100,0	0,0	0,0	25,0	25,0
Professional, scientific and technical activities	25,0	25,0	25,0	0,0	25,0
Agriculture, forestry ans fisheries	33,0	0,0	0,0	33,0	25,0
Wholesale and retail trade; repair of motorcycles	76,9	38,5	46,2	46,2	76,9
Construction	83,3	50,0	50,0	75,0	75,0
Electricity, gas, steam and air conditioning supply	100,0	80,0	80,0	100,0	80,0
Information and communication technology	84,6	61,5	76,9	69,2	69,2
Manufacturing	80,0	60,0	70,0	70,0	65,0
Hotels and tourism	66,7	55,6	66,7	55,6	55,6
Human health and social work activities	60,0	40,0	40,0	60,0	40,0
Administrative and support service activities	66,7	33,3	33,3	33,3	66,7
Transportation and storage	88,9	66,7	77,8	66,7	77,8
Total	78,5	52,9	58,7	65,3	66,9

Source : UNESCO (2021: 45)

According to the Mapping Research and Innovation in the Republic of Mozambique (2021), conducted by UNESCO, Ministry of Science, Technology and Higher Education of Mozambique and the Islamic Development Bank – IsDB the share of women researchers among total researchers in Mozambique has remained fairly static between 2008 and 2010, both full-time equivalent and headcounts. Indeed, women represented 33.3% of the researchers in 2008, both full-time equivalent and headcounts. This percentage increased to 33.70% in 2009. Then in 2010, women researchers represented 33% of the total researchers in Mozambique, falling to 29.0% in 2015. It is worth noting that the percentages of women researchers in full time equivalent and in headcounts remained steady over the time period. Women comprise 22.60% of doctorate holders, 26.0% of those with master's degrees, and 44.0% of those with the Licenciatura. So, there is a female qualification gap (UNESCO, 2021:42).

FUGURE : Headcount of Researchers, Technicians and Other Personnel by Gender in Mozambique : 2016-2017

Indicator	**2016**			**2017**		
	Male	**Female**	**Total**	**Male**	**Female**	**Total**
Researchers	2326	842	**3168**	1874	1004	**2878**
Technicians, Assistants and Equivalent Personnel	918	599	**1517**	462	477	**939**
Administrative and Support Staff	920	676	**1596**	987	726	**1713**

Source : MCTESTP (2018)

The science, technology and innovation policy in Mozambique have a gender issue as one of its structural aspects and pillars and women perform various activities such as researchers, technicians, assistants and equivalent personnel or administrative and support staff. According to the data shown in the chat, we can see that, 38% of researchers involved on Science, Technology and Innovation development in Mozambique, are women, with a 42 % concentration among support staff.

Final Remarks

The innovation system and governance in Mozambique have a long way to go. The analysis of the Mozambican science, technology and innovation system and governance shows that it is in a process of construction and consolidation. The Mozambican system of innovation includes the necessary set of public sector institutions, actors and intermediaries that are needed for a functional ecosystem. However, these institutions and actors, including public universities, centers, department-based research institutes and regulators may be operating in coordination and cooperation for the scientific and innovation production process can be robust and respond to the current and future challenges of society and the Mozambican State.

The colonial historical legacy and recurrent armed conflicts created an unfavourable legacy in matters related to science, technology and innovation in Mozambique. This scenario began to change in the early 2000s, with the creation of a favourable legal and institutional framework for scientific production and technological innovation. Despite the fact that the Government of Mozambique places Science, technology and innovation on its political agenda, there is still little investment in this sector. The professional and technical skills production falls short of demand and dependence on foreign skills. We have gains in infrastructure and systems for health, but these gains are unevenly distributed. So, the discovery and exploitation of strategic resources such as mineral coal, natural gas, graphite, heavy sands, among others, requires a robust and ambitious national program in the science, technology and innovation sector.

According to the national strengths and limitations, there are three pivotal and strategic areas that the Mozambican government can concentrate on promoting science, technology and innovation, namely, science, technology, engineering and mathematics; science, technology and innovation national policy; oil and gas sector; and agriculture. Thus, it is necessary to define the national agenda, the financing, monitoring and evaluation mechanisms, in a holistic, integrated and incremental approach.

References

Bonate, Liazzat J. K. (2022). **O Jihadismo Transnacional e a Insurgência em Cabo Delgado, Moçambique.** Afro-Ásia, nº 65, p. 519-553.

Cabrita, João M. (2000). **Mozambique: The Tortuous Road to Democracy**. Palgrave Macmillan, London.

Decree nº 13/2005, 4 February – Creation of the Ministry of Science and Technology. Imprensa Nacional, Maputo.

Habib,E Saide; FORQUILHA, Salvador and Pereira, João (2019). **Radicalização Islâmica no Norte de Moçambique : O Caso de Mocímboa da Praia.** Cadernos IESE nº17/2019. IESE, Maputo.

Mahtani, Dino; Walle, Nelleke Van De; Pigou, Piers; Elias, Meron (2021). **Understanding the New U.S. Terrorism Designations in Africa.** International Crisis Group, Washington, D.C.

Morier-GenouD, Eric (2020). **The Jihadi Insurgency in Mozambique: Origins, Nature and Beginning.** Journal of Eastern African Studies. volume 14, nº 3, p. 396-412.

Nair-Bedouelle, Shamila (2021). **Foreword by the Assistant Director-General for Natural Sciences, UNESCO. In UNESCO** – United Nations Educational, Scientific and Cultural Organization. Mapping Research and Innovation in the Republic of Mozambique. GO – SPIN Country Profiles in Science, Technology and Innovation Policy. Volume 9. UNESCO, Paris.

Nivagara, Daniel Daniel (2021). **Science, Technology and Innovation for Promotion of Social and Economic Development.** In UNESCO – United Nations Educational, Scientific and Cultural Organization. **Mapping Research and Innovation in the Republic of Mozambique.** GO – SPIN Country Profiles in Science, Technology and Innovation Policy. Volume 9. UNESCO, Paris.

OECD – Organization for Economic Co-operation and Development (2015). **Guidelines for Collecting and Reporting Data on Research and Experimental Development.** OECD, Paris.

Peter, Fabricius (2022). Is **another Boko Haram or al-Shabaab erupting in Mozambique?** Institute for Security Studies, Pretoria.

Presidential Decree nº 1/2015, 16 January – Creation of the Ministry of Science and Technology, Higher Education and Vocational Training. Imprensa Nacional, Maputo.

Resolution nº 23/2003, of July 22 – Approves the Science and Technologies Policy and the Strategy for its Implementation. Imprensa Nacional, Maputo.

Schwartz, Stephanie (2010). **Youth and Post-Conflict Reconstruction: Agents of Change.** United States Institute of Peace Press, Washington, D.C.

SINDI, Hayat (2021). **Foreword by the Senior Advisor to the IsDB President for Science, Technology and Innovation.** In UNESCO – United Nations Educational, Scientific and Cultural Organization. **Mapping Research and Innovation in the Republic of Mozambique.** GO – SPIN Country Profiles in Science, Technology and Innovation Policy. Volume 9. UNESCO, Paris.

UNESCO – United Nations Educational, Scientific and Cultural Organization (2021). **Mapping Research and Innovation in the Republic of Mozambique.** GO – SPIN Country Profiles in Science, Technology and Innovation Policy. Volume 9. UNESCO, Paris.

The Economist (2020). **More Misery, Few Answers**. Volume 436, nº. 9209. p. 37.

Vines, Alex (1997). **Still Killing : Landmines in Southern Africa.** Human Rights Watch. New York.

DEGITAL STRATEGY FOR ETHIOPIA : INCLUSIVE PROSPERITY

Mrs Shitaye Haile Lemma

Why does digital transformation matter ?

Technological change has been the primary driving force for innovation, social development, productivity improvements and inclusive and sustainable growth.

As a developing country, Ethiopia recogniser that its aspirations and intentional journey to realising a prosperous Ethiopia, conducive and inclusive for all, is intimately tied to advancements in technology.

Five years ago, Ethiopia adopted a national digital strategy which laid out a unified vision for Ethiopia's progress to an inclusive digital economy. The strategy focused on developing infrastructure enabling systems, digital platforms and building the digital ecosystem.

According to the Ethiopian Government, the implementation of a set of medium-term national development goals to be achieved by 2025 (Vision 2025) include :

- Achieving inclusive growth and sustainable development ;
- Attaining middle-income status and a prosperous society ;
- Doubling, if possible, tripling, the country's total export capacity ;
- Becoming a leading manufacturing hub in Africa ;
- Ensuring that the manufacturing sector contributes 40% of exports ;
- Creating 14 million jobs by 2025 ;
- Achieving a double-digit growth rate and sustaining it beyond 2025.

Ethiopia, a digital transformation strategy is aligned with :

National Economic Reform Agenda and the Ten-Year Development Plan (2020-2030)

United Nations Sustainable Development Goals (SDGs), in particular the goal of leaving no one behind (2030 Agenda) ;

African Union's continental digital transformation strategic framework for the socio-economic transformation of the continent over the next 50 years strategy (Agenda 2063).

Ethiopia's drive to advance digital transformation two pathway

- The application of digital technology to promote both domestic and international trade through ecommerce platforms to strengthen domestic supply chains and implement an export-led industrialisation strategy;
- Use technology/ICT park to attract and facilitate investment in IT-related activities and kick-start of digital transformation in the country.

Key Objectives of the Digital Ethiopia by 2025

The Ministry of Innovation and Technology designed the strategy to focus on four sectors that can create the most jobs : **Agriculture, Manufacturing, ICT and Tourism.**

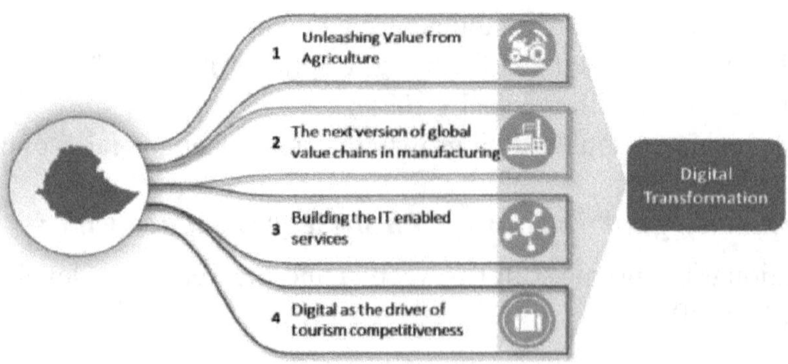

Sector 1 : Unleashing value from agriculture

- Building a Digital Agriculture platform;
- Support Ag-Tech Entrepreneurship.

Sector 2 : Global value chains in manufacturing

- Fast and Reliable Internet Connectivity to Enable the adoption of new communication technologies;
- Enhance digitally enabled logistics.

Sector 3 : Building the IT-enabled services

- Provide infrastructure to high potential talent centres;
- Identify and attract leading Business Process Outsourcing (BPO), specifically Impact Sourcing Service Providers (SSPs).

Sector 4 : Digital as the driver of tourism competitiveness.

- Set up a tourism digitalisation task force;
- Targeted digital marketing strategies;
- Building capacity of tourism SMEs to 'go digital' and adopt digital technologies.

Unleashing value from agriculture

Agriculture is the main pillar of Ethiopia's economy, employing 75% of the labour force, accounting for 40% of GDP, and 80% of the national export value.

Ethiopia has made significant progress in laying the groundwork to build a digital agriculture platform to offer decision-making tools and support, and boost agri-tech entrepreneurship.

The Ethiopian government has adopted a national economic policy that mainly focuses on implementing the Agricultural Development Led Industrialisation (ADLI). The objectives of ADLI include promotion of economic efficiency and growth, development of domestic technological capacities and capabilities for the promotion and development of small, intermediate and capital goods.

Global Network of Digital Agriculture Innovation Hubs

The "Global Network of Digital Agriculture Innovation Hubs" project is part of a broader FAO's Flexible Multi-Partner Mechanism (FMM) global programme also being implemented in Dominica, Grenada and Morocco.

Food and Agriculture Organization (FAO) in close collaboration with Ethiopia's Agriculture and Finance Ministries launched a digitisation project to improve the productivity and digital transformation of Ethiopia's agriculture sector.

The network of Ethiopian innovation hubs is a subprogramme of the Global Network of Digital Agriculture Innovation Hubs, aims to contribute to the digital transformation of agrifood systems, increasing productivity, managing climate risks and diversifying rural economies.

Advancing the digitalisation of Ethiopia's agriculture sector : Objective of Ethiopia Programme :

- Facilitate knowledge exchange and sharing within the national Hub and across the global network through organising joint events and platforms;
- Create national digital agriculture innovation hub models to spearhead digital innovation programs in agriculture that meet local needs;
- Facilitate the creation of sustainable business models to support innovation projects through Public-Private Partnerships (PPP);
- Develop digital agriculture solutions at the national or regional level to support the agri-food systems transformation;
- Formulate digital agriculture strategies, policies, or programmes to mainstream digital innovation in agri-food systems;
- Provide farmers with reliable marketing information that helps them reach their markets more effectively, at lower cost;
- Enhance agricultural digital skills and literacy by providing targeted training for farmers, particularly for women, and extension agents;
- Empowering women in agriculture using ICTs.

International Telecommunication Union, Digital Transformation Centre's in Ethiopia (DTC)

The Ethiopian digital transformation strategy recognises digital literacy and digital skills as a foundation for building an inclusive digital economy. The Digital Transformation Centres (DTC) Initiative was introduced three years ago by the International Telecommunication Union (ITU) in partnership with Cisco, an American-based multinational digital communications technology company.

As part of phase two of ITU's Digital Transformation Center (DTC) Initiative, the Digital Transformation Program office (DTP) within the Federal Democratic Republic of Ethiopia (FDRE) Ministry of Innovation and Technology became part of the global network.

Within its mandate to support citizens' innovation and technology capabilities, the Ministry of Innovation and Technology is undertaking a wide range of digital capacity-building initiatives.

To implement the DTC initiative, the Ministry of Innovation and Technology has selected 11 DTC satellite training centres across the country to reach a wider population.

The government aims to train 5,000 citizens with different levels of digital skills in the year 2022 and thus, contributing to national efforts to achieve Sustainable Development Goal (SDG)

Digital Transformation Centres (DTC) Initiative Objectives of the DTC Initiative :

- Contribute towards the goal of an inclusive digital society by ensuring that lack of digital skills is no longer a barrier to digital participation
- Narrow the digital divide by developing digital skills for the most underprivileged groups
- Improve the capacity of policymakers to design and implement digital transformation programmes
- Improve livelihoods of citizens through the use of digital technologies and services

Target groups :

- People in rural communities (farmers, local artisans, etc.);
- General public requiring digital skills that enable them to engage in the digital economy;
- Policymakers are responsible for the development and implementation of digital policies;
- start-up, SMEs and emerging Entrepreneurs;
- Youths and school leavers;
- Women and girls.

ICT Park as a driver of digital transformation

In 2011, the government of Ethiopia established an ICT (Information and Communication Technology) Park in Addis Ababa to:

- Attract Foreign Direct Investment (FDI); boost exports of IT-related products and services;
- Provide an innovative business environment for start-ups; and enable the development of the digital economy.

Ethiopia's ICT and digital transformation journey have been marked by key progress milestones aligned with the following five Internet Governance Forum (IGF's) subthemes:

- Connecting All People and Safeguarding Human Rights;
- Avoiding Internet Fragmentation ;
- Governing Data and Protecting Privacy;
- Enabling Safety, Security and Accountability;
- Addressing Advanced Technologies, including Artificial Intelligence. The Artificial Intelligence Institute (AI) is one of the governmental institutions undertaking initiatives to support the country's digital transformation endeavour.

October 2022, the government of Ethiopia has inaugurated a dome-shaped state-of-the-art Science and Technology Museum. that displayed local solutions in healthcare, finance, cybersecurity, Geographic Information Systems (GIS), service industries, data analytics, manufacturing, and robotics among others

The museum contains an exhibition hall dedicated to scientific and developmental research.

The first Pan-African Artificial Intelligence Conference in Ethiopia was held at the newly inaugurated Science Museum.

The conference mainly focused on solving African problems with an African digital alternative. Scholars and Researchers from various African countries have participated in the conference.

Internet Uptake has accelerated during the pandemic

The latest International Telecommunication Union (ITU) data show that uptake of the Internet has accelerated during the COVID-19 pandemic. In

2019, 4.1 billion people (or 54 percent of the world's population) were using the Internet.

4.9 billion people used the Internet in 2021. That means that roughly 63 percent of the world's population was now online – an increase of 17 percent – with almost 800 million people estimated to have come online since 2019.

Internet/ Mobile use in Ethiopia

Internet coverage shows an increase from 19 million users in 2017 to 31 million in 2022. However, despite the recent growth of mobile and internet subscribers, a significant part of the Ethiopian population still does not have accesses to the internet, 4G and 5G network has been rolling out in populated towns throughout major cities of the country, accelerating connectivity; adding over 2,300 high schools throughout the country have internet access.

Microsoft has collaborated with the Ethiopian Ministry of Education to implement a Higher Educational Management Information System supporting the successful digital transformation of the education sector

According to Groupe Special Mobile Association (GSMA), smartphones will constitute 58 percent of internet connections in Ethiopia by 2025 and will play a critical role in facilitating the delivery of digital financial services to consumers.

Considering Ethiopia-s large and growing population, improving connectivity and expanding accessibility have been a priority with investment being made in infrastructure expansion by opening up the telecom sector to private investors and building government data infrastructure,

Kenya-based Safaricom is working in partnership with the Ethiopian government for transforming the digital landscape of the country.

Safaricom PLC is a technology company providing a wide range of services and solutions, including mobile voice, messaging, data, financial and digital services that enable commercial and personal platforms.

Ethio telecom, a publicly owned telecom and internet services providing company, in May 11, 2021 launched the first ever mobile money transfer platform brand name "telebirr".

DYNAMIQUE DE LA RECHERCHE-DÉVELOPPEMENT ET DE L'INNOVATION AU MAROC

Mohamed Smani

Introduction

En matière de recherche-développement et d'Innovation, chaque pays peut être décrit par ce qui est désigné communément par son Système National de Recherche – SNR. Le SNR du Maroc est relativement jeune et a connu deux périodes d'évolutions importantes :

• Première période : avant 1957

• Deuxième Période :1957- à nos jours

Première période de la construction du Système

La Première période de La construction du Système commence avec l'édification par une femme de l'Université AL KARAOUYNE de FÈS en l'an 859 APR. J.-C. a peu prêt à la même période que l'université de La Sorbonne et celle de Bologne notamment. C'est une université encore en activité aujourd'hui.

Au cours de la période coloniale (1912 – 1956) la priorité étant donnée au développement agricole et en particulier à l'acclimatation des espèces nouvelles avant la généralisation de leur plantation, deux structures de recherche-développement furent créées à Rabat et à Fès :

• 1914 : « Jardin d'essais » de Rabat

• 1916 : « la ferme expérimentale » de Fès,

Il était aussi impératif à cette même époque coloniale de connaître les ressources du sol et du sous-sol en vue de leur exploitation. Ainsi fut créé

• Le 24 janvier 1920 : l'Institut Scientifique Chérifien

Cet Institut a joué un rôle fondamental dans le développement de la recherche scientifique au Maroc dans plusieurs domaines : Géologie, minéralogie, zoologie, botanique, géophysique ... etc. C'est le plus ancien établissement universitaire de recherche au Maroc qui existe encore aujourd'hui, intégré à la Faculté des Sciences de Rabat de l'Université Mohammed 5.

- C'est l'ancêtre de la première Faculté des Sciences créée en 1957.

S'agissant de la protection sanitaire, il fut créé en 1929 : L'Institut Pasteur du Maroc.

- En 1938 : Mise en place d'une structure de gouvernance, le Comité Mixte Franco - Marocain de la recherche scientifique qui ne fut opérationnelle qu'en 1947.

Deuxième période de la construction du Système

C'est en 1959 que fut créée la première université moderne marocaine, l'université de Rabat. À partir de 1976 le Maroc a connu la création progressive des 12 universités publiques actuelles et de plusieurs établissements d'enseignement supérieur publics et privés.

Dans le domaine du partenariat on peut noter plus particulièrement :

- 1983 : démarrage du programme « actions intégrées » pour encourager la mobilité des chercheurs entre la France et le Maroc pour contribuer ainsi à la formation des enseignants-chercheurs dans toutes les disciplines
- et en 2016, lancement des Premières CIFRE France Maroc pour promouvoir la recherche-développement dans les entreprises et renforcer leur relation avec les universités.
- 2000, la création d'une antenne de l'Institut français de Recherche pour le Développement - IRD - au Maroc
- 2013 à 2020 : implantation de plusieurs établissements d'enseignement supérieur (Université Internationale de Rabat, l'école centrale à Casablanca, l'ENSA de Fès et École de Management de LYON à Casablanca, l'Université Euro-méditerranéenne de Fès, l'Université des Sciences de la santé Mohammed 6, l'Université Mohammed 6 de Ben Grir)

II- Évolution de la gouvernance et du cadre législatif du système

- 1976 : Création du Ministère de l'Enseignement Supérieur et la Recherche Scientifique
- 1999 : création d'un Secrétariat d'État à la recherche scientifique qui en

- 2003 a été relevé au rang d'un ministère délégué chargé de la recherche et en 2006 : suppression de l'autorité en charge de la recherche et son intégration dans le Ministère de l'Enseignement Supérieur
- La loi 01 - 00 du 1er juin 2000 portant organisation de l'enseignement supérieur est toujours en vigueur à ce jour. Cette loi a été élaborée à la suite de la Charte Nationale d'Éducation et Formation préparée par une commission spéciale.
- 2000 : instauration de la Provision pour Recherche Développement pour le financement de la R&D dans les entreprises et en 2009 sa suppression par le gouvernement
- 1er janvier 2001 : création du Fonds de soutien à la R&D alimenté par la contribution des entreprises de Telecom à raison de 0,25% du CA
- 2003 : Adoption du système LMD
- 2009 : stratégie nationale pour le développement de la Recherche Scientifique à l'horizon 2025 et sa mise en œuvre à travers le plan d'urgence 2009-2012 par une contractualisation avec les 12 universités publiques
- 2015 : le Conseil Supérieur de l'Éducation, de la Formation et de la Recherche Scientifique élabore une vision à l'horizon 2030 qui sera traduite par une loi-cadre en 2016

Cette loi d'orientation est en cours de mise en œuvre par le Ministère chargé de la recherche. Elle vise à répondre aux défis scientifiques, techniques et sociaux. Sa mise en œuvre ayant une dimension interministérielle indispensable à la consolidation d'une vision nationale cohérente tant sur le plan stratégique que dans sa déclinaison programmatique, il a été adopté :

- En juin 2021 : Un Conseil National de la recherche présidé par le chef de gouvernement et composé de tous les départements ministériels concernés ainsi que des institutions publiques constitutionnelles et le patronat marocain
- En septembre 2021 : une Commission Technique Permanente de suivi et d'accompagnement présidée par l'autorité en charge de la recherche et composée des acteurs opérationnels

Les recommandations de la Stratégie Nationale à l'horizon 2035 élaborée par la Commission Spéciale pour un Nouveau Modèle de Développement pour le Maroc, à l'initiative du Chef de L'État, sont en cours de mise en œuvre par le gouvernement issu des élections du 8 septembre 2021.

En octobre 2021 : Création d'un Ministère de l'Enseignement Supérieur de la Recherche scientifique et de l'innovation. Notons que c'est la première fois que la compétence innovation est attribuée à un département ministériel. Ceci est l'expression de la prise de conscience par la nouvelle équipe gouvernementale issue des élections de 2021 de l'importance de l'innovation et en particulier dans les entreprises pour le développement économique et social du pays.

III- Les principaux acteurs du système

- 12 Universités publiques, une par région, comprenant :
    - 170 établissements d'enseignement supérieur (72 Facultés, 50 Grandes Écoles… etc.)
    - 17 Établissements publics et instituts de recherche (CNRST, MASCIR, IRESEN, INRA, INRH, CNESTEN, INPAM … etc.)
- 7 universités publiques privées et 5 universités privées (176 Établissements privés d'enseignement supérieur)
- Des organismes institutionnels : Académie Hassan 2 des Sciences et Techniques, le Conseil Supérieur de l'Éducation, la Formation et la Recherche Scientifique
- Des entreprises privées et des fondations

IV- Les principaux indicateurs de la R&D et de l'innovation

Les principaux indicateurs pris en considération à l'échelle internationale pour caractériser les performances d'un SNR portent essentiellement sur :

- Le personnel de la R&D
- Les ressources financières
- La production scientifique (base web of science)
- Les dépôts de brevet

Le personnel de la R&D
Effectifs estimés en 2016 (source : Ministère)

Établissements	Nombre	Effectif	%
Universités publiques (72 facultés, 50 Grandes Écoles, 6 instituts de recherche)	12 après la fusion	13 329 Enseignants Chercheurs, 28 167 Doctorants Total : 41 496	76,72
Établissements publics d'enseignement supérieur non universitaire	72	3106	5,74
Établissements privés d'enseignement supérieur	176	1704	3,15
Établissements publics de recherche	17	4516	8,34
Entreprises privées	PM	PM	PM

Répartition du personnel de recherche par domaine disciplinaire : Total : 49 118

- Sciences humaines et sociales : 20 443 (37,79 %)
- Sciences exactes et naturelles : 18 260 (33,75%)
- Sciences de l'ingénieur : 10 487 (19,38 %)
- Sciences médicales : 4 897 (9,05%)

Personnel de la R&D ramené à la population totale au Maroc et dans d'autres pays (2015- 2014) - Source : statistique UNESCO

Pays	Personnel total	Personnel de la R&D par million d'habitants
Corée du Sud	619 907	12 325
France	575 830	8 980
Maroc	49 840	1 469
Tunisie	36 070	3 206
Jordanie	11 908	1 568

Effectif des inscrits en doctorat et des doctorats délivrés au Maroc (2012 – 2016)

Année	2012	2013	2014	2015	2016
Inscrits	22 736	19 585	20 908	27 505	28 492
Délivrances	981	701	1624	2309	1723
% de délivrances	4,3	3,5	7,76	8,40	6,05

B. Les ressources financières

- La part du PIB consacrée à la R&D au Maroc est estimée à 0,75 % et reste loin des objectifs de la loi 01-00 adoptée en 1999 qui recommandait d'atteindre 1 % du PIB à l'horizon 2010.
- La France se situe à 2,23 %, la Corée du Sud à 4,23 %, le Portugal et l'Espagne : 1,28 % et 1,22 %
- Le financement de la recherche est fait à travers le fonds de soutien à la recherche et le développement technologique alimenté par l'État et le fonds créé dans le cadre de la loi sur la libéralisation du secteur des télécoms par 0,25 % du CA des sociétés concernées.
- L'État finance exclusivement les établissements universitaires par des aides directes ou subventions et à travers des appels à projets lancés par le Centre National pour la Recherche Scientifique

- À ce jour, aucun mécanisme public n'est mis en place pour le financement des travaux de R&D et d'innovation des entreprises.

C. La production scientifique (base web of science)

Pays	2010	2016
Maroc	1 217	1 858
Algérie	1 560	3 188
Tunisie	2 396	3 893
Égypte	5 154	10 091
Kenya	830	1 291
Portugal	7 814	11 338
France	53 541	60 288
Turquie	19 165	25 878
Malaisie	5 128	9 091
Corée du Sud	37 725	50 462

Co-publications du Maroc :

- Nombre de publications : en 2010 et 2016 : 846 et 1342
    - France : 53,8 % et 54,5%
    - Espagne 18,4% et 24,0%
    - Tunisie : 3,4% et 0,0

D. Les dépôts de brevets (source OMPIC)

	2012	2013	2014	2015	2016
Universités	58	138	158	109	131
Centres de recherche	16	25	32	31	24
Entreprises marocaines	26	26	36	14	21
Personnes physiques	96	96	127	70	64
Total Maroc	196	315	353	224	237
Non-Résidents				797	1066

V- La recherche et d'innovation dans les entreprises : un Maroc à deux vitesses

Un tissu de PME/ PMI très peu innovant :

Le Maroc occupe la 77ème place sur 128 pays concernés par l'Édition 2021 du GII. Dans la catégorie des économies à revenu moyen inférieur, il est classé dans la catégorie des pays faiblement innovants.

Les enquêtes réalisées au Maroc auprès des entreprises en 2000, 2004, 2010, 2022, confirment la faiblesse de l'innovation dans les entreprises marocaines, le secteur privé marocain, moteur de l'innovation dans les autres pays, participe peu à l'effort de recherche et d'innovation :

- Le nombre de brevets déposés est insignifiant ; il est le fait de moins de dix entreprises
- Faible niveau de technologies dans les produits importés ou exportés
- Absence totale de doctorants et postdocs dans les entreprises
- Relation université entreprises quasi inexistante ;
- Les entreprises ne contribuent pas à la dépense intérieure de recherche qui est le fait uniquement des pouvoirs publics
- Aucun incitatif n'est mis en place, à ce jour, en faveur de l'innovation dans les entreprises

Des succès indéniables dans certains domaines
Secteur de l'automobile

- Capacité de production de 700 000 véhicules/an
- 147 000 emplois créés
- 250 équipementiers alignés sur les normes des constructeurs

Le Maroc est aujourd'hui le 2ème exportateur en Afrique, derrière l'Afrique du Sud (Usines implantées à Casablanca (Renault), à, Kenitra (Peugeot), Tanger (Renault)

Secteur de l'aéronautique :

- 142 entreprises en 15 ans
- 11 313 emplois
- Maitrise au fur et à mesure de nouveaux métiers à forte valeur ajoutée (composites, assemblage mécanique, chaudronnerie, câblage.)
- Principales entreprises du secteur : EADS, BOEING, Safran

Monter en gamme dans les Chaines de valeur mondiales : un nouveau défi

Les deux secteurs ont connu une constante montée en gamme technologique. Le taux d'intégration est supérieur à 34%. Ce taux est supérieur à celui de pays comme le Chili (15,5%), le Brésil (11,6%) et inférieur à celui de pays comme la Hongrie (46 %) la République Tchèque (42%)

De nouveaux efforts sont à faire pour passer à des niveaux supérieurs en investissant en particulier dans le capital intellectuel pour améliorer la productivité et différencier par la R&D et l'innovation le produit fini de la chaine L'état et les opérateurs se sont engagés à assurer la formation de 100000 cadres, techniciens et ingénieurs d'ici 2025

Les deux industries espèrent s'appuyer sur la recherche et l'innovation pour accroître le taux d'intégration et atteindre 65% pour l'automobile et 50% pour l'aéronautique

Le Maroc a réussi à allier ses points forts traditionnels avec le développement de nouvelles filières d'activités dont l'automobile et l'aéronautique font figure d'exemples sur tout le continent africain

Des faiblesses à corriger

La faiblesse de l'innovation et la structure du tissu productif ne favorisent rien par la montée en gamme vers des produits à plus forte valeur ajoutée. De nouvelles sources de compétitivité doivent être recherchées telles que l'innovation. Or l'investissement et la promotion de l'innovation sont encore marginaux :

- Les montants investis en R&D s'élèvent à 0,75% du PIB depuis 2016
- La part du secteur privé est négligeable dans l'effort de recherche
- Aucune incitation fiscale n'est disponible, le Crédit Impôt Recherche n'existe pas

Le monde de la recherche publique est faiblement structuré, peu productif: publications scientifiques, doctorats soutenus, très peu de production technologique (prototype, brevets)

Les performances en innovation sont très modestes et le niveau de création technologique faible

Tout cela s'observe par une baisse des exportations de biens manufacturés et de la part des exportations de hautes technologies : depuis 2000 les exportations ont baissé de 11% à 6%.

La part des produits manufacturés à technologie moyenne ou élevée s'est toutefois renforcée pour atteindre 40%. Ce qui s'explique principalement par la hausse des exportations de véhicules et des produits de l'aéronautique

IV- La relance de la recherche et l'innovation : Une nouvelle vision stratégique

• Les fondements de la nouvelle vision stratégique

Le conseil supérieur de l'éducation, la formation et la recherche dont les instances ont été renouvelées en 2015 a élaboré une vision stratégique à l'horizon 2030 que le gouvernement a traduit dans une charte et dans une loi-cadre adoptée en 2016 par le parlement marocain. Objectif : réformer le système éducatif (école, université, formation professionnelle)

La commission spéciale sur le nouveau modèle de développement du Maroc à l'horizon 2035, approuvé par le Chef de l'État place le capital humain, la recherche, l'innovation au cœur du modèle de développement proposé

Le nouveau modèle de développement est une réforme majeure élaborée à la demande du Chef de l'État. Le rapport a été rendu public en septembre 2021. Le gouvernement, issu des élections du 8 septembre 2021 et constitué le 20 février 2022, s'attèle à sa mise en œuvre ;

• Les leviers du changement : Les mesures en cours de préparation

1. Création d'un conseil national de la Recherche Scientifique et de l'innovation qui dans sa composition tient compte de la dimension interministérielle indispensable à la consolidation d'une vision nationale cohérente tant sur le plan stratégique que dans la déclinaison programmatique ; ce conseil est présidé par le chef de gouvernement.
2. Un comité technique permanent créé auprès du conseil est constitué par les acteurs du système et présidé par la Direction Générale de la Recherche et de l'Innovation
3. Instauration de mesures fiscales en faveur de la RDI dans les entreprises (Crédit Impôt Recherche)
4. Augmentation progressive de la part du PIB consacré à la recherche : 1% en 2022, 1,5% à 2% en 2030

5. Participation aux Chaines de Valeur Mondiales avec l'ambition d'atteindre un taux d'intégration de 60% voire plus au lieu de 43% aujourd'hui dans le secteur de l'automobile
6. Augmenter la valeur ajoutée de la production industrielle moyenne ou haute technologie
7. Mettre en place un cadre favorable pour promouvoir l'innovation au sein de l'entreprise et faire émerger des start-up de dimension régionale voire mondiales
8. Promouvoir le made in Morocco pour répondre aux besoins de la société

V- Conclusion

Le Système national marocain de recherche et d'innovation a connu des avancées et des reculs au cours de son histoire moderne. À ce jour nous avons relevé que de nombreuses insuffisances subsistent malgré les succès indéniables enregistrés.

Les engagements au plus haut niveau de l'état et les nouvelles orientations stratégiques adoptées permettent d'espérer que les nouvelles avancées attendues seront à la hauteur des défis et seront au rendez-vous à l'horizon 2030 fixé.

LE PARTENARIAT UNIVERSITÉ-ENTREPRISE ET LA PROBLÉMATIQUE DE L'INNOVATION AU MAROC

Driss Guerraoui

L'Entreprise et l'Université constituent les deux acteurs clés des enjeux fondamentaux de la création de la richesse. L'Entreprise parce qu'elle est le lieu de la production de la valeur et l'Université en raison de son statut d'espace de la production du génie, de l'intelligence, de la connaissance et du savoir indispensables pour la production des innovations et des technologies dont l'économie et la société ont besoin.

Par conséquent, renforcer la relation Université-Entreprise c'est être en phase avec cette réalité, particulièrement en cette deuxième décade du XXI^{éme} siècle où le capital immatériel émerge pour devenir un levier essentiel des nouveaux modèles de croissance et de développement.

Dans ce cadre se pose une question fondamentale. Quels sont les défis que cette relation est appelée à relever aujourd'hui ?

À ce niveau trois défis paraissent être au cœur de cette relation :

1. Gérer la complexité économique générée par l'obsolescence rapide des savoirs, des savoir-faire, des qualifications, des technologies et des métiers, phénomène impulsé par l'exacerbation de la concurrence entre les firmes et les centres de recherche, annonçant de ce fait la fin des droits acquis et l'émergence d'une forme nouvelle de compétitivité se construisant chaque jour par la connaissance, l'intelligence et l'innovation.
2. Maîtriser les insécurités économiques du fait que les entreprises et les universités évoluent de plus en plus dans des environnements empreints d'aléas, d'incertitudes et de risques majeurs liés aux fluctuations imprévisibles des marchés, à la fréquence des phénomènes naturels extrêmes, elles-mêmes imprévisibles, et à l'évolution de guerres d'un genre nouveau et à leur tête la guerre du génie et de

l'intelligence qui met les entreprises et les universités devant des insécurités réelles.

3. Répondre à la raréfaction des ressources à fois naturelles, humaines et financières à la mesure des exigences de l'entreprise et de l'université en matière de production d'innovations pouvant contribuer à faire face à des réalités imposées par l'entrée des économies et des sociétés du XXIéme siècle dans une véritable ère de la rareté, dans un contexte de pression vertigineuse des besoins des entreprises, des territoires et des populations. Face à ces défis, la réalité de la recherche scientifique et de l'innovation, qui est l'ont-pu de cette relation Université-Entreprise, souffre de nombreux dysfonctionnements rendant difficile la réalisation de raccourcis technologique.

I- Les dysfonctionnements majeurs

Pour le Maroc, ces dysfonctionnements sont de plusieurs ordres. :

- La recherche scientifique et l'innovation offrent l'image d'un système éclaté, porté par une multitude d'acteurs et d'intervenants, avec comme conséquence un déficit de convergence, de cohérence et de coordination, et in fine de mutualisation des ressources humaines et matérielles. Cette réalité est due à l'absence d'un pilotage institutionnel unifié de l'ensemble des programmes de recherche et d'innovation. Ce faisant, il n'y a pas un écosystème national d'innovation, mais des pôles d'excellence disséminés à travers le territoire porté soit par des clusters, par des technopôles soit ou des Technoparcs.

- La faiblesse et la dispersion des moyens. En effet, si la part de la recherche scientifique et de l'innovation n'est que de 0.8 % du PIB du pays en 2013, cette part connaît une répartition différenciée qui s'apparente à une vraie dispersion des moyens entre la recherche universitaire fondamentale qui rentre pour 45,28% et la recherche appliquée des secteurs de l'activité économique qui est de 36,11% pour l'énergie, les mines et les industries de transformation , de 5,47% pour l'agriculture, de 3,1% pour la communication et les nanotechnologies, de 2,33 pour la pêche, de 1,17% pour les sciences de la santé et de 0,85 % pour l'équipement et les transports.

- Le nombre limité de partenariats entreprise-université qui est passé de 17 projets en 2008, à 28 en 2010 pour s'établir à 13 en 2013, à 12 en 2015 et à 11 en 2017.

- Une production scientifique très faible par rapport aux besoins immenses de l'économie nationale. À ce niveau, si la part du Maroc dans la production scientifique mondiale n'est que de 0.12% en 2010, le nombre d'articles scientifiques publiés par million d'habitants en 2011 n'est que de 73 contre 784 pour le Portugal, 392 pour la Turquie, 361 pour la Tunisie, 211 pour l'Afrique du Sud, 112 pour l'Égypte et 62 pour l'Algérie.

- La prédominance des sciences humaines et sociales dans la recherche scientifique nationale que mesure le nombre de diplômes de l'enseignement supérieur délivrés par les Universités marocaines et qui est pour 2011 de 62.52% pour les Sciences Sociales et Humaines, 20.73% pour les sciences exactes et naturelles, 5.36 % pour les sciences de la santé et 11,35% pour l'ingénierie.

- La recherche appliquée et l'innovation dans le secteur privé n'est pas structurée et demeure de l'apanage de quelques grands groupes multinationaux et quelques champions nationaux publics et privés comme le Groupe de l'Office Chérifien des Phosphates.

- Le cloisonnement de la recherche appliquée et de l'innovation entre les secteurs public et privé que matérialise si non l'absence du moins l'insuffisance des passerelles entre les deux secteurs.

- Les thèmes de recherche abordée par les chercheurs marocains comprennent des financements assurés par la coopération internationale avec le souvent des problématiques sans impact ou un impact faible sur l'économie et la société marocaines et avec un risque en termes de sécurité nationale du fait de l'usage des résultats des recherches des scientifiques marocains dans le cadre du renseignement et de l'espionnage scientifique, technologique et en termes d'innovation.

- Quand les financements nationaux existent, ils sont souvent faibles et objet de procédures complexes rendant difficile leur obtention. Ce qui décourage le plus souvent les chercheurs et innovateurs nationaux, causant ainsi des manques à gagner pour nos entreprises et pour notre économie. Au-delà de ces réalités, il y en a deux autres formes de dysfonctionnements qui semblent extrêmement importants parce qu'ils correspondent à deux données structurelles qui impactent aujourd'hui et impacteront demain de façon significative la relation entre l'Université et l'Entreprise, et donc la dynamique de l'innovation si aucune solution n'est trouvée pour les résoudre :

- La crise de production et de reproduction des scientifiques et des savants d'un niveau d'excellence et de compétence et d'une masse critique à la mesure des ambitions du pays dans tous les domaines et pour tous les chantiers structurants rentrant dans le cadre de la stratégie nationale de modernisation généralisée de l'économie et de la société.

- Et, la crise du modèle de croissance et de développement qui a atteint ses limites et dont la dynamique actuelle ne permet pas de générer la création d'un volume d'entreprises conforme à la diversité et à l'importance des grands chantiers structurants lancées par le pays. De ce fait, force est de constater que la relation entre l'Université et l'Entreprise souffre d'un déficit de création annuel d'entreprises par et dans l'économie nationale. Aussi, le volume de création n'est que de 80.0000 entreprises par an au moment où celui-ci est de 2.500.000 aux États-Unis et de près de 750.000 en France. Ce chiffre reste en dessous du potentiel de création d'activités économiques nouvelles. Il peut connaître une augmentation significative si la démographie des entreprises a été adossée aux grands chantiers structurants prioritaires autour desquels se doit de s'organiser la relation Université- Entreprise au Maroc.

Ces grands chantiers structurants prioritaires sont :

- Les nouveaux métiers mondiaux du Maroc qui font partie d'un pacte dit pacte national pour l'émergence industrielle. Il comprend les secteurs de l'offshoring, l'automobile, l'aéronautique, l'électronique, le textile, le cuir et l'agroalimentaire. Pour tous ces secteurs et métiers, le Maroc entend devenir une plateforme régionale de choix non seulement en Afrique, mais dans le monde.

- Les secteurs pour lesquels le Maroc dispose d'un avantage comparatif traditionnel : l'agriculture, la pêche, l'artisanat, le tourisme et l'industrie des phosphates. Pour tous ces secteurs, le pays dispose d'un plan fixant la stratégie, définissant les moyens pour sa réalisation, précisant l'horizon et la visibilité temporelle et les objectifs chiffrés datés à atteindre. Il s'agit, entre autres, du Plan Maroc Vert pour l'agriculture, du Plan Halieutis pour la pêche, de la vision 2030 pour le tourisme, le Plan artisanat et la nouvelle politique de valorisation des phosphates.

- Les secteurs stratégiques correspondant aux défis que le Maroc aura à affronter dans un avenir proche. Il s'agit des secteurs de l'énergie, l'eau,

- Les biotechnologies liées à la préservation et à la protection du patrimoine végétal et animal national, de la santé et des médicaments, des nouvelles technologies de l'information et des télécommunications et de l'environnement avec ses multiples composantes (assainissement, traitement des déchets solides et liquides, lutte contre la désertification et la déforestation, la prévention et la gestion des risques et des catastrophes naturelles,). Trois plans méritent d'être signalés à ce niveau : le plan solaire, la charte de l'environnement et du développement durable, la stratégie nationale pour la société de l'information et de l'économie numérique.

- Les secteurs de la banque, la finance, l'assurance et la bourse qui connaissent une modernisation soutenue, une concentration-centralisation avancée et une internationalisation poussée.

- Les grands chantiers d'infrastructures, notamment les plateformes industrielles intégrées, les routes, les autoroutes, les ports, les aéroports, les chemins de fer, la logistique de transport et les plateformes de logistique en général, le logement, l'électrification et l'adduction d'eau potable.

- Les chantiers relevant de l'économie sociale et solidaire pour la promotion et le développement de l'entrepreneuriat social, notamment les activités génératrices de revenus dans le cadre de l'Initiative Nationale pour le Développement Humain, les activités des associations et fondations de la microfinance et les activités des coopératives et des mutuelles.

- Les chantiers rentrant dans le cadre de l'agenda national pour le climat et le développement durable.

- Les chantiers ouverts dans le cadre de la feuille de route économique Africaine.

- Les grands chantiers d'accompagnement économique de la régionalisation avancée, notamment ceux inscrits dans le cadre des engagements pris en matière de mise en œuvre du Nouveau Modèle de Développement des Provinces du Sud du Royaume.

- Enfin, les chantiers ouverts dans le cadre de la promotion du capital immatériel, et notamment dans les domaines de la culture, des arts et du patrimoine.

C'est autour de ces chantiers prioritaires que doivent s'organiser et se structurer des partenariats Universités-Entreprises solides, avec leurs déclinaisons territoriales au niveau des douze régions du pays, en vue de hisser toutes ces régions au rang de véritables pôles de compétitivité et d'excellence par le renforcement de leurs capacités en matière de recherche et de l'innovation.

Cette perspective doit conduite, cependant, à élargir le champ du partenariat entre les Universités et les Entreprises pour inclure les Régions, ainsi que par un décloisonnement de la recherche appliquée et de l'innovation entre les secteurs publics, privés et les territoires par l'institutionnalisation et la pérennisation de leurs relations de coopération par l'établissement de passerelles au moyen de la contractualisation.

II- Pistes pour l'avenir

L'examen des dysfonctionnements que connait le partenariat Universités-Entreprises dans ses relations avec l'innovation et la présentation des grands chantiers structurants pouvant et devant faire l'objet de ce partenariat montrent que les défis sont immenses, nombreux et complexes à maitriser et à réguler. Par conséquent, il faut changer radicalement de démarche et explorer de nouveaux axes d'amélioration et des pistes audacieuses pour l'avenir de ce partenariat pour l'innovation.

Ces axes d'améliorations et ces pistes de transformation sont de plusieurs ordres.

1. Il faut d'abord une volonté politique nationale plaçant la recherche et l'innovation à un haut niveau de la décision à savoir celui du Chef de l'État ou du Chef du Gouvernement, comme c'est le cas dans tous les pays qui ont réussi à hisser la recherche et l'innovation à des niveaux mondiaux élevés.
2. La traduction de cette volonté politique par la création d'une instance nationale qui s'érige en un cadre permanent assurant un pilotage institutionnel unifié qui coordonne entre tous les intervenants et mutualise les ressources humaines et matérielles mobilisées par l'ensemble des composantes de l'écosystème national de recherche et d'innovation. C'est le cas de la Jordanie avec le Conseil Supérieur des Sciences et de la Technologie, de Mauritius Recherche Council pour les Iles Maurice et du Conseil National de la science, et de la Technologie présidé par le Président de la République de Corée du Sud pour ne citer que ces trois exemples.
3. Cette instance nationale doit élaborer une véritable stratégie nationale de la recherche et de l'innovation qui part des dysfonctionnements identifiés, des priorités économiques nationales fixées et des exigences imposées par la nouvelle révolution postindustrielle.
4. Cette stratégie doit être portée pas des programmes phares fixant des objectifs précis, comme c'est le cas au Rwanda, en Malaisie, en Turquie, au Portugal et au Brésil, mais aussi de la Chine avec le programme

« Made in China 2015 », de l'Allemagne avec « industrie 4.0 », des États-Unis avec « National Network for manufacturing innovation » du Royaume-Uni avec la « High Value Manufacturing Catapult », de la Corée du Sud avec « Manufactoring industrie innovation3.0 stratégie » ou encore de la France avec le très ambitieux programme dit « Industrie du futur ». Comme on peut le constater, tous ces programmes ne concernent que le secteur industriel et les entreprises de ce secteur.

5. Cette stratégie nationale doit être portée par une nouvelle ambition pour le Maroc en matière de recherche et d'innovation, compatible avec les objectifs en termes de modernisation économique généralisée et en phase avec les nouvelles responsabilités régionales et internationales du pays.
6. Enfin, former des scientifiques et produire des inventeurs. À ce niveau les besoins du pays sont importants, mais ses capacités sont limitées et les moyens alloués à la recherche et à l'innovation sont insuffisants.

Pour réussir à relever ces défis, il est nécessaire et au préalable, d'identifier les besoins en concertation avec les entreprises et les territoires, valoriser davantage l'apport des Marocains du Monde et arrêter un financement conséquent pour réaliser les grands chantiers industriels structurants.

Quand on voit que la Corée du Sud, la Chine, l'Allemagne et la France consacrent à leurs industriels respectivement 1.5, 1100, 200, et 2,3 Milliards d'euros, avec 0,8% du PIB seulement consacré par le Maroc à toute la recherche scientifique et technologique, on se rend bien compte qu'on est très loin des ambitions du pays en matière d'industrialisation.

Par conséquent, le pays doit augmenter de façon substantielle et volontariste le volume du financement public alloué à l'innovation, réorganiser le système actuel d'incitations adresser aux chercheurs et au secteur privé et promouvoir davantage le partenariat public-privé, public public, et Etat-Régions.

Enfin, il est impératif de bâtir des bases solides d'une gouvernance stratégique, compétitive, partenariale et responsable de la recherche scientifique et de l'innovation par un État stratégie qui définit de façon concertée avec les acteurs nationaux et territoriaux concernés les options, coordonne les actions et les programmes, en assure le suivi permanent, évalue les résultats et les retombées sur la compétitivité des secteurs concernés, opère les ajustements nécessaires en temps réel, contrôle la régularité, la conformité et l'usage de la valorisation de ces résultats. Le tout devant déboucher sur la reddition des comptes sur la base d'un système de récompense et de sanction si les objectifs ne sont pas atteints. La forme la plus appropriée de ce mode de gouvernance devrait être la contractualisation entre l'État, les structures de la recherche et l'innovation, les entreprises et les territoires.

C'est à partir de ces pistes et conformément à cette approche que le partenariat entre les entreprises et les universités pourra devenir un véritable levier futur de l'innovation au Maroc.

Références

Centre National de la Recherche Scientifique et Technique (CNRST), 2021, Production scientifique nationale en comparaison avec d'autres pays Scopus et Web of Science2016-2020, Rabat.

Commission Spéciale sur le Modèle de Développement, Le Nouveau Modèle de Développement, Avril 2021, Rabat.

Conseil Économique, Social et Environnemental, Rapport annuel 2017, Rabat.

Conseil Supérieur de l'Éducation, de la Formation et de la Recherche scientifique, 2014, la mise en œuvre de la Charte Nationale d'Éducation et de Formation 2000-2013, Acquis, déficits et défis, Rapport analytique, Rabat

Conseil Supérieur de l'Éducation, de la Formation et de la Recherche scientifique, 2017, Évaluation du cycle doctoral, pour promouvoir la recherche et le savoir, rapport thématique, Rabat.

Conseil Supérieur de l'Éducation, de la Formation et de la Recherche scientifique, 2017, Évaluation des facultés polydisciplinaires, Quelle politique, quel impact et quelle perspective, Rapport thématique, Rabat

Conseil Supérieur de l'Éducation, de la Formation et de la Recherche scientifique, 2018, l'évaluation de la recherche scientifique, Actes du colloque international des 6-7 décembre 2017, Rabat.

Conseil Supérieur de l'Éducation, de la Formation et de la Recherche scientifique, 2022, La recherche scientifique au Maroc, Analyse évaluative, Rapport sectoriel, Rabat.

Cherkaoui Mohamed (Sous la direction de), 2007, L'évaluation du système national de la recherche dans le domaine des sciences humaines et sociales, Ministère de l'Éducation Nationale, de l'Enseignement Supérieur, de la Formation des cadres et de la Recherche Scientifique, Rabat.

Janjar Mohamed-Sghir, 2019, Recherche scientifique au Maroc, Données et éléments structurels, Rapport au Conseil Économique, Social et Environnemental, Rabat.

Ministère de l'Industrie, du Commerce, de l'Investissement, et de l'Économie Numérique, 2015, Données sur la recherche scientifique et l'innovation au Maroc, Rabat.

Ministère de l'Enseignement Supérieur, la recherche Scientifique et l'Innovation, Intervention du Ministre à la Chambre des Conseillers, 2023, 28 avril, Rabat.

Secrétariat d'État chargé de la recherche scientifique, 2002, Recherche scientifique, bilan 1998-2002, Rabat.

Secrétariat d'État chargé de la recherche scientifique, 2007, Enquête nationale sur le potentiel scientifique et technique, Rabat.

The Economiste Intelligence Unit, 2018, Preparing for disruption, Technological Readiness Ranking, London.

QUELLE PLACE POUR L'INNOVATION TECHNOLOGIQUE DANS LA PLANIFICATION ET LA GESTION DES VILLES AFRICAINES ?

Caroline Sack Kendem

Plus de 50 % de la population mondiale vit en ville (UN, 2011) et les gouvernements des villes sont confrontés à toute une série de défis : ils doivent produire de la richesse et de l'innovation, mais aussi assurer la santé et la durabilité. Les villes doivent être vertes et sûres, mais aussi dynamiques sur le plan culturel (Landry, 2006). En outre, les villes doivent être en mesure d'intégrer des populations toujours plus nombreuses aux origines (ethniques, religieuses, socio-économiques) variées. Il y a peu, Barber (2013) soutenait et affirmait que « les maires gouvernent le monde ». L'accent actuellement mis par les administrations sur les villes en tant que centres de gouvernance s'accompagne d'un intérêt de la part du monde universitaire. La gouvernance urbaine est devenue un domaine capital, mais on commence à mettre cette discipline en rapport avec des disciplines axées sur la technologie et l'innovation. Les études sur l'innovation sont peu à peu reliées à la gouvernance urbaine en vue de définir des approches susceptibles de rendre les villes plus intelligentes (Nam & Pardo, 2011).

Rendre les villes plus intelligentes est une chose à laquelle personne ne peut s'opposer à partir du moment où cela se traduit par des solutions plus efficaces à tout un éventail de problèmes sociétaux. Les technologies intelligentes, les collaborations intelligentes, une population instruite et des institutions efficaces seraient nécessaires pour relever les défis des villes modernes. Ce discours sur les villes intelligentes se propage rapidement dans le monde entier. L'idée selon laquelle les villes sont le noyau du développement économique est répandue et, pour la gouvernance de la ville, cela signifie que les politiciens et les administrateurs de la ville devraient, au lieu d'essayer de résoudre tous les problèmes de la ville, renforcer la capacité des systèmes urbains à faire face à toute une série de problèmes et produire un vaste éventail de valeurs publiques (Landry, 2006).

L'urbanisation galopante en Afrique est l'une des transformations les plus importantes que les pays africains subiront au cours de ce siècle. En termes de population, elle devrait atteindre 60 % en 2050.

D'ici 2030, près d'un milliard d'Africains vivront en milieu urbain. Les embouteillages qui génèrent une pollution abondante deviennent problématiques pour la santé de ses habitants et ont un impact négatif direct sur l'activité économique.

Les conséquences d'une telle urbanisation peuvent être complexes et se recouper avec d'autres questions de politique de développement telles que le changement climatique, le logement, l'accès à l'eau, la migration, la mobilité...

Toutefois, si elle est bien gérée, l'urbanisation en Afrique a le potentiel de propulser la croissance, de créer des emplois, et de mettre fin à la pauvreté généralisée.

Le constat que l'on peut faire, c'est que l'urbanisation du continent africain est majoritairement subie et informelle.

Depuis 50 ans, des plans d'urbanisme ont été développés dans les villes d'Afrique subsaharienne sans résultat probant. Une des principales explications de cet échec est l'absence de mise à disposition de données de base sur la ville et ses habitants.

Des données existent, mais elles ne sont ni gérées ni utilisées. Or, l'information est une condition essentielle d'une planification urbaine maîtrisée. Elle permet de bâtir des systèmes fonciers et donc fiscaux assurant le fonctionnement et le financement des services communs des villes. Le financement des services commun de la ville est un élément essentiel pour un développement harmonieux de la ville permettant en retour un impact sur l'activité économique de la ville, mais aussi favorisant le bien-être des citoyens de ces villes.

En tant que pratiques de planification et de gestion des territoires, l'aménagement et l'urbanisme sont traversés par une transition numérique sans précédent, offrant un cadre intéressant pour analyser les transformations en cours.

La notion de ville intelligente s'entrecroise avec les enjeux contemporains de nos espaces habités et en premier lieu la ville et l'urbain. Depuis trente ans, l'usage des technologies numériques dans la vie quotidienne, l'économie et l'environnement ont construit un autre rapport aux espaces habités. Cette transition numérique de la société touche les organisations urbaines à divers titres : les communications et le « faire société », les rapports aux écosystèmes naturels et anthropiques, la valeur et la définition des ressources, les pratiques quotidiennes de l'espace, mais aussi le rapport au temps et à l'avenir.

La ville intelligente entraîne des modifications profondes au sein des villes actuelles sur des aspects organisationnels, sociétaux ou encore techniques et technologiques. Les nombreuses possibilités d'application offertes par les technologies numériques alimentent les capacités d'innovation et bousculent les systèmes, organisations et processus existants, notamment pour les collectivités territoriales..

En mobilisant les nouvelles technologies numériques, la ville intelligente cherche à répondre de manière transversale aux **enjeux du développement durable** au travers de ses différents piliers (économique, sociétal, environnemental et gouvernance).

Il en découle une approche systémique permettant d'optimiser services et ressources de la ville tout en replaçant l'humain et l'usager au centre des attentions.

Les termes et thématiques concernant la ville intelligente sont nombreux. Comment dès lors s'y retrouver, et quelles sont ses caractéristiques principales ? Soulignons encore une fois l'importance de la gestion des données, et les évolutions induites pour les collectivités territoriales en matière de service public, de relation aux citoyens, d'évolution des métiers et compétences et de cybersécurité.

La diffusion d'un modèle de ville « intelligente » est observable dans de nombreux territoires (grandes métropoles d'abord, puis métropoles intermédiaires, et aujourd'hui petites agglomérations), qui optent ou ont opté pour la mise en place de politiques ou démarches explicites favorisant certains principes de la ville « intelligente » : numérisation, recueil, stockage et partage de données urbaines, plateformes, dispositifs sociotechniques de gestion urbaine, en amont ou en aval des projets d'aménagement, à des échelles diverses (bâtiment, projet urbain, espace urbain dans son ensemble), etc.

Les avancées digitales et numériques offrent de nouvelles perspectives en matière de planification dans les villes en très forte croissance. Les technologies urbaines intelligentes peuvent ainsi apporter une contribution significative au développement durable des villes. On parle alors de ville intelligente.

Le concept de ville intelligente signifie qu'une ville utilise efficacement les NTIC, pour intégrer les besoins de sa communauté urbaine, en termes d'énergie et d'autres services publics (production, distribution et utilisation), de protection de l'environnement, de mobilité et de transport, de services aux citoyens (santé, éducation, services d'urgence, etc.) ; ceci dans le respect de la sécurité, tant des personnes que de leurs données personnelles, et l'utiliser comme moteur d'amélioration économique et sociale.

Ce concept de ville intelligente augmenterait également le déploiement de technologies et de solutions intelligentes dans les communautés rurales, contribuant au développement des entreprises et créant les conditions pour rendre les communautés intelligentes et attrayantes pour la population.

C'est ainsi que les nouvelles technologies intelligentes mises au service d'une ville créent de facto des conditions nécessaires pour le développement économique de nos villes.

Il est à noter que les stratégies de ville intelligente commencent par les gens, pas par la technologie. L'intelligence ne consiste pas seulement à installer des interfaces numériques dans les infrastructures traditionnelles ou à rationaliser les opérations de la ville. Il s'agit également d'utiliser la technologie et les données de manière ciblée pour prendre de meilleures décisions et offrir une meilleure qualité de vie.

Trois couches fonctionnent ensemble pour faire grandir une ville intelligente :

1/ Premièrement, la base technologique qui comprend une masse critique de smartphones et de capteurs connectés par des réseaux de communication à haut débit.

2/ Les applications spécifiques. La traduction des données brutes en alertes, informations et actions nécessite les bons outils, et c'est là qu'interviennent les fournisseurs de technologie et les développeurs d'applications.

3/ l'utilisation par les villes, les entreprises et le public. De nombreuses applications ne réussissent que si elles sont largement adoptées et parviennent à modifier les comportements.

L'objectif visé étant entre autres par exemple :

- d'encourager les gens à utiliser les transports en commun pendant les heures creuses,
- à changer d'itinéraire ;
- à se garer non plus en centre-ville surchargé, mais dans des rues annexes un peu plus loin ;
- à utiliser moins d'énergie et d'eau et/ ou à le faire à différents moments de la journée ;
- à réduire les contraintes sur le système de santé grâce à des soins personnels préventifs ;
- À donner à certains endroits (près de zones à haute densité scolaire par exemple) l'accès à internet gratuitement et pendant certaines heures…
- …..

Les villes deviennent donc intelligentes non seulement en ce qui concerne la manière dont elles peuvent automatiser certaines fonctions habituelles au service des particuliers, des bâtiments et des systèmes de circulation, mais aussi en ce qui concerne les solutions qui leur permettent de surveiller, de comprendre, d'analyser et de programmer la ville afin d'améliorer l'efficience, l'équité et la qualité de vie de ses citoyens.

Les recherches sur la question ne cessent dès lors de se multiplier dans les revues internationales et les livres. Cette littérature est riche, mais elle est aussi fragmentée.

La fragmentation se retrouve également dans la notion de gouvernance des villes intelligentes. Tout le monde s'accorde pour dire que les politiques des gouvernements ont un rôle majeur à jouer dans la promotion des villes intelligentes (Yigitcanlar et al., 2008). Cette idée s'intègre bien dans la perspective propre à la gestion publique, laquelle souligne que la résolution des problèmes sociétaux n'est pas simplement une question de définition des politiques appropriées, mais bien plus une question managériale d'organisation de collaborations solides entre le gouvernement et les autres parties prenantes (Torfing et al., 2012).

Des organismes institutionnels ont évalué comment les applications de la ville intelligente pourraient affecter diverses dimensions de la qualité de vie : sécurité, temps et commodité, santé, qualité de l'environnement, connectivité sociale et participation civique, emplois et coût de la vie.

Le large éventail de résultats reflète le fait que les applications fonctionnent différemment d'une ville à l'autre en fonction de facteurs tels que les systèmes d'infrastructure existants, la gestion des données…

Enfin, il est à signaler que l'utilisation d'une gamme d'applications à leur effet maximal pourrait potentiellement réduire les décès (d'homicide, de circulation routière et d'incendies) de 8 à 10 % selon certains experts. Dans une ville à forte criminalité avec une population de cinq millions d'habitants, cela pourrait signifier sauver jusqu'à 300 vies chaque année. Les incidents d'agression, de vol, de cambriolage et de vol de voiture pourraient être réduits de 30 à 40 %. En plus de ces mesures, il y a les avantages incalculables de donner aux résidents la liberté de mouvement et la tranquillité d'esprit.

Sur le plan de la sécurité d'une ville, la technologie même si elle n'est pas une solution miracle au crime, elle peut permettre l'utilisation des données pour déployer plus efficacement des ressources et du personnel rares. La cartographie de la criminalité en temps réel, par exemple, utilise l'analyse statistique pour mettre en évidence les tendances, tandis que la police prédictive va encore plus loin en anticipant la criminalité pour éviter les incidents avant qu'ils ne se produisent.

Lorsque des incidents se produisent, des applications telles que la détection de coups de feu, la surveillance intelligente et les systèmes de sécurité à domicile peuvent accélérer la réponse des forces de l'ordre.

Mais la police basée sur les données doit être déployée de manière à protéger les libertés civiles et à éviter de criminaliser des quartiers ou des groupes démographiques spécifiques.

Il est à retenir que l'essor des technologies numériques devrait avoir un impact significatif sur la gestion et la planification efficace de nos villes.

Les nouvelles technologies de l'information réconcilient les attentes et les besoins, parfois divergents, des acteurs de la ville : secteur public, secteur associatif, habitants, entreprises. La ville intelligente informe davantage ses habitants et les responsabilise. Connectés, ceux-ci deviennent, à leur tour, émetteurs d'information en utilisant les réseaux et les services urbains. L'intelligence de la ville est ainsi partagée avec ses habitants, dans le souci d'inscrire le développement de la ville dans la durée, la sobriété et l'optimisation des ressources.

Bien que le véritable impact de ces innovations et de bien d'autres à venir reste encore à découvrir, ces technologies ont le potentiel de transformer profondément notre façon de faire gérer et planifier nos villes.

Toutefois, il est à relever que si elles offrent de nouvelles possibilités, les nouvelles technologies ne peuvent cependant pas être considérées comme la panacée de la planification urbaine, qui reste une question éminemment politique, humaine, et très liée aux finances publiques.

HARNESSING OF TECHNOLOGY AND INNOVATION AFRICA: A CASE STUDY OF A VERTICALLY INTEGRATED COFFEE FRAMER ORGANISATION IN UGANDA

James Kizito-Mayanja

I- Introduction

Technology and innovation are critical factors of production. With climatic change taking root with significant impacts on the livelihood of mankind,,technology and innovation becomes very important. They both have a bearing on the United Nations Sustainable Development Goals (SDGs), more specifically SDGs 1, 2, 4, 5, 7, 8 ;12, 13, 15, 16 and 17 which put thrust on reducing poverty and hunger, gender equality, sustainable economic growth, industrialisation, reduction in inequality, sustainable production and consumption, inclusive societies, combating climatic change and its impacts, agroforestry as well as a global partnership for sustainable[5]. Africa Agenda 2063[6] also gives thrust on technological transformation if Africa is to unlock its potential. Reducing poverty and hunger especially in developing countries requires investment in agricultural research to develop short maturing and disease-resistant and drought tolerant varieties, agro-processing to add value to primary products which Africa is exporting to the developed world on one hand, and also provide employment to the ever-increasing number of graduates,, tax revenue as well as improved infrastructure on the other. Governments have strived to put in place a conducive enabling environment for the private sector to innovate, industrialise through new technologies including Information Communication Technology (ICT), Artificial Intelligence (AI) and strategic and business intelligence. For farmers, the need to strengthen their capacity

---

5. 2030 Agenda for Sustainable Development web.pdf (un.org)

6. Our Aspirations for the Africa We Want | African Union (au.int)

to produce, bulk, market, export competitively and also innovate through the use of solar energy to power their businesses is underpinned.

In Uganda, and more specifically in the coffee subsector, incremental production has been achieved in recent years on account of a conducive policy framework (National Coffee Policy, the Coffee Road map[7], National Trade Policy[8], Coffee Subsector Strategy) and more importantly political will. The National Development Plan 3 (Agro-industrialisation programme) which fits within the overall goal of Vision 2040 that is envisaged transforming the economy from a subsistence one to the lower middle-income status by 2040. This would require a transformative technology policy and strategy.

These initiatives adopted by Uganda are in line with Forum for African Economic Intelligence Associations' (FAAIE) objectives of contributing to the promotion of Economic Intelligence practices in Africa; disseminating scientific knowledge, strategic intelligence and African economic security information towards companies, administrations, territories, universities and research centers; development cooperation, share knowledge and know-how between the members of the forum; deepening the knowledge of the geostrategic dimensions of the African continent; assisting in the creation of national associations dedicated to Economic Intelligence in African countries; providing training in strategic intelligence and economic security for the benefit of public and private institutions, administrations, local authorities and universities; conducting studies and research in strategic intelligence and economic security; organising scientific, cultural activities and other events according to the objectives of the forum as well as creating an African Center for Studies and Research on Economic Intelligence.

1) This paper articulates what Ugandan government has done to harness technology and innovation in terms of an enabling policy and institutional environment. It focuses on a coffee farmers' organisation, National Union of Coffee Agribusinesses and Farm Enterprises (NUCAFE[9]) that has been able to mobilise farmers, added value to their coffee without losing their ownership along the value chain. NUCAFE has integrated vertically.

7. https://ugandacoffee.go.ug/coffee-roadmap

8. National Trade Policy (enhancedif.org)

9. https://www.nucafe.org

Along the coffee value chain and exported to both conventional and niche markets as well as engaging in roasting and branding with a number of coffee brands on the market.

II- National Policy and Development Frameworks for technology and Innovation

The government of Uganda has a deliberate strategy to transform the economy through Vision 2040[10] whereby Ugandan Society would be transformed from a Peasant to a Modern and Prosperous Country within 30 years. The Vision 2040 is conceptualised around strengthening the fundamentals of the economy to harness the abundant opportunities around the country. The opportunities include; oil and gas, tourism, minerals, ICT business, abundant labour force, geographical location and trade, water resources, industrialisation and agriculture. Government has (and is still) invested significantly in infrastructure for energy, transport, water, oil and gas and ICT; Science, Technology, Engineering and Innovation (STEI); urban development; human resource; peace, security and defence. The 2040 Vision would be achieved through Six (6) 5-year National Development Plans (NDPs).

Currently Uganda is implementing NDP 3 which has 18 development programmes. Its goal is 'To Increase Average Household Incomes and Improve the Quality of Life of Ugandans'.

> *'This goal is to be achieved under the overall theme of "Sustainable Industrialisation for inclusive growth, employment and sustainable wealth creation". This is in line with Uganda Vision 2040, EAC Vision 2050, Africa Agenda 2063 and the Sustainable Development Goals (SDGs)*[11]'.

Three (3) of the 18 development programmes of the NDP 3 emphasise (i) **Innovation, technology development and transfer** that aims to increase development, adoption, transfer and commercialisation of Technologies & Innovations through the development of a well-coordinated STI ecosystem (ii) **Digital Transformation** which aims to increase ICT penetration and use of ICT services for social and economic development. Expected results relate to : increasing ICT penetration; reducing the cost of ICT devices and services; creating more direct jobs in the sector; and increasing government services online

---

10. https://www.npa.go.ug/vision2040

11. https://www.npa.go.ug/development-plans/national-development-plan-ndp

(iii) **Agro-industrialisation** whose goal is to increase commercialisation and competitiveness of agricultural production and agro-processing. The expected results are: Increased total export value of processed agricultural commodities; coffee, tea, fish, dairy, meat, and maize (and its products) from USD 1 Billion to USD 4 Billion; Increased agricultural sector growth rate from 3.8 percent to 6.0 percent; Increased labour productivity in the agro-industrial value chain (value added, USD per worker) from USD 616 to USD 850; Increased number of jobs created in agro-industry along the value chain by 500,000; Reduction in the percentage of households dependent on subsistence agriculture as the main source of livelihood from 68.9 percent to 55 percent; Increased proportion of households that are food secure from 60 percent to 80 percent.

Uganda has also developed a National Industrial Policy (NIP)[12] which hinges on identifying strategic value chains and interventions that will contribute significantly to employment creation, increased value addition, promotion of import substitution and exports. The NIP prioritised 3 investment areas : (i) Agro-based industries including coffee (ii) Extractive-Based Manufacturing including fertilisers and (iii) Knowledge-Intensive Industries including pharmaceuticals, electronics, electricals and automobiles.

The specific objectives of the NIP include, among others, to increase and sustain the supply of quality raw materials for value addition; develop and to strengthen skills/human resource as well as accelerate development and use of research innovations and adoption of appropriate technologies. These are cemented by promoting resource-efficient and environmentally sustainable industrialisation. This paper falls directly under these objectives of the NIP and is also in line with the SDG of promoting inclusive, and sustainable industrialisation (efficient use of natural resources, clean production, and ways of combating climatic change effects and impacts.

In terms of technology infrastructure, there is the existence of Uganda Industrial Research Institute (UIRI[13]), Uganda National Council for Science & Technology (UNCST[14]) and CURAD (Consortium for University's

---

12. https://www.mtic.go.ug/national-industrial-policy-2020

13. https://www.uiri.go.ug

14. https://www.uncst.go.ug

Responsiveness for Agribusiness Development[15]) which handle research and value addition related interventions.

III. National Union of Coffee Agribusinesses and Farm Enterprises (NUCAFE[16])

NUCAFE is a coffee farmer organisation, legally registered as a company limited by guarantee. It is a union of about 155 Members (farmer associations, cooperatives, coffee estates, coffee-related companies) located throughout the country. It was established in 2003 after an evaluation of the services which were hitherto being delivered to members by Uganda Coffee Farmers Association. The outcome of the evaluation necessitated the change of name of the association and service portfolio to ensure that farmers retain ownership of their coffee along the coffee value chain in what is commonly known as the **Farmer Ownership Model (FOM)**. The model emphasises capacity building of the farmers to know the dynamics of the global coffee market and therefore be in position to make prudent decisions to sell coffee when they have added value to it. This has resulted into high returns to members of NUCAFE compared to those who are not members.

NUCAFE's mission is **"to develop and establish a sustainable market-driven system of coffee farmer associations and groups that are empowered to enhance their household incomes"**.

In 2008, NUCAFE advocated for a National Coffee Policy which, together with UCDA, MAAIF and other actors developed it in a participatory manner. It was approved in 2013 to guide the industry. NUCAFE has also innovated in other areas such as the use of solar power on the farm and also powering the coffee export and roasting facility at Kiwanga, Mukono District, Uganda.

Innovation and creativity have enabled the organisation to pioneer the first Geographical Indications (GI) project in the coffee subsector in Uganda where it has exported coffee from a specific location as a GI after registration with Uganda Registration Services Bureau (URSB), a government agency responsible for registering a trade mark. This initiative will bring more

---

15. https;//curadincubator.org

16. https://www.nucafe.org

money in the pockets of small farmers. NUCAFE has also pioneered the use of solar power to run an export processing and roasting facility.

1 Diagnosis of the Farmers' Situation : What was the Problem?

The first step was to identify which problem(s) coffee farmers were facing. These were followed by interventions. Farmers were selling unprocessed coffee to middlemen at less than 5% of the global value. They didn't have appropriate financing sources. At the global level, Uganda was earning less than 10% of the coffee trade value. This would result in a vicious cycle of poverty among farmers with no decent jobs and therefore insignificant contribution to the millennium development goals (MDGs) then.

Arrangements were made to mobilise farmers into viable economic units, assist them register legally as associations and then build their capacity in production, bulking and marketing. NUCAFE acted as a marketer of members' valued added coffee looking for attractive (niche) markets abroad. The FOM addresses the linkage between farmers/farmer groups and other actors such as processors, traders, exporters, foreign buyers, banks, insurance companies, agro-input suppliers, government ministries and agencies, and development partners. It also reflects how information flows among stakeholders. The services provided by the different service providers would be paid (except extension services provided by the government). Once the farmers know the clients they are to work with and are also linked to the market through NUCAFE, they would get better returns. This is what has transformed NUCAFE membership.

NUCAFE has also innovated by providing solar power to some of the members' coffee farms. This has also been pioneered at export and roasting facility in Kiwanga, Mukono District as illustrated in figure 7. These initiatives show innovation and use of technology on one hand but also visionary and result-oriented leadership. NUCAFE is led by relatively young agripreneurs who are able to do diagnostics of their clientele, look for lucrative markets and link their members to those markets. NUCAFE has Figure a state-of-the-art roasting and packaging unit for value-added coffee producing different roast and ground coffee brands (Omukago and Nucafe). All these initiatives show innovativeness and ability to know what the buyer's tastes and preferences are and the type of product which should be supplied.

IV- Lessons Learnt

- Innovation to address Climatic Change (Solar Energy) is critical
- Strong Policies & Development Frameworks on Technology and Innovation using a Public Private Partnership Approach and Academia/ research institute is pertinent
- Effective leadership of Organisations (visionary & succession planning) is a prerequisite for innovation
- Benchmarking with other countries (best practices) is crucial through experiential learning
- Increased investment in Education, Science, Technology and Research and Development is key
- Prioritising Strategic Areas for Investment and Innovation by both the public and private sectors is very vital
- There is need for increased Oversees Development Assistance through partnerships with development partners (SDG 17).

Conclusion

Harnessing technology and innovation in Africa are among the driving forces of the social and industrial transformation on the African continent. Prudent policies and strategies are key in achieving this. Linking Uganda's efforts to the regional and global development agenda is also critical to ascertain how the country together with other African countries are contributing to the African Agenda 2063 and the UN Sustainable Development Goals. A farmer organisation which has been able to influence policy, innovate and also link its member associations to niche markets is applauded. Visionary, result oriented and innovative leadership is key to social and economic transformation. The need to benchmark with countries which have successfully developed and implemented an innovation and technology transformation agenda is important. The FAAIE and the Open University of Dakhla become extremely important and relevant conduits in sharing knowledge about different innovations and technology in Africa and beyond. The digital transformation which is being embraced in Africa should target improved land and labour productivity especially in the agricultural sector that would spur agro-industrialisation, creation of jobs, economic growth and hence development.

II
INNOVATIONS ET DÉVELOPPEMENT ÉCONOMIQUE EN AFRIQUE

TRANSFORMATION NUMÉRIQUE EN MAURITANIE : OPPORTUNITÉS ET DÉFIS

El Moustapha Sidi Mohamed

Introduction

La Mauritanie vise à saisir les opportunités du digital pour transformer en profondeur les administrations publiques et mettre en place un cadre et des leviers incitatifs pour favoriser l'accès à la digitalisation au niveau des entreprises et des citoyens, générant ainsi un impact positif significatif sur les plans économique et social.

Le pays dispose d'un potentiel fort dans le domaine du numérique notamment par sa position géostratégique et par rapport aux pays du Sahel ayant des défis et des contraintes pour développer la connectivité Internet et accéder à la bande passante internationale.

La stratégie numérique de la Mauritanie serait de i) -appuyer les secteurs économiques clés dans leur transformation numérique pour une meilleure compétitivité et ii) - Développer un *écosystème* de l'innovation et une industrie du numérique centrée sur le capital humain, créateurs de forte valeur ajoutée et d'emplois.

Les technologies numériques ont la capacité d'élargir l'accès aux marchés et d'ouvrir plus de perspectives. C'est pour ces raisons que l'investissement dans le développement numérique constitue une part importante de l'action du gouvernement en faveur de la promotion de la croissance économique, de la réduction de la pauvreté et des inégalités.

Des études récentes ont démontré que l'aptitude d'un pays à utiliser les nouvelles technologies disponibles et à innover détermine sa performance économique et pourrait procurer d'immenses bénéfices socio-économiques (Banque mondiale, 2021).

La présente réflexion vise à passer en revue les piliers fondamentaux de la transformation numérique (I), d'apprécier les incidences de la transformation numérique (II), de faire l'état de lieux du numérique en Mauritanie (III) et enfin de présenter l'agenda national de développement en matière de la transition numérique (IV).

Piliers fondamentaux de la transformation numérique

La transformation numérique d'un pays (aussi appelée transformation digitale ou digitalisation) désigne le processus d'intégration des technologies numériques dans l'ensemble des activités économiques et sociales. Tous les pays du monde sont concernés par cette évolution qui s'applique aussi bien aux ménages (utilisation d'internet pour communiquer, télétravail, achats en ligne…), aux entreprises (e-commerce, solutions informatiques et d'Intelligence Artificielle…) et aux administrations publiques (dématérialisation des démarches administratives, identité numérique, open data…).

La transformation numérique des pays, notamment les pays africains dont la Mauritanie, n'est donc pas une fin en soi, mais représente un levier important pour leur développement économique qui se traduit par la croissance économique, la création d'emploi, le développement de compétences et le développement de nouvelles opportunités commerciales.

À l'échelle microéconomique, la digitalisation appelle l'ensemble des entreprises à se transformer afin de tirer avantage des opportunités qu'elle offre, plutôt que de la subir. Cette transformation digitale est au cœur des stratégies d'entreprise actuelles.

Sur le plan macroéconomique, la transformation numérique représente l'occasion, pour les pays, de dynamiser la croissance économique et l'industrialisation, de réduire la pauvreté et d'améliorer la vie des populations..

Pour accélérer la transformation digitale, cinq piliers sont fondamentaux :

1. Élaboration d'une stratégie numérique ;
2. Mise en place des *infrastructures* numériques ;
3. Innovation pour développer une offre riche de services ;
4. Formation et développement des compétences ;
5. Réglementation du commerce et du paiement électronique.

1/ Élaboration d'une Stratégie Numérique

Si les objectifs des stratégies numériques convergent vers l'amélioration de la qualité de vie, le développement économique, ou la simplification des procédures administratives, les voies de réalisation sont propres à chaque pays et prennent en compte de paramètres multiples qu'ils soient sociétaux, économiques, géographiques, réglementaires…

2/ Mise en place des infrastructures numériques

Il faut des infrastructures numériques pour assurer une connectivité partout et il s'agit notamment de :

- Backbones domestiques ou régionaux ;
- Réseaux d'accès mobile ou fixe ;
- Réseaux d'accès très haut débit avec la fibre sur des agglomérations importantes ;
- Réseaux d'accès pour les objets connectés.

Il faut des réseaux, mais il faut aussi développer et mettre en place des plateformes de services qui seront le support des offres de services numériques pour les clients grand public ou entreprises.

3/ Innovation et développement d'une culture collaborative

L'émergence d'écosystèmes numériques forts passera par des interactions fortes associant entreprises, start-up, universités, opérateurs, pouvoirs publics et financiers.

4 / Formation et développement des compétences

Les moyens pour parvenir à la digitalisation des services sont multiples, mais sans les compétences humaines nécessaires, nous ne pourrons réussir. Le constat montre que les pays les plus en avance dans la transformation digitale sont ceux qui ont le plus misé sur la formation et le développement des compétences de leurs jeunes et de leurs citoyens. Les compétences sont la clé pour pouvoir contribuer au processus d'innovation, mais aussi pour permettre le bon usage des nouveaux services numériques. La promotion de l'entrepreneuriat dans les domaines de l'informatique est cruciale pour la transformation numérique.

5/La réglementation du commerce et du paiement électronique

Dans le contexte de l'économie numérique, l'environnement réglementaire est un catalyseur de l'adoption des technologies numériques. Il englobe des domaines vastes et divers comme les transactions et les signatures électroniques, la protection des consommateurs, la législation antitrust, la protection des données, la cybersécurité et la réglementation en matière de responsabilité. Un cadre de réglementations plus complet peut encourager le recours aux transactions numériques en instaurant une plus grande confiance à l'égard des services numériques.

II- Impact de la transformation numérique sur les résultats économiques

La transformation numérique peut influencer la productivité, l'emploi et la croissance. L'amélioration de la connectivité numérique favorise la spécialisation de la production et les économies d'échelle, qui peuvent toutes deux augmenter la productivité et la croissance. De plus, elle peut contribuer à la résilience des pays en permettant aux entreprises et aux travailleurs de maintenir une partie de leur activité durant les crises (l'illustration parfaite durant la pandémie de COVID-19).

Les outils numériques peuvent améliorer l'efficience, la transparence et l'impact de la politique budgétaire en renforçant le recueil et l'analyse des données par les autorités, ainsi que leur efficacité dans la prestation des services publics et l'accroissement des recettes (*FMI, 2020)*.

La transformation numérique n'est pas pour autant une solution miracle pour obtenir de meilleurs résultats budgétaires, mais elle peut compléter et renforcer les réformes budgétaires structurelles sous-jacentes. Des progrès majeurs sont à réaliser pour généraliser les usages numériques et développer une industrie du numérique impactant.

III- Aperçu du Numérique en Mauritanie : les Principaux indicateurs

La Mauritanie regorge de potentialités économiques énormes. La Recherche & Développement (R&D) et l'innovation peuvent servir à exploiter et valoriser ce potentiel. La digitalisation, transversale à tous les secteurs économiques, offrant un grand potentiel d'innovation, surtout en ce qui concerne le développement, la création de plateformes, et l'utilisation de technologies numériques innovantes.

Le pays dispose d'un potentiel fort dans le domaine du numérique notamment par sa position géostratégique et par rapport aux pays du Sahel ayant des défis et des contraintes pour développer la connectivité Internet et accéder à la bande passante internationale.

Selon les différents index internationaux relatifs au numérique et comparativement au pays du G5 Sahel, la Mauritanie présente un potentiel d'amélioration important :

Tableau 1 : Indice de participation électronique 2020

Rang	Pays	Score
1	États Unis/Estonie/ Corée du Sud	1,00
74	Tunisie	0,69
107	Maroc	0,51
107	Burkina Faso	0,51
127	Sénégal	0,44
156	Mali	0,32
165	Niger	0,29
170	Tchad	0,26
186	Mauritanie	0,10

Source : ONU

Tableau 2 : Indice de développement des TIC 2017

Rang	Pays	Score
1	Islande	8,98
99	Tunisie	4,82
100	Maroc	4,77
142	Sénégal	2,66
151	Mauritanie	2,26
155	Mali	2,16
162	Burkina Faso	1,90
174	Tchad	1,27
–	Niger	–

Source : ITU

Tableau 3 : Network Readiness Index 2016-2021

Rang	Pays	Score
1	États Unis	100
45	Tunisie	86,23
50	Maroc	82,41
95	Tchad	40,44
96	Burkina Faso	39,98
100	Sénégal	35,85
132	Mauritanie	19,12
156	Niger	11,38
160	Mali	10,14

Source : WEF

Tableau 4 : Indice de cybersécurité 2020

Rang	Pays	Score
1	Singapore	6
78	Maroc	3,9
81	Tunisie	3,9
107	Sénégal	3,4
127	Mali	2,9
136	Mauritanie	2,5
139	Tchad	2,2
–	Burkina Faso	–
–	Niger	

Source : ITU

En dépit des avancés ces dernières années, en Mauritanie la qualité de service des réseaux Télécom et la couverture des réseaux mobiles « 4G » nécessitent des efforts d'amélioration supplémentaires. La Mauritanie reste en deçà de la moyenne des pays comparables en termes d'administration numérique. Le secteur privé du numérique essentiellement composé des opérateurs Télécom et timidement présentant quant au niveau des services numériques. Enfin, un besoin de développement des compétences et du capital humain en matière du numérique est indispensable.

IV- Agenda mauritanienne de transition numérique à l'horizon 2025

La stratégie de la Mauritanie à l'horizon 2025 vise de faire du Numérique et de l'Innovation un levier clé de modernisation de l'Administration, d'inclusion sociale et de renforcement de la compétitivité.

Cette vision est déclinée en trois leviers stratégiques : i) - Gouvernance et Cadre Réglementaire & Juridique, ii) - Compétences Numériques et iii) - Culture & Confiance Numérique (MTNIMA, 2022).

i- Gouvernance et cadre Réglementaire & Juridique

Le développement du secteur du numérique sur la période 2022-2025 devra être porté par une gouvernance qui permettra de coordonner au mieux l'action gouvernementale et les entités impliquées (agences, autorités, observatoires, institutions). Ce dispositif nécessite par ailleurs l'adaptation et la mise à jour du cadre législatif et réglementaire.

- **Sur le plan de la Gouvernance,** l'État mauritanien s'est doté d'un Haut Conseil du Numérique (HCN) qui permettra de suivre l'exécution de l'Agenda numérique 2022-2025. À court et moyen terme, la mise en place effective de l'Agence Numérique de l'État (AN-ETAT), de l'Agence Nationale de la Cybersécurité et de Certification électronique (ANCC), de l'Autorité de Protection des données à caractère personnel (APD) et de l'Observatoire National du Numérique (ONN) renforcera l'arsenal administratif national engagé dans l'exécution des projets de l'Agenda numérique 2022-2025 ;
- **Le cadre juridique relatif au numérique** a connu d'importantes avancées ces dernières années avec l'adoption de la loi d'Orientation relative à la Société Mauritanienne de l'Information (loi n° 2016-006), sur la cybercriminalité (loi n° 2016-007), sur la protection des données personnelles (loi 2017-020), sur les transactions électroniques (loi n° 2018-022), sur les moyens de paiement électroniques (loi n° 2021-014);

- De nouveaux textes sont également prévus comme la loi sur les start-up visant à promouvoir les start-up locales, et la loi sur l'Open-Gouvernement visant à organiser la relation entre les Mauritaniens et leur administration (avec des services publics dématérialisés et un accès élargi aux données publiques) ;
- Le secteur des télécommunications en Mauritanie est régulé par l'Autorité de Régulation (ARE) –agence multisectorielle dont la plupart des effectifs est dédiée à la régulation des télécoms. L'autorité effectue des contrôles sur le plan économique et technique, comme la qualité de services voix et data et les catalogues des offres de gros des opérateurs. L'ARE peut également imposer des remèdes aux acteurs du secteur pour encadrer la concurrence du marché.

ii- Compétences Numériques

Le développement des compétences numériques est un prérequis et un levier majeur pour :

✓ Sécuriser la mise en œuvre du programme de développement de l'économie numérique mauritanienne des cinq prochaines années ;
✓ Pouvoir généraliser les usages du numérique à travers toute la population, l'administration et les acteurs économiques ;
✓ Assurer un développement d'une industrie et d'un écosystème d'innovation & d'entrepreneuriat forts et durables.

Afin de pallier les faiblesses actuelles en matière de compétences numériques en Mauritanie, le plan de développement des compétences nécessite une synergie et une complémentarité forte entre plusieurs axes à savoir :

- L'adaptation et développement du cursus de formation universitaire et professionnelle en adéquation avec les besoins du marché ;
- Le renforcement des compétences numériques pour les usagers (administration, entreprises et citoyens) ;
- Le développement des compétences numériques comme un levier d'inclusion sociale, de reconvention professionnelle et plus généralement rendre l'éducation, l'enseignement et le savoir accessible à tous.

iii-Culture & Confiance Numérique

L'adoption du numérique passe avant tout par une culture généralisée et une confiance suffisante à l'usage du numérique.

La modification des pratiques pour intégrer l'usage du numérique ne devrait pas dépendre de l'âge, du niveau de formation, ni de la catégorie socio professionnelle. Il est important de développer cette culture pour toutes les franges de la population à travers deux axes importants :

- Le rapprochement du numérique à la population notamment la moins favorisée depuis leur jeune âge ;
- La sensibilisation à travers une communication étudiée et des programmes de formation spécifiques.

L'instauration de la confiance numérique passe par une garantie d'un haut niveau de confiance régissant les transactions dans l'espace cybernétique afin de permettre aux usagers, citoyens et entreprises de bénéficier des services en ligne et d'accepter le partage à distance de leurs données. Le Gouvernement Mauritanien est en train de se doter d'une stratégie nationale de sécurité de l'information et d'un cadre juridique permettant de lutter contre la cybercriminalité et aussi de protéger les données à caractères personnels.

Conclusion

Le rôle central que la Science, la Technologie et l'Innovation (STI) et la numérisation jouent dans le monde contemporain est surtout devenu évident au plus fort de la pandémie de COVID-19. La STI a été essentielle, entre autres : pour la prévention et le traitement de la crise sanitaire, y compris la mise au point de nouveaux vaccins ; pour fournir des moyens nouveaux et innovants d'apprentissage, de travail et de communication ; et pour permettre une croissance accélérée du commerce électronique et de la finance mobile.

L'économie numérique doit devenir une préoccupation majeure dans l'ensemble des politiques. Si l'économie numérique n'est considérée que comme l'affaire des régulateurs des technologies de l'information et de la communication ou d'un seul ministère de tutelle, sa capacité à contribuer à la transformation structurelle a peu de chances de se concrétiser. Tous les acteurs concernés devraient donc réfléchir à la numérisation et à la manière dont elle affecte leurs portefeuilles.

La Mauritanie possède un vivier humain de jeunes qui, par le développement de ses compétences dans le numérique, pourra constituer une véritable force du développement économique et social du pays.

Afin de se concentrer sur la réalisation de la transformation économique et des emplois de qualité en facilitant l'adoption et l'utilisation des technologies par les entreprises, le Gouvernement Mauritanien doit mettre en œuvre des réformes permettant, un partenariat avec le secteur privé, d'intégrer la culture de l'adoption et de l'utilisation des technologies, ainsi que le développement continu des compétences dans l'application des technologies de l'information et de la communication (TIC) et l'adoption des technologies par les entreprises.

Références bibliographiques

Banque européenne d'investissement (2021) « L'essor de l'économie numérique africaine », Document de travail février.

Banque mondiale (2021) « Les avantages du numérique pour les pays du Moyen-Orient et d'Afrique du Nord » Ouvrage.

Banque mondiale (2022) « Le secteur privé au centre de la transformation économique et de la création d'emplois » Rapport sur la situation économique en Mauritanie.

Commission Economique des Nations Unies pour l'Afrique (2019)

« Transformation numérique et diversification économique en Afrique centrale : enjeux, défis et opportunités » RAPPORT DE LA RÉUNION, Malabo, septembre.

Digital Impact Alliance (2020) « Libérer l'économie numérique en Afrique : Analyse comparative de la transformation numérique » Août.

Fonds Monétaire International (2020) « La transformation numérique en Afrique subsaharienne » Avril.

Ministère de la Transition numérique, de l'Innovation et de la Modernisation de l'Administration (2022) « Agenda National de Transition Numérique 2022-2025 » Mars.

Organisation des Nations Unies pour le développement industriel (2015)

« Rôle de la technologie et de l'innovation dans le développement inclusif et durable », Rapport sur le développement industriel 2016, Vue d'ensemble.

Secrétariat OEACP (2022) « MSP Rapport de recommandations politiques Mauritanie » - Programme OEACP R&I Mécanisme de soutien aux politiques (MSP), Bruxelles. Janvier

Union Africaine, « Stratégie de Transformation Numérique pour l'Afrique 2020-2030 ».

CARENCES ET OPPORTUNITÉS DE L'INNOVATION AU TCHAD

Adoum Youssouf Ibrahim

Introduction

L'innovation peut être définie comme le processus de création, de développement et de mise en œuvre de nouvelles idées, de produits, de services ou de processus, qui génèrent de la valeur pour les individus, les entreprises et la société dans son ensemble. Les apports de l'innovation pour un pays comme le Tchad sont nombreux, notamment en termes de développement économique, de création d'emplois, d'amélioration de la qualité de vie, de renforcement de la compétitivité, et de promotion du progrès social.

Cependant, malgré ces avantages, le Tchad reste en retard dans les différents indicateurs de l'innovation au niveau mondial. Selon le Global Innovation Index de 2021, le Tchad se situe à la 151ème place sur 132 pays évalués, avec des performances relativement faibles dans les domaines tels que les infrastructures, la formation, la recherche, les dépenses en R&D, et les résultats économiques liés à l'innovation. Ce retard peut s'expliquer par divers facteurs, tels que le manque de financement, la faible capacité d'absorption des nouvelles technologies, le manque d'infrastructures adaptées, le faible niveau d'éducation et de formation, ainsi que les contraintes institutionnelles et réglementaires.

Par conséquent, pour relever ce défi et améliorer son niveau d'innovation, le Tchad doit renforcer ses politiques et stratégies nationales en matière d'innovation, favoriser l'émergence de nouvelles entreprises innovantes, renforcer les partenariats public-privé, promouvoir l'éducation et la formation en sciences et technologies, et renforcer son cadre institutionnel et réglementaire. Cela permettra de stimuler l'innovation dans le pays et de contribuer à son développement économique et social.

Dans ce contexte, une analyse des carences et des opportunités de l'innovation au Tchad s'avère nécessaire. La première partie de notre étude dresse un état des lieux de l'innovation au Tchad, en identifiant les différents domaines d'application de l'innovation et les acteurs impliqués. La seconde partie met en évidence les principales carences et causes qui empêchent l'innovation de se développer au Tchad, notamment le manque de financement, d'infrastructures et de compétences techniques, ainsi que l'instabilité politique et sécuritaire. Nous soulignons ainsi les trois facteurs majeurs qui entravent le développement de l'innovation au Tchad : le manque de financement, l'absence d'un environnement favorable à l'innovation et la faible capacité de recherche et développement. Ce texte apporte ainsi un éclairage sur les défis à relever pour développer l'innovation au Tchad.

I- Contexte de l'innovation au Tchad

Dans cette partie, nous allons dresser un état des lieux de l'innovation au Tchad. Nous allons identifier les différents domaines d'application de l'innovation ainsi que les acteurs impliqués dans ce processus.

a. État des lieux de l'innovation au Tchad

Le Tchad est un pays en développement qui fait face à de nombreux défis économiques et sociaux. L'innovation est encore à ses balbutiements au Tchad. En effet, le pays est confronté à de nombreux défis, tels que l'instabilité politique, l'insuffisance de financement, le manque de ressources humaines qualifiées, ainsi que l'accès limité aux technologies de l'information et de la communication.

Malgré ces défis, le Tchad a réalisé quelques progrès en matière d'innovation ces dernières années, notamment dans le domaine de la santé, où des initiatives locales ont été lancées pour améliorer l'accès aux soins de santé dans les zones rurales. De plus, des start-up ont émergé dans des domaines tels que la technologie de l'information et de la communication, l'agriculture et l'énergie.

Cependant, le pays reste en retard dans de nombreux indicateurs de l'innovation, tels que l'investissement dans la recherche et développement, la formation de personnel qualifié, l'adoption des technologies de pointe, la protection des droits de propriété intellectuelle, et l'ouverture aux échanges internationaux.

En termes de recherche et développement, le Tchad ne dispose pas d'un système de recherche structuré et performant, avec un faible financement public et peu de collaboration entre les universités et les entreprises. En outre, le manque de personnel qualifié dans les domaines de la science, de la technologie et de l'innovation constitue un obstacle majeur au développement de l'innovation dans le pays.

En ce qui concerne l'adoption des technologies de pointe, le Tchad est confronté à des problèmes de connectivité limitée à Internet et de faible utilisation des technologies mobiles. Par conséquent, la transformation numérique des entreprises et des administrations est très limitée.

Enfin, en ce qui concerne l'ouverture aux échanges internationaux, le Tchad est l'un des pays les moins intégrés dans l'économie mondiale. Le pays a peu de liens commerciaux avec d'autres pays, et la propriété intellectuelle est faiblement protégée, ce qui décourage les investissements étrangers.

En somme, l'innovation au Tchad reste un défi majeur pour le développement du pays. Des mesures doivent être prises pour renforcer les capacités de recherche et développement, améliorer l'accès aux technologies de pointe, encourager l'entrepreneuriat et la création de start-up, et renforcer l'intégration économique internationale.

b. Les domaines d'application de l'innovation

Au Tchad, l'innovation peut être appliquée dans divers domaines tels que l'agriculture, l'énergie, la santé, l'éducation, les TIC, le tourisme, etc. ci-dessous quelques exemples concrets d'application :

- Agriculture : Au Tchad, l'agriculture occupe une place prépondérante dans l'économie nationale. Les agriculteurs locaux peuvent bénéficier de technologies innovantes pour améliorer leur productivité et leur rentabilité. Par exemple, l'utilisation de semences améliorées et de fertilisants organiques peut augmenter les rendements agricoles. Les systèmes d'irrigation modernes peuvent également permettre aux agriculteurs de produire plus de cultures dans des zones arides.
- Énergie : L'énergie est un enjeu majeur pour le développement économique et social du Tchad. Les innovations peuvent aider à fournir une énergie abordable, fiable et propre pour les populations

locales. Par exemple, l'utilisation de panneaux solaires peut fournir de l'énergie électrique pour les zones rurales éloignées qui ne sont pas connectées au réseau national.

- Santé : Les innovations dans le domaine de la santé peuvent aider à améliorer l'accès aux soins de santé pour les populations du Tchad. Par exemple, la télémédecine peut être utilisée pour permettre aux patients d'avoir des consultations avec des médecins spécialistes à distance. Des applications mobiles peuvent également être développées pour aider à diagnostiquer et à traiter les maladies.
- Éducation : L'innovation peut également être appliquée pour améliorer l'éducation au Tchad. Par exemple, les technologies éducatives peuvent aider à fournir un accès à l'éducation à distance pour les populations éloignées. Des logiciels d'apprentissage en ligne peuvent également aider les élèves à améliorer leurs compétences en mathématiques, en sciences et en langues étrangères.
- TIC : Le secteur des TIC est en pleine croissance au Tchad. Les innovations peuvent aider à stimuler le développement de ce secteur en fournissant des solutions pour les entreprises locales et en créant de nouveaux emplois. Par exemple, des start-up peuvent développer des applications mobiles pour les consommateurs locaux ou des solutions de paiement en ligne pour les entreprises.
- Tourisme : Le tourisme est un secteur clé pour l'économie du Tchad. Les innovations peuvent aider à développer le potentiel touristique du pays en améliorant les infrastructures et les services touristiques. Par exemple, des applications mobiles peuvent être développées pour aider les touristes à planifier leur voyage ou à trouver des attractions locales. Des solutions innovantes peuvent également être développées pour la gestion des déchets et la préservation de l'environnement dans les zones touristiques.

En résumé, l'innovation peut être appliquée dans de nombreux domaines au Tchad pour aider à résoudre les défis économiques, sociaux et environnementaux du pays. Les exemples ci-dessus montrent comment les innovations peuvent améliorer la productivité, la rentabilité, l'accès aux soins de santé, l'éducation, le développement du secteur des TIC et du tourisme.

c. Les acteurs de l'innovation au Tchad

Les acteurs de l'innovation au Tchad comprennent des institutions publiques, des organisations de la société civile, des entreprises privées et des universités. Cependant, la plupart de ces acteurs ont des capacités limitées en matière d'innovation et ont besoin d'un soutien accru pour développer leur potentiel.

Il existe au Tchad plusieurs institutions publiques qui s'occupent de l'innovation et de la recherche. Parmi les plus importantes, on peut citer :

- Le Ministère de l'Enseignement Supérieur, de la Recherche et de l'Innovation : il est chargé de la coordination et de la supervision de la recherche scientifique et technologique dans le pays.
- Le Ministère des Postes et de l'Économie Numérique du Tchad joue un rôle important dans la promotion de l'innovation dans le pays. Il est chargé de développer et mettre en œuvre la politique du gouvernement en matière de développement des technologies de l'information et de la communication (TIC) et de l'économie numérique. Le Ministère travaille en étroite collaboration avec les acteurs du secteur privé, les universités et les instituts de recherche pour stimuler l'innovation et le développement de l'écosystème numérique au Tchad. Il soutient également la création de start-up et d'entreprises innovantes, en leur offrant des facilités fiscales et administratives. En outre, le Ministère est en charge de la réglementation et de la supervision du secteur des TIC et de l'économie numérique, ce qui contribue à créer un environnement favorable à l'innovation et à l'entrepreneuriat.
- Le Ministère de l'Économie et de la Planification du Tchad a un rôle important dans la promotion de l'innovation au Tchad. Il est responsable de l'élaboration et de la mise en œuvre des politiques économiques et de développement du pays. Dans ce cadre, il peut soutenir financièrement des projets innovants, promouvoir l'investissement dans des secteurs clés de l'innovation, faciliter la création d'entreprises innovantes et encourager la recherche et le développement technologique. Il peut également travailler en collaboration avec d'autres ministères et institutions pour promouvoir l'innovation de manière transversale et intégrée dans le développement économique du pays.

- Le Centre National de la Recherche Scientifique et Technologique (CNRST) : il a pour mission de coordonner et de promouvoir la recherche scientifique et technologique au Tchad.
- L'Agence de Développement des Technologies de l'Information et de la Communication (ADETIC) : elle est chargée de la promotion et de la régulation des technologies de l'information et de la communication dans le pays.
- L'Agence Nationale des Investissements et des Exportations (ANIE) : elle a pour mission de promouvoir les investissements privés et publics dans les secteurs économiques du pays, y compris dans les domaines de la recherche et de l'innovation.
- La Chambre de Commerce, d'Industrie, d'Agriculture, des Mines et d'Artisanat du Tchad : elle a pour mission de promouvoir le développement économique du pays, y compris par la promotion de l'innovation et de la recherche.
- Les différentes universités et les centres de recherches publics.

À côté de ses institutions publiques, nous pouvons également citer quelques initiatives associatives qui contribuent à impulser l'innovation au Tchad :

- Wenaklabs est un incubateur de start-up tchadien fondé en 2018 à N'Djamena. Il vise à soutenir les entrepreneurs et les jeunes talents tchadiens en leur fournissant un espace de travail, des formations et des ressources pour développer leurs idées d'entreprise. Wenaklabs organise également des événements pour favoriser l'échange d'idées et les collaborations entre entrepreneurs.
- La Maison de l'Innovation Sociale Numérique du Tchad est une initiative mise en place par l'association AIESEC N'Djamena en partenariat avec l'incubateur tchadien GoTIC. Elle a pour objectif de promouvoir l'innovation sociale et numérique au Tchad en offrant des formations, des ateliers, des événements et un espace de coworking aux jeunes entrepreneurs et innovateurs tchadiens. La Maison de l'Innovation Sociale Numérique du Tchad est située à N'Djamena et a été inaugurée en 2019.
- L'Association Tchadienne d'Intelligence Economique (ATIE) joue un rôle important dans la promotion de la culture de l'innovation au Tchad.

Depuis sa création, elle a travaillé à sensibiliser les entreprises, les organisations publiques et la société civile à l'importance de l'innovation pour le développement économique et social du pays. L'ATIE a mis en place des initiatives pour promouvoir l'entrepreneuriat et l'innovation, telles que des programmes de formation pour les jeunes entrepreneurs et des concours de plan d'affaires pour encourager l'émergence de projets innovants. Elle organise également des événements de networking pour permettre aux acteurs du secteur de l'innovation de se connecter et de collaborer. De plus, l'ATIE joue un rôle de conseil auprès des entreprises et des organisations publiques pour les aider à développer des stratégies d'innovation et à mettre en place des processus d'innovation efficaces. Elle fournit des informations sur les tendances et les développements du marché, ainsi que sur les nouvelles technologies et les meilleures pratiques en matière d'innovation. L'ATIE travaille à sensibiliser les décideurs politiques à l'importance de l'innovation et à la nécessité de créer un environnement propice à l'innovation au Tchad. Elle plaide pour des politiques et des réglementations qui favorisent l'innovation et l'entrepreneuriat, ainsi que pour des investissements publics et privés dans la recherche et le développement. Dans l'ensemble, l'ATIE apporte une contribution précieuse à la promotion de la culture de l'innovation au Tchad. Son travail contribue à stimuler l'entrepreneuriat, à encourager l'émergence de projets innovants et à favoriser le développement économique et social du pays.

Il convient de noter cependant que la plupart de ces institutions souffrent d'un manque de financement et de ressources humaines, ce qui limite leur capacité à mener des projets de recherche et d'innovation à grande échelle.

II- Les carences de l'innovation au Tchad

Dans cette partie, nous allons mettre en évidence les principales carences et causes qui empêchent l'innovation de se développer au Tchad.

Il existe plusieurs causes à la faiblesse de développement de l'innovation au Tchad, notamment :

Le manque de financement : le financement de l'innovation est essentiel pour la recherche et le développement de nouvelles technologies. Cependant, le Tchad fait face à un déficit de financement de l'innovation en raison de la faiblesse de l'économie nationale.

Le manque d'infrastructures : l'innovation nécessite des infrastructures modernes telles que des laboratoires de recherche, des centres d'incubation et des espaces de coworking. Le Tchad souffre du manque d'infrastructures adéquates pour soutenir la recherche et le développement.

Le manque de compétences techniques : pour innover, il est nécessaire de disposer de compétences techniques solides. Cependant, le système éducatif tchadien ne met pas suffisamment l'accent sur le développement de ces compétences, ce qui limite la capacité de la jeunesse à innover.

L'instabilité politique et sécuritaire : l'instabilité politique et sécuritaire au Tchad peut avoir un impact négatif sur l'environnement des affaires et l'innovation. Elle peut décourager les investisseurs et les partenaires de collaborer avec des entreprises tchadiennes.

Principalement, nous relevons trois facteurs qui entravent le développement de l'innovation au Tchad :

a. Le manque de financement de l'innovation :

Le financement est un élément clé pour encourager l'innovation. L'un des principaux obstacles à l'innovation au Tchad est le manque de financement. Les institutions financières sont souvent réticentes à investir dans des projets innovants en raison de l'incertitude quant à leur rentabilité. De plus, la plupart des entreprises et des entrepreneurs n'ont pas accès à des sources de financement suffisantes pour développer leurs idées et leurs projets.

b. L'absence d'un environnement favorable à l'innovation :

Un autre obstacle majeur à l'innovation au Tchad est l'absence d'un environnement favorable à l'innovation.

Un environnement favorable à l'innovation est essentiel pour stimuler la créativité et l'innovation. Malheureusement, le Tchad ne dispose pas d'un tel environnement. Les politiques gouvernementales en matière d'innovation sont limitées et peu coordonnées, et le cadre réglementaire est souvent instable. Par ailleurs, le manque de ressources humaines qualifiées, notamment en matière de recherche et développement, limite également la capacité d'innovation du pays.

c. La faible capacité de recherche et développement :

Le Tchad souffre d'un manque de capacités en recherche et développement. Les universités et les centres de recherche manquent souvent de financement et de ressources pour mener des recherches de qualité.

La faible capacité de recherche et développement est donc un défi majeur pour l'innovation au Tchad. La plupart des entreprises et des institutions publiques n'ont pas suffisamment de personnel qualifié pour mener des activités de R&D, ce qui limite leur capacité à développer de nouvelles technologies et à innover. Le secteur privé, quant à lui, est peu enclin à investir dans l'innovation en raison des risques élevés et de la faible rentabilité à court terme.

III. Les opportunités pour l'innovation au Tchad

Malgré les carences susmentionnées, le Tchad dispose d'un certain nombre de potentialités économiques et technologiques qui peuvent favoriser l'innovation. Ces potentialités comprennent notamment la richesse en ressources naturelles, la diversité culturelle, les opportunités dans le domaine des TIC, etc.

Bien que le Tchad soit confronté à des carences importantes en matière d'innovation, il existe des opportunités considérables pour stimuler l'innovation et favoriser le développement économique et social du pays. Pour y parvenir, il est crucial de combler les lacunes en matière de financement, de créer un environnement propice à l'innovation et de favoriser la collaboration entre les acteurs de l'innovation.

a. Les potentialités économiques et technologiques du Tchad

Le Tchad dispose de plusieurs potentialités économiques et technologiques qui peuvent être développées grâce à l'innovation. En voici quelques exemples :

- L'agriculture : Le Tchad possède un potentiel agricole important grâce à son climat favorable et ses terres fertiles. Cependant, le secteur agricole est confronté à plusieurs défis tels que le manque d'infrastructures, le manque de financement et le manque de technologies modernes. L'innovation dans ce domaine peut contribuer à l'amélioration de la productivité agricole, à la modernisation des infrastructures et à la création de nouvelles filières de production. Des exemples de projets innovants en agriculture comprennent l'utilisation de drones pour la surveillance des cultures, la mise en place de systèmes d'irrigation modernes et la création de coopératives agricoles pour améliorer la commercialisation des produits.

- Les énergies renouvelables : Le Tchad dispose d'un potentiel important en énergies renouvelables, en particulier l'énergie solaire. L'innovation dans ce domaine peut contribuer à la mise en place de systèmes d'énergie solaire à grande échelle pour alimenter les zones rurales en électricité, ainsi qu'à la création de nouvelles industries liées aux énergies renouvelables. Des exemples de projets innovants dans ce domaine comprennent l'utilisation de mini-grids solaires pour fournir de l'électricité aux communautés rurales et l'installation de panneaux solaires sur les bâtiments publics pour réduire les coûts énergétiques.
- Les technologies de l'information et de la communication : Le Tchad dispose d'un marché des TIC en croissance avec un potentiel de développement important. L'innovation dans ce domaine peut contribuer à la création d'emplois, à l'amélioration de l'accès à l'information et l'assistance technique.
- Les ressources minières : Le Tchad possède des ressources minières importantes, telles que le pétrole, le gaz et l'uranium. L'innovation dans ce domaine peut contribuer à l'amélioration de l'exploration et de l'exploitation des ressources, ainsi qu'à la création de nouvelles industries liées à l'exploitation minière. Des exemples de projets innovants dans ce domaine comprennent l'utilisation de drones pour la cartographie géologique et la surveillance de l'environnement, ainsi que l'utilisation de technologies de pointe pour l'extraction et le traitement des minerais.

En résumé, le Tchad dispose de nombreuses potentialités économiques et technologiques qui peuvent être développées grâce à l'innovation. Car elle peut contribuer à améliorer la productivité, à créer des emplois, à moderniser les infrastructures et à stimuler la croissance économique. Cependant, pour réaliser pleinement ce potentiel, il est nécessaire d'investir dans la recherche et le développement, de favoriser l'entrepreneuriat et d'améliorer l'accès à la formation et au financement.

b. La création d'un cadre propice à l'innovation

La création d'un cadre propice à l'innovation est essentielle pour stimuler l'innovation au Tchad. Cela implique des politiques gouvernementales coordonnées en matière d'innovation, des réglementations claires et stables, ainsi que des investissements dans la recherche et le développement. La promotion de la collaboration entre les différents acteurs de l'innovation, tels que les entreprises, les universités et les centres de recherche, est également essentielle.

Il est essentiel de souligner que la création d'un cadre propice à l'innovation nécessite une volonté politique forte et un engagement à long terme. Les politiques publiques doivent encourager l'innovation en offrant des incitations fiscales et financières, en facilitant l'accès aux financements et en favorisant la collaboration entre les acteurs de l'innovation. La mise en place d'un écosystème favorable à l'innovation nécessite également une sensibilisation et une éducation accrues à l'importance de l'innovation pour le développement économique et social du pays.

c. Les partenariats public-privé pour le développement de l'innovation

Les partenariats public-privé peuvent être un moyen efficace de stimuler l'innovation au Tchad. Les partenariats entre les entreprises et les institutions publiques de recherche peuvent contribuer à combler le déficit de financement de l'innovation en partageant les risques et les coûts liés à la recherche et au développement, et ainsi de bénéficier d'une expertise et de ressources complémentaires. Les entreprises peuvent de ce fait accéder à des connaissances et des technologies de pointe, tandis que les institutions publiques de recherche peuvent obtenir des financements pour leurs projets.

Conclusion

En conclusion, l'innovation est un enjeu majeur pour le développement économique et social du Tchad. Cependant, plusieurs obstacles entravent son développement, notamment le manque de financement, l'absence d'un environnement favorable et la faible capacité de recherche et développement. Malgré ces carences, le Tchad dispose de nombreuses opportunités pour stimuler l'innovation, notamment grâce à ses potentialités économiques et technologiques et à la création d'un cadre propice à l'innovation. Les partenariats public-privé peuvent également être un moyen efficace pour stimuler l'innovation et combler le déficit de financement.

Pour l'avenir de l'innovation au Tchad, il est crucial de poursuivre les efforts visant à renforcer les capacités de recherche et développement, à améliorer l'environnement réglementaire et à promouvoir les partenariats public-privé. Les autorités doivent également encourager les initiatives innovantes en fournissant des incitations financières, des formations et des compétences nécessaires pour la réussite de l'innovation.

En somme, l'innovation est une clé de voûte pour le développement économique et social du Tchad. Il est impératif pour le gouvernement et les partenaires internationaux de travailler ensemble pour surmonter les obstacles à l'innovation et créer un environnement favorable à son développement afin de réaliser le plein potentiel de l'innovation pour le bien-être de la population tchadienne.

Références bibliographiques

«Au Tchad, un laboratoire d'innovations pour développer l'agriculture» (Le Monde, 15/06/2017) - Consulté le 14/10/2022 sur : https://www.lemonde.fr/afrique/article/2017/06/15/au-tchad-un-laboratoire-d-innovations-pour-developper-l-agriculture_5144651_3212.html

«Innovation : Les start-up tchadiennes ont leur espace de coworking» (Alwihda Info, 16/12/2020) - Consulté le 10/10/2022 sur : https://www.alwihdainfo.com/Innovation-Les-start-up-tchadiennes-ont-leur-espace-de-coworking_a94317.html

"Innovation systems in Africa: the Chad case study" de Abdelkader Djeflat et Khaled Bouabdallah, International Journal of Innovation and Regional Development, vol. 5, n° 2, 2013.

«Innovation: Quelles perspectives pour l'Afrique?» (Jeune Afrique, 13/06/2020), Consulté le 02/12/2023 sur : https://www.jeuneafrique.com/1006754/economie/innovation-quelles-perspectives-pour-lafrique/

«Innovative entrepreneurship in Chad: conceptualisation, context and practice» de Sanoussi Toudou, Journal of Entrepreneurship in Emerging Economies, vol. 8, n° 1, 2016.

« Le secteur privé tchadien et l'innovation : une analyse exploratoire » de Kévin Guillaume Pioch, mémoire de master, Université de N'Djamena, 2018.

« L'innovation au service du développement durable en Afrique subsaharienne » de l'Organisation de coopération et de développement économiques (OCDE).

« Rapport sur le développement humain 2019 » du Programme des Nations Unies pour le développement (PNUD).

« Stratégie nationale de développement du Tchad 2017-2021 » du gouvernement tchadien.

« Tchad : la formation et l'innovation, clés de la modernisation de l'agriculture » (Afrik21, 09/08/2021) - Consulté le 29/11/2022 sur : https://www.afrik21.africa/tchad-la-formation-et-linnovation-cles-de-la-modernisation-de-lagriculture/

« Tchad : les défis du développement économique et social » de Djimet Adoum, éditions L'Harmattan, 2013.

« Tchad : l'innovation pour sortir de la crise » de Sylvie Kpodar, Jeune Afrique, 18 octobre 2019.

L'INNOVATION EN AFRIQUE ENTRE DÉVELOPPEMENT, CHALLENGES ET OPPORTUNITÉS

Mounir Rochdi

Penser pouvoir ou croire savoir, pourquoi choisir ? Explorer, expérimenter, analyser, appliquer et partager sont les voies vers l'innovation. Des postures très souvent présentes en Afrique. En effet le continent ne cesse d'explorer de nouvelles solutions pour répondre à ses contraintes ; expérimenter de nouveaux outils pour réduire les difficultés ; analyse les situations pour mieux anticiper ; appliquer les enseignements pour se développer ; et partager les expériences pour apprendre collectivement. Quelle est aujourd'hui l'évolution de l'innovation en Afrique ? Quelles sont les solutions développées de manière concrète, qu'elles soient technologiques, sociales, énergétiques ou éducatives ? Nous allons tenter de présenter une vue d'ensemble de ces sujets en Afrique.

Les innovations en Afrique sont souvent développées dans un contexte difficile lié aux manques de moyens financiers, technologiques, humains, législatifs ou lié encore au manque d'infrastructures favorisant cette activité. Cela n'a pas empêché le continent de connaître la création d'entreprises innovantes axées sur la digitalisation, les technologies propres, l'AgriTech, la santé, l'éducation et l'énergie, pour ne citer que ces secteurs. Ces créations ont été motivées par le désir de répondre aux besoins locaux et de résoudre les problèmes les plus urgents, tels que la pauvreté, la malnutrition, l'accès limité aux soins de santé, l'éducation et l'énergie.

Par ailleurs, l'augmentation de la population jeune a contribué à stimuler l'innovation. Selon les chiffres 2020 des Nations Unies, plus de 60% des Africains sont âgés de moins de 25 ans. Ceci représente près de 800 millions d'individus. Un terreau de créativité, qui, avec l'accès à Internet ainsi que les politiques d'encouragement à l'entrepreneuriat, a permis la création de plusieurs entreprises innovantes.

La place actuelle de l'Afrique

Selon l'Indice mondial de l'innovation 2022 de l'OMPI[17] (Organisation Mondiale de la Propriété Intellectuelle), la Suisse, les États-Unis d'Amérique et la Suède sont en tête du classement mondial de l'innovation ; la Chine se rapproche des 10 premiers pays, l'Inde et la Turquie progressent rapidement. Et l'Afrique alors ?

Selon ce classement, le top 5 des pays africains présents est l'Ile Maurice (45e position), l'Afrique du Sud (61e), Le Maroc (67e), la Tunisie (73e) et le Botswana (86e), sur 132 pays évalués dans le monde.

Ce classement montre aussi la relation entre l'innovation et le développement économique. Il démontre que plus le pays possède un indice élevé, plus son PIB est important. Cependant, malgré cette relation, plusieurs économies à revenu élevé ont du mal à obtenir un meilleur équilibre entre le niveau d'investissement et les résultats, souvent au détriment de leur performance globale en matière d'innovation. Ce groupe d'économies comprend notamment les producteurs et exportateurs de pétrole et de gaz naturel : le Canada (15e), la Norvège (22e), les Émirats arabes unis (31e), l'Arabie saoudite (51e), Bahreïn (72e) et le Brunei Darussalam (92e). Parmi les autres économies qui peinent à transformer les intrants en extrants, citons Singapour (7e), l'Australie (25e), l'Ouzbékistan (82e) et le Rwanda (105e). Un pays peut donc avoir les moyens financiers, mais ne va pas pour autant performer (proportionnellement à son investissement) en innovation. L'innovation n'est donc pas qu'une question d'argent.

Un petit tour de quelques innovations africaines

Citons quelques exemples d'innovation liés à des secteurs particuliers :

Le paiement mobile

En 2007, a été lancé le système mobile de paiement M-Pesa au Kenya. Il permet aux utilisateurs de transférer de l'argent et de payer des factures à partir de leur téléphone portable. Le système a transformé le paysage financier en Afrique, permettant aux personnes qui n'ont pas accès à des

---

17. https://www.wipo.int/edocs/pubdocs/en/wipo-pub-2000-2022-section3-en-gii-2022-results-global-innovation-index-2022-15th-edition.pdf

services bancaires traditionnels d'effectuer des transactions financières en toute sécurité. Le système M-Pesa est désormais utilisé dans plusieurs pays africains et a inspiré d'autres innovations financières, telles que les prêts peer-to-peer et les assurances.

Le développement de logiciels et la formation

Andela, une entreprise technologique qui forme des développeurs de logiciels africains et les met en relation avec des entreprises américaines pour des projets à distance. Son objectif est de lutter contre la pénurie de talents en sélectionnant et formant les développeurs les plus doués d'Afrique. Andela a été créé en 2014 et a rapidement attiré l'attention des investisseurs, levant plus de 180 millions de dollars de financement. L'entreprise a contribué à renforcer les capacités de développement de logiciels en Afrique, créant des emplois et stimulant la croissance économique. Andela compte trois campus technologiques dans des pays anglophones : Nigéria, Kenya et Ouganda.

L'Énergie renouvelable

650 millions d'Africains n'ont pas accès à l'électricité, soit plus des deux tiers de la population. Les pénuries d'électricité coûteraient quelque 2 à 4% du PIB (Produit Intérieur Brut). C'est dans ce contexte de contrainte énergétique que le Maroc avait lancé le projet de centrale solaire Noor-Ouarzazate au Maroc. Doté d'une capacité de 580 mégawatts répartie sur quatre centrales, ce complexe figure parmi les plus grands parcs solaires au monde. Il permet de produire de l'électricité à partir de sources renouvelables, réduisant ainsi la dépendance à l'égard des combustibles fossiles. Le Maroc a l'ambition de porter à 52% la part du renouvelable dans son mix énergétique en 2030. La centrale permet d'alimenter près de deux millions de Marocains en électricité et d'éviter le rejet, dans l'atmosphère, de près d'un million de tonnes par an de gaz à effet de serre.

L'AgriTech

En ce qui concerne l'AgriTech, de nombreuses innovations ont vu le jour en Afrique, visant à améliorer la productivité agricole, à réduire les pertes post-récolte et à faciliter l'accès aux marchés. Des start-up telles que Farmcrowdy et Hello Tractor ; Twiga Foods au Kenya, ont développé des technologies pour connecter les agriculteurs aux marchés, fournir des services de financement et d'assurance et faciliter la logistique de transport. Hello Tractor, par exemple, met en relation les agriculteurs et les propriétaires de tracteurs. Ainsi, un agriculteur qui n'a pas les moyens de mécaniser sa récolte peut le faire. Les propriétaires de tracteurs quant à eux peuvent rentabiliser leur investissement. Il ne s'agit pas d'ailleurs de tracteurs uniquement, mais de moissonneuses aussi. Ces dernières coûtent plus cher encore à l'acquisition puisque leur prix commence à 100 k€.

La santé

Voici un secteur stratégique qui est sensible, celui de la santé. Le développement d'un pays se mesure, en partie, par l'efficacité de son système santé. MPharma (Ghana) et LifeBank (Nigéria) sont des start-up HealthTech qui ont développé des solutions pour améliorer l'accès aux médicaments, réduire les coûts et améliorer la logistique de la chaîne d'approvisionnement. En outre, des start-up ont également créé des applications mobiles pour faciliter l'accès aux soins de santé et la consultation à distance avec des médecins. Pour se rendre compte des capacités d'investissements, mPharma, a été cofondé en 2013 et avait 30 millions $ en capitaux propres et 5 millions $ sous forme de prêt. En 2022, avec une levée de 35 millions $.

L'accès Internet dans les zones rurales

60% d'Africains n'ont pas accès à internet et moins d'un tiers ont accès au haut débit. S'ajoute à cela une très forte disparité à l'accès Internet entre les pays du continent. Par ailleurs, dès que l'on s'éloigne des grandes villes, une connexion devient plus difficile à avoir. C'est pour cela que la société kényane BRCK a développé une solution de connectivité Internet hors réseau pour les zones rurales qui ne disposent pas d'une infrastructure Internet fiable. La technologie fournit une connectivité fiable et abordable dans les zones les plus reculées du continent. La solution consiste en un routeur portatif de la taille d'une brique qui permet d'accéder au Web sous toutes les latitudes. Seule condition, avoir un réseau 3G. C'est peut-être l'une des bonnes nouvelles pour BRCK qui est le fort développement du Web Mobile et de la 3G / 4G en Afrique.

Des programmes de formations pour soutenir l'innovation

Face à la demande croissante pour des compétences en innovation et en entrepreneuriat, de nombreuses institutions d'enseignement supérieur en Afrique ont commencé à proposer des programmes axés sur l'innovation et l'entrepreneuriat.

Le Rwanda, par exemple, a créé un écosystème d'innovation dynamique qui comprend plusieurs universités et institutions de recherche, dont l'Université du Rwanda et le Centre d'excellence en TIC de l'Institut des sciences et technologies de Kigali. Ces institutions ont mis en place des programmes de formation pour les entrepreneurs et les innovateurs en herbe, ainsi que des laboratoires de recherche et de développement pour les projets innovants.

Le Ghana a également lancé plusieurs programmes de formation axés sur l'innovation et l'entrepreneuriat. L'Université du Ghana a créé un programme de formation sur l'entrepreneuriat social pour les étudiants de premier cycle, qui vise à aider les étudiants à développer des compétences en leadership, en résolution de problèmes et en prise de décision. L'université a également mis en place un incubateur d'entreprises pour aider les étudiants à transformer leurs idées en projets concrets.

En Afrique du Sud, la Stellenbosch University Graduate School of Business a lancé un programme de formation sur l'entrepreneuriat social en 2011, qui aide les étudiants à développer des compétences en matière de développement de produits, de marketing et de gestion de projet. L'université a également créé un incubateur d'entreprises pour aider les étudiants à lancer des entreprises innovantes.

Au Maroc, l'université Mohammed VI Polytechnique (UM6P) est un Hub de Recherche & Innovation. À titre d'exemple, l'institution avait lancé l'Innovation Lab for Operations (ILO) dont le programme a pour vocation de développer et gérer des infrastructures démonstrateurs et outils de test axés sur la digitalisation industrielle, ou encore le programme UM6P Explorer, lancé en collaboration avec le MIT Sandbox permettant de présenter des projets innovants.

D'autres institutions telles que l'Académie africaine des sciences, le Tony Elumelu Foundation Entrepreneurship Programme visant à autonomiser les entrepreneurs africains et à soutenir la croissance d'entreprises durables sur le continent ou encore le programme de bourses de l'Institut africain des sciences mathématiques pour soutenir la formation des jeunes entrepreneurs en Afrique, ont été créés dans un esprit de renforcement des capacités axées sur l'innovation en Afrique.

Dans l'ensemble, les programmes de formation axés sur l'innovation et l'entrepreneuriat en Afrique offrent plusieurs possibilités pour les jeunes entrepreneurs et les innovateurs en herbe. Ces programmes leur permettent de développer des compétences essentielles pour innover et créer des entreprises durables et rentables..

Quelles perspectives ?

L'innovation en Afrique continuera à évoluer dans les années à venir, et les défis et les opportunités qui se présentent continueront d'inspirer de nouvelles idées et de nouvelles solutions. Voici quelques pistes possibles pour l'avenir de l'innovation en Afrique :

L'essor de la technologie de l'intelligence artificielle (IA) : Les pays africains ont pris conscience des avantages de l'IA, tels que la gestion de l'agriculture, la santé, l'énergie, la finance et l'éducation. L'IA permettra également de trouver des solutions innovantes pour résoudre des problèmes sociaux et environnementaux.

La croissance de l'économie verte : Les pays africains cherchent de plus en plus à développer des économies vertes pour résoudre les problèmes environnementaux tout en créant des emplois et de la croissance économique. Les innovations en matière d'énergie solaire, d'agriculture durable, de gestion des déchets et de recyclage sont quelques exemples de la façon dont l'innovation peut contribuer à l'économie verte en Afrique.

La connectivité numérique accrue : La connectivité numérique en Afrique est en constante évolution, et il y a des efforts pour améliorer l'infrastructure des télécommunications, ainsi que l'accès à Internet. Une connectivité renforcée permettra aux entreprises, aux particuliers et aux communautés de bénéficier des avantages de la technologie, en améliorant l'efficacité, l'accessibilité et la qualité de vie.

L'importance de la collaboration : L'innovation en Afrique sera de plus en plus axée sur la collaboration et la création de partenariats public-privé pour maximiser les ressources et les efforts. Les gouvernements, les entreprises et les organisations de la société civile devront travailler ensemble pour identifier les opportunités et les défis, et pour développer des solutions innovantes.

En conclusion

Malgré les avancées significatives réalisées ces dernières années, l'innovation en Afrique est confrontée à des défis importants. Le manque de financement, l'instabilité politique, la corruption et les faiblesses des infrastructures sont autant d'obstacles qui entravent le développement de l'innovation en Afrique. Pourtant, malgré ces défis, les innovateurs africains continuent de proposer des solutions novatrices pour résoudre les problèmes les plus pressants auxquels font face les communautés locales.

Les gouvernements africains doivent travailler à améliorer les conditions nécessaires pour encourager l'innovation, telles que l'investissement dans l'éducation et les infrastructures, ainsi que la création d'un environnement réglementaire favorable. Les investisseurs étrangers doivent également considérer l'Afrique comme un marché attractif pour les innovations.

Si l'on surmonte les obstacles, le futur de l'innovation en Afrique sera prometteur et devra passer par le développement d'une culture de l'innovation durable. L'innovation en Afrique continuera d'être un domaine de croissance et de transformation, avec des avantages sociaux, économiques et environnementaux pour les pays africains.

Finalement, l'innovation est la clé de la transformation de l'Afrique.

Bibliographie :

Ludovic Temple, Ludovic Temple, Nadine Machicou Ndzesop, «Système National de Recherche et d'Innovation en Afrique : le cas du Cameroun», Innovations 2017/2 (n° 53).

François Wassouni, « L'innovation dans le secteur de l'artisanat africain: l'émergence et le développement de l'artisanat des cornes de bœufs à Maroua dans l'extrême nord du Cameroun », Marché et organisations 2015/3 (n° 24).

Christian Le Bas, « L'innovation frugale peut-elle être un levier de croissance économique pour les pays en développement ? (Caisse d'émission, transferts de fonds, transport urbain, prix de l'eau, innovation frugale) », Mondes en développement 2021/2 (n° 194).

André Dumas Tsambou, Benjamin Fomba Kamga, « Adoption d'innovations et productivité des entreprises en Afrique subsaharienne francophone : cas du Cameroun, de la Côte d'Ivoire et du Sénégal », Revue d'économie industrielle 2021/1 (n° 173).

Henri Dou, Hamidou Koné, « L'innovation frugale dans les pays en développement et la nécessité d'une protection intellectuelle appropriée », Mondes en développement 2016/1 (n° 173).

Mekonnen KinduThorne Peter J., "Africa RISING: Innovation for development highlights", CGIAR System Organization, 2019.

Hollanders Hugo Iizuka Michiko Unu-Merit 政策研究大学院大学, "Innovation Indicators: for a critical reflection on their use in Low- and Middle-Income Countries (LMICs)", GRIPS Policy Research Center, 2020.

Gurib-Fakim Ameenah, "Innovation, Entrepreneurship and Governance for Sustainable Development of Africa's Agri-food System", Technical Centre for Agricultural and Rural Cooperation, 2020.

Nicolas Friederici, "Innovation Hubs in Africa: An Entrepreneurial Perspective", Oxford Internet Institute 2018.

Solomon Nwaka, "Social and Technological Innovation in Africa: Sustaining a Post COVID-19 Research for Development". ‎Palgrave Macmillan; 1st ed. 2021 edition.

Calestous Juma, "The New Harvest: Agricultural Innovation in Africa. Oxford University Press, 2nd edition, 2015.

Nnamdi Oranye, "Disrupting Africa: The Rise and Rise of African Innovation Paperback". Nnamdi Oranye Second Edition, 2018).

Clapperton Chakanets Mavhunga, "What Do Science, Technology, and Innovation Mean from Africa?", The MIT Press (June 16, 2017).

Philip Franklin, African American Inventor Package: The Unsung Heroes of and Innovation", ‎Independently published, 2022.

Mammo Muchie, "Creating Systems of Innovation in Africa". Country Case Studies, Africa Institute of South Africa, 2013.

Landry Signé, « L'innovation en stratégies de développement en Afrique - acteurs nationaux, régionaux et internationaux de 1960 à nos jours, KARTHALA, 2015.

Joël Stephan Tagne, « Digitalisation et innovation en Afrique subsaharienne », Éditions universitaires européennes, 2020.

Goli Lucien Zan VAMI, «La gouvernance des PME de l'innovation technologique en Afrique: La gouvernance, une autre approche de solution à la problématique de performance des PME des TIC en contexte ivoirien», Éditions universitaires européennes, 2020.

Emmanuel Kamdem , « Innovation entrepreneuriale et développement durable en Afrique : défis et opportunités », Éditions L'Harmattan, 2016.

Mboungou Mouyabi Seke, « L'impact de l'innovation sur la croissance économique en Afrique: Un regard sur les cas de l'Éthiopie et du Rwanda », Éditions Notre Savoir, 2020.

Jean-Louis Martinez, Serge Guerin, « Afrique, Jeunesse, Innovations : Des Pistes Pour Inventer Le Xxie Siecle », MA, 2020

ENTRE FRUGALITÉ ET AGILITÉ, L'INNOVATION COMME LEVIER DE DÉVELOPPEMENT ÉCONOMIQUE EN AFRIQUE

Siham Harroussi

L'Afrique est un continent en pleine expansion qui fait face à des défis économiques, sociaux et environnementaux croissants. Dans cette dynamique, l'innovation représente un levier important pour relever ces défis en encourageant l'entrepreneuriat et développant des solutions durables.

Une approche émergente consiste à associer le principe d'agilité et de frugalité aux démarches d'innovation pour augmenter le potentiel d'impact positif et contribuer au développement économique.

I- L'agilité, pour une performance augmentée et une transformation accélérée

Dans un monde en constante évolution, les entreprises sont confrontées à des défis de plus en plus complexes et imprévisibles. Pour relever ces défis, de nombreuses organisations se tournent vers l'agilité, une approche novatrice qui favorise l'itération, la collaboration, la flexibilité et l'adaptabilité.

1- L'origine de l'agilité

Initialement développée dans le domaine informatique, l'approche agile a connu un succès retentissant notamment dans le développement des logiciels de manière itérative, collaborative et plus efficace.

Désormais, l'approche agile ne se cantonne plus au monde informatique et se généralise au sein des organisations. Ces dernières l'utilisent comme un levier pour réussir les transformations organisationnelles en l'intégrant dans leur culture, leurs bonnes pratiques et leurs processus pour encourager l'innovation, l'adaptabilité et la flexibilité face aux changements de leur écosystème.

2- L'agilité pour faire face à un monde VUCA

Le monde d'aujourd'hui est souvent décrit comme étant VUCA (acronyme pour Volatilité, Incertitude, Complexité et Ambiguïté). La volatilité se réfère aux changements rapides et imprévisibles, l'incertitude englobe le manque de prévisibilité, la complexité fait référence à la multitude de facteurs interconnectés et l'ambiguïté se réfère, quant à elle, à la difficulté d'interpréter les informations.

Dans cet environnement VUCA, les entreprises sont donc confrontées à des défis sans précédent, nécessitant une adaptation et une agilité constantes. Elles sont ainsi obligées de prendre des décisions rapides et éclairées, de s'adapter rapidement aux changements, de gérer l'incertitude, de naviguer dans des environnements complexes et de trouver des solutions dans des situations ambiguës.

C'est pour cette raison que les entreprises ont adopté une stratégie impliquant la promotion de l'agilité organisationnelle, le renforcement de la flexibilité et la résilience, l'adoption d'une approche itérative et expérimentale, et la mise en place d'une culture d'apprentissage continu.

Ainsi, l'agilité devient une des principales Soft Skills (concept désignant les compétences comportementales liées au savoir-être) que les entreprises cherchent à développer au sein de leurs organisations, et qui peine encore aujourd'hui à se généraliser au-delà de la gestion de projets informatiques.

II- La frugalité, pour une innovation responsable et accessible

Dans une société axée sur la surconsommation et la recherche du toujours plus, la frugalité émerge comme un contre-mouvement conscient et réfléchi. Elle consiste à adopter un mode de vie économe et plus respectueux de l'environnement, et à valoriser la simplicité, l'efficacité et la sobriété.

1- L'origine de l'innovation frugale

L'innovation frugale trouve son inspiration dans le « Jugaad », un concept indien (autrement dénommé Juggaar ou Jugar) qui signifie littéralement « détournement ». En pendjabi, « Jugaad » désigne un camion de fortune bricolé avec un moteur Diesel monté sur un chariot.

Ainsi, le frugal est né de l'adaptation des populations les plus démunies ou reculées à des conditions de vie extrêmes ou à des environnements difficiles. Elles ont déployé des trésors d'ingéniosité pour répondre à des besoins quelques fois vitaux par des solutions simples et peu coûteuses.

L'innovation frugale consiste donc à innover mieux avec moins, en répondant à un besoin de la manière la plus simple et efficace possible.

2- Quelques principes du frugal

Ils reposent sur la recherche de la simplicité tout au long de la vie d'un produit en utilisant un minimum de moyens. Ces principes font écho aux enjeux de RSE (Responsabilité Sociale et Environnementale) des entreprises pour faire face aux problèmes de consommation excessive et de gaspillage des ressources.

On s'attache alors à réduire la complexité et le coût de la chaîne de conception, de réalisation et de mise en œuvre de la solution. Aussi, une connaissance des besoins réels des utilisateurs cibles est indispensable pour aller à l'essentiel dans la recherche de solutions.

Aussi, la flexibilité, l'inclusivité, l'agilité, l'intelligence collective, l'intuition, l'économie d'échelle, la recherche de nouveaux modèles économiques, l'inspiration... sont autant de principes qui fondent l'innovation frugale.

Nous pouvons noter ces dernières années un engouement pour l'innovation frugale de la part des grands groupes et laboratoires de R&D dans les pays les plus développés. Ils y voient un intérêt pour remédier au manque d'agilité et de flexibilité lié à la taille importante des équipes et à des processus rigides.

Aussi, et contrairement à ce que l'on pourrait imaginer, l'innovation frugale ne tend pas vers une innovation incrémentale qui consiste à améliorer l'existant en y ajoutant de nouvelles fonctionnalités ou en l'optimisant. L'innovation frugale s'intègre plutôt dans des démarches d'innovation, de rupture en allant chercher de nouvelles perspectives et de nouvelles façons de faire.

De la même manière qu'il ne s'agit pas d'une approche low cost, puisque les solutions issues de processus d'innovation frugale sont épurées à leur maximum sans sophistication, mais également sans concession sur la réponse aux besoins ciblés. Il ne s'agit donc pas de proposer moins de services, mais plutôt de répondre de manière exhaustive à un besoin sans ajouts superflus.

Exemples d'innovations frugales en Afrique

Zipline (Rwanda) : entreprise de livraison de produits médicaux par drones. Au Rwanda, elle fournit des produits sanguins essentiels et d'autres fournitures médicales aux régions éloignées et difficilement accessibles. Cette innovation permet ainsi de surmonter les défis logistiques liés aux infrastructures limitées et aux mauvaises conditions routières.

Les éco-villages solaires (Maroc) : il s'agit d'éco-villages développés pour fournir un accès à l'énergie propre et abordable aux communautés rurales éloignées. Ils sont équipés de systèmes solaires photovoltaïques, offrant ainsi une alternative durable aux sources d'énergie traditionnelles.

M-Pesa (Kenya) : il s'agit d'une plateforme de services financiers mobiles développée au Kenya. Elle permet aux utilisateurs de transférer de l'argent, de payer des factures et d'accéder à des services bancaires de base via leur téléphone portable. Cette innovation a révolutionné l'accès aux services financiers dans les zones rurales et les communautés non bancarisées en Afrique.

3- Le frugal, le meilleur allié pour continuer à innover dans les périodes de crise

L'expérience que nous avons vécue tout récemment avec la crise pandémique provoquée par le Covid 19 a démontré l'efficacité du frugal pour trouver des solutions peu coûteuses, agiles et efficaces en réponse à des situations d'urgence.

En effet, pendant la crise, nous avons vu émerger une multitude d'initiatives frugales consistant à développer de manière agile des solutions nouvelles en utilisant des ressources déjà disponibles. C'est ainsi que L'Oréal, Dior ou Ricard ont pu produire du gel hydroalcoolique ou encore des industriels comme Renault, PSA, Valeo et Schneider Electric se sont associés à la production de respirateurs artificiels.

Un exemple marquant a été l'utilisation des masques de plongée Easybreath de Decathlon par un médecin italien pour en détourner l'usage en les équipant d'éléments imprimés en 3D pour servir de respirateurs.

Au-delà de la réponse à des situations d'urgence dans des temps très courts et avec peu de moyens grâce notamment à la réutilisation des ressources disponibles, l'innovation frugale devient indispensable dans le contexte actuel marqué par des incertitudes liées à différentes crises sanitaire, géopolitique, économique, sociale, etc., qui nécessiteront inéluctablement une réallocation des moyens pour répondre à des besoins autres que l'innovation.

L'Afrique, berceau du frugal et de l'agilité

Nous noterons que l'agilité et le frugal sont intimement liés à un état d'esprit, au-delà des méthodes et outils, et donc peuvent-être quelques fois difficilement acquérable par le biais du simple apprentissage par la voie des formations.

Certains pays, à l'instar des pays africains, ont naturellement développé cet esprit d'agilité et de frugalité pour répondre à des environnements difficiles et disposant de peu de ressources.

Ainsi, ce qui pouvait paraître comme une contrainte hier peut constituer une vraie force pour faire face aux défis d'aujourd'hui.

GLOBAL RISKS FROM PERPETUAL DISRUPTION AND THE CHALLENGES TO INTELLIGENCE ORGANIZATIONS

Paul Santilli

Today's businesses are faced with unprecedented business upheaval and investment uncertainty, as the industrial climate of today is unlike anything we have seen. The onslaught of never-ending data, the proliferation of perpetual disruption activity, and the rise of industry-changing digital transformation requirements overnight - all this has a dramatic effect on the data intelligence professional ability to not only acquire the right data, but to be able to synthesise the analytics in order to drive it to the right conclusions, all while navigating through a non-stop, fluid information environment.

The COVID-19 pandemic completely disrupted the global economic landscape, creating new, undefined opportunities and subsequently unforeseen challenges and threats. The COVID-19 pandemic wasn't the first major disruption, neither will it be the last. As a matter of fact, to view this pandemic as a "disruptive event in time" is seriously flawed! We must view our global socio-economic dynamic as something that is **continuously under a perpetual disruption** landscape. Disruption must be viewed as always being a part of society and that the magnitude of the disruption over time is what varies across geographies, industries, and related business environments. And this level of magnitude consequently results in a corresponding level of response from business and industry – something we are all experiencing on a global scale.

Unfortunately, intelligence communities are often times stuck into the same mold of consistent use of common legacy methodologies, fragmented infrastructure hierarchy, and limited ability to influence company direction. In order for intelligence to be truly applied universally, corporations have to take a pragmatic approach of leveraging the data analytics and intelligence efforts throughout the company and recognise the value of a systemic perspective to integrating data intelligence into the overall strategy of the company.

Economic Risks

Based on an analysis by Allianz Trade in 2022, there are 5 main factors associated with the Macroeconomic risks present in global economies :

1. Economic Risk – Indebtedness, monetary policy, economic policy
2. Political Risk – Institutional independence, political effectiveness, power concentration
3. Structural Business Environment – Ease of doing business, regulatory framework.
4. Commercial Risk – Short-term demand disruption
5. Financing Risk – risk of short-term disruptions of accounts receivables

Globally, there are key African communities that have high-risk factors associated with their business and socio-economic infrastructure (Fig 1). These factors have a high degree of impact to competitiveness, innovation, and business growth within these societies.

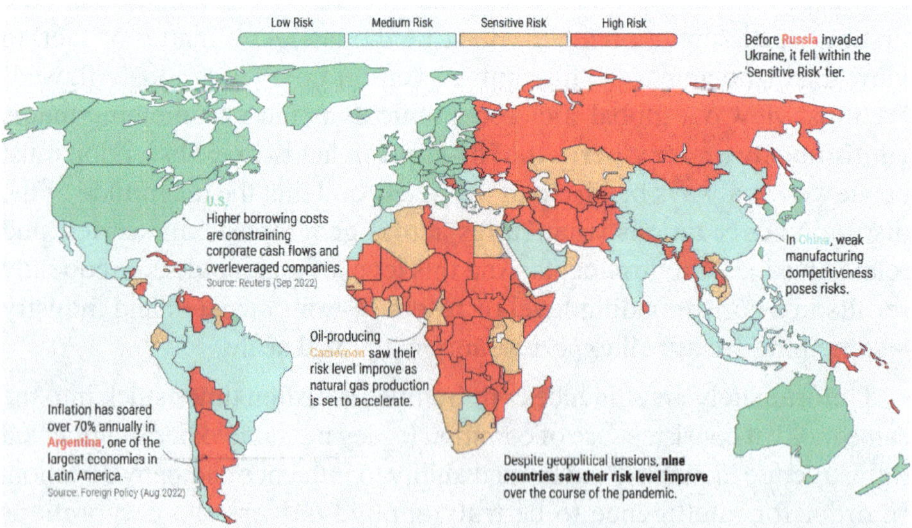

Simultaneously, there is a growing shift in revenue in the Business to Business (B2B) marketplace over the next decade. More business opportunities are investing in Disruptive Technology, Cloud-based analytics, Smart Infrastructure and related advanced technology applications in Healthcare, Aerospace, and Chemical products. (MarketsandMarkets, 2022). This $25 Trillion opportunity potential is centred around the burgeoning growth in post Covid pent-up demand in major industralised regions.

The Digital Divide

The strategic problem most organisations face is the growth of digital divide between those leaders that have sprinted ahead from the rest of the pack; those leaders that have integrated digital transformation into their infrastructure – both internal and external facing business models. Significant investment in internal IT systems as well as developing a digital interface to their customer and supplier community has allowed these organisations to be the preferred choice among those doing commerce in a Covid and post-Covid environment.

Despite tremendous amounts of investment in digital transformation, many companies are still falling behind, failing to achieve the business breakthroughs that deliver differentiated outcomes.

The problem we're seeing across industries is a digital transformation divide that is widening – a gap in performance between those at the top of the market and those at the bottom.

The leaders have sprinted ahead, while 67% of CEOs agree that acting with agility is the new currency of business – if we are too slow, we will be bankrupt. In the *KPMG 2019 Global CEO Outlook Survey of 400 CEOs, a majority of the 400 U.S. CEOs* surveyed told KPMG that being too slow can lead to obsolescence, a marked increase from those who thought so last year. U.S. CEOs face a choice : agility or irrelevance.

What has changed ? The answer is clear : The speed of change is only getting faster.

Those who have sprinted ahead are seeing double the growth. Source : *McKinsey The Great Acceleration July 2020*

McKinsey's report found the combined profit of the top-performing companies grew their total market-implied annual economic profit by

$335 billion, while companies in the bottom quintile lost over $303billion between December 2018 and May 2020; this gap widened even further into 2021 as the pandemic continues.

Companies with resilient, future-ready business models positioned to ride these trends have pulled further away from their industry peers, while those with legacy business models have, for the most part, fallen further behind.

This failure of companies to employ resilient and flexible operating systems have led to corresponding self-introspective priorities during the Covid lockdown – focusing on ensuring infrastructure and security systems could support the most important business applications, while relying less on customer-facing or growth application development.

Ecommerce

The aspect of eCommerce growth during this timeframe cannot be ignored. Ecommerce has grown 2 to 5 times (and in some cases, 10 times) faster than before the pandemic; obvious to understand given the restrictions on face-to-face engagements and in-person purchasing of B2C customer relationships.

This has resulted in a now-more-than-ever reliance on implementing a digital transformation platform as a foundational **must** for sustained organisational health and growth.

IT Digital Transformation

Complementing this digital transformation platform with shifts in IT infrastructure investment will enable enterprise organisations to be more nimble and have better agility to continually evolve to capture market opportunities while highly engaging their employees.

There are 5 fundamental IT shifts that can help companies compete with digital natives, accelerate time to market, and improve customer experience (McKinsey, April 15, 2021)

1. Collaboration – Agile BizDevOps teams form cross-functional units co-managed by business and IT leads.
2. Applications and services – Granular application and services owned by "teams of teams" supported by a leaner core.

3. Sourcing and People – Larger, more experience, in-house IT workforce balanced with strategic use of partners and vendors.
4. Delivery process – Fully automated, continuous software delivery with thousands of releases per year.
5. Infrastructure – Could and containers at scale with provisioning within seconds and autoscaling.
6. This formulation requires a paradigm shift in how organisations view information, data and usage – one towards Instantaneous Transformation of IT infrastructure.

The 3 A's

The result addresses major disruption-based business implications around acceleration of company lifecycles and exploitation of strengths and weaknesses in company design.

I have identified 3 categories of company behavior that stems from major disruption magnitudes :

1. Amplification – strengths and weakness in company business model are amplified while under unforeseen stresses in the marketplace and changes in customer demand. Those organisations that have strong business models, experienced digital transformation platforms, and efficient yet flexibly supply chains will not only maintain their business through these perpetual disruption activities, but will potentially grow share of wallet due to the competition's inability to manage these challenges.
2. Acceleration – the trajectory of the organisational value proposition and company roadmap will accelerate. This behavior tests the fundamental strategies that the organisation had in place to determine if and how they were equipped to prepare for and compete in tumultuous times. Sound business strategies that took into consideration different competitive and social threats will perform better than those relying on predictable and narrow value propositions in this model.
3. Augmentation – the requirements around an organisation's flexibility to augment and change their product and service portfolio. This is extremely critical in having organisations that are nimble enough

4. to pivot their business offerings to accommodate fast-changing customer demands. Those organisations that have this flexibility not only in their IT and manufacturing infrastructure, but also in their culture and organisational structure will be best suited for challenging business conditions.

Strategic Partnerships

Partner ecosystems are a critical component in the development of sound business strategies to survive in this environment. Investing in partner relationship with other groups that either share similar applications and use cases around your products and services, or can complement your portfolio with added value and maybe event service an expanded customer set gives you a significant advantage in the marketplace. These partnerships can be generated via consultative services, contractor partnerships, mergers & acquisitions or even project or geography-based. The ability to supplement your value proposition to better suit your existing and **future** customer needs will differentiate yourselves from the competition.

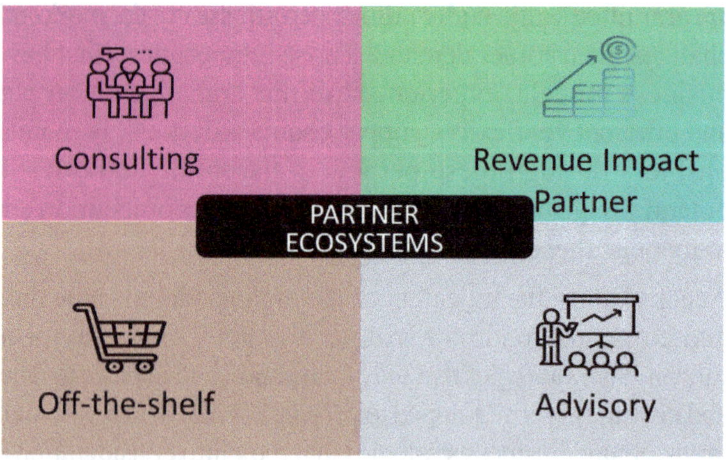

There are many challenges that organisations must contend with in the ever-expanding data ecosystem that has become a fundamental currency in our global economic platforms. However, many evolving societies that are attempting to develop better Intelligence management systems have the advantage of adopting proven and Best-in-Class practices from a number of solution providers in this discipline. Developing partnerships with a multitude of both local and international players can make many organisations more efficient in their data-management efforts, which can lead to extremely effective and productive outcomes for their environment.

Governmental organisations can also benefit extremely from these best learning, to better equip their infrastructure players with the right knowledge and to support through legislation and related governmental policies that promote data-driven and intelligence-based practices. This will encourage organisations and private sector to invest in further development and partnerships to carry out these intelligence objectives.

COMPRENDRE LES RUPTURES : INNOVATION ET INTELLIGENCE DES RISQUES ?

Philippe Clerc

« *Nous nous retrouvons finalement, en ce XXIème siècle, dans un état de surprise permanent, où tout est devenu incongru parce que nous sommes en état de vide [...]* »

Philippe Baumard, Le vide stratégique, Cnrs, 2012.

« *Au cœur de cet espace qui se dévoile sans perspective ni fin, les boussoles s'affolent, les gyroscopes se détraquent et les compas ne servent plus à rien. Les cartes manquent de ce territoire qui s'enfuit...* »

Yves Stourdzé, Les ruines du futur, Sens & Tonka, Paris, 1979.

Introduction

Nous changeons d'ère. Nos sociétés et nos économies développées comme émergentes, l'économie-monde basculent dans l'ère de « l'innovation intensive[18]», puissant moteur du développement et d'une transformation parfois radicale. D'où qu'ils soient, organisations, hommes et femmes, territoires, sont confrontés à des situations inédites marquées par des crises locales et mondiales, des ruptures et des chocs, situations chaotiques caractérisées par « l'incertitude de toutes les données[19] ». « L'état de surprise est permanent » et « la puissance de l'imprévisible » règne en maître. Nos

18. Armand Hatchuel, enseignant chercheur à Mines Paris Tech,

19. Carl von Clausewitz, De la guerre, livre 2, chapitre 2, § 24, Berlin Ferdinand Dümmler, 1832.

modèles stratégiques volent en éclat[20]. La fracture cognitive qui s'installe plonge nos agirs et nos décisions dans l'immobilisme, aboutissement inéluctable de la tentation au repli vers les schémas du passé, le mimétisme des processus, les tactiques de « report »[21]. S'inscrire dans cette nouvelle réalité de la dynamique d'innovation schumpétérienne, c'est-à-dire de destruction créatrice, nécessite de comprendre la situation – ce qui est à l'œuvre.

Pour ce faire nous interrogerons nos capacités d'intelligence de ces situations nouvelles, des ruptures et des risques, et ce, plus particulièrement en ce qui concerne les dynamiques d'innovation. Pour agir et ne pas subir, ces ruptures peuvent-elles être anticipées avec les démarches et les méthodes dont nous disposons ? Ainsi nous visiterons des démarches d'intelligence des situations et leur dimension anticipatrice. Pour aboutir , nous tenterons l'articulation entre intelligence économique et « agir prospectif ».

Poussant plus loin l'investigation, nous constaterons que l'appareillage conceptuel, technique et institutionnel s'inscrit encore dans la posture du « prévisible » et de « la remise en état » - le relèvement, la résilience. Pour tenter le dépassement et « sortir du cadre des situations prévisible » nous explorerons un chemin esquissé vers un nouveau paradigme[22], celui de « l'incertitude radicale[23]» et de l'imprévisibilité au cœur des nouvelles dynamiques d'innovation sociales, organisationnelles et technologiques. Tel est au fond l'objet principal de notre communication.

I - Retrouver « la soif de définir »

Afin de sortir nos « intelligences aveugles[24] » de l'ornière, il convient de retrouver « la soif de définir » et de remettre en débat les définitions comme y invite Philippe Baumard qui appelle à « une reprise en main »

---

20. Philippe Baumard, le vide stratégique, CNRS Editions, Paris 2012.

21. Ibid, p.17

22. Philippe Clerc, « Crises et catastrophes : comment anticiper et s'adapter. Vers un nouveau paradigme », Médecine de catastrophe – Urgences collectives. Société Française de Médecine de Catastrophe, Elsevier Masson, Août 2021.

23. « La caractéristique propre de l'histoire humaine est l'incertitude radicale de l'avenir » Michel Aglietta, La preuve dans les sciences économiques, L'Économie politique, n°78, P. 97.

24. Edgar Morin

de nos « agirs stratégiques », c'est-à-dire de ce qui fait « la particularité du genre humain – sa capacité à résoudre stratégiquement des problèmes qui dépassent son échelle individuelle d'entendement[25] ». Dès lors trois termes nous intéressent : l'innovation, le risque, la rupture. Nous voulons les définir comme processus – en dynamique en quelque sorte – mais aussi comme outils d'entrée en stratégie en osant l'innovation, en osant le risque.

L'innovation, enjeu de puissance

L'innovation devient l'enjeu économique et social de la nouvelle forme de conflictualité mondiale que les Chinois définissent comme une « guerre des intelligences » principalement vis-à-vis des États-Unis [26] à la conquête de la suprématie technologique. Cette dernière vise la maîtrise des technologies critiques[27] moteurs des dynamiques d'innovation transformatrices de nos modes de vie, de production et d'échanges. L'enjeu devient géopolitique. L'ancien dirigeant de Google, Eric Schmidt[28] parle désormais du « pouvoir d'innovation » soit « une nouvelle force déterminante de la politique internationale… » ou « la capacité d'inventer, d'adopter et d'adapter de nouvelles technologies. Il contribue à la fois au hard et au soft power. »

L'innovation a toujours été au cœur des modèles de développement-y compris dans les pays à faible capacité de développement. Elle se situe également dans celui que nous devons bâtir , fondé sur les ruptures écologiques, énergétiques et numériques. Armand Hatchuel en dresse les réalités : « Nous entrons dans l'ère de l'innovation intensive... Une ère dans laquelle les compétiteurs innovants débarquent de façon surprenante ». Il convient de retenir ici deux conséquences remarquables de l'innovation intensive. La première consiste dans le caractère disruptif – hors des règles du marché - qui crée la « surprise » et plus encore la rupture. En second

---

25. Philippe Baumard, le vide stratégique, CNRS Editions, Paris 2012.

26. Après des stratégistes tels que Hervé Couteau-Bégarie « *La stratégie est la dialectique des intelligences, dans un milieu conflictuel…* »

27. ASPI, Australian Strategic Policy Institute, Jamie Gaida, Jennifer Wong-Leung, Stephan Robin and Danielle Cave « Who is leading the critical technology race », ASPI's Critical Technologies Trackers, Policy Brief, Report 69/2023.

28. Eric Schmidt, « Innovation Power - *Why Technology Will Define the Future of Geopolitics* », *Foreign Affairs,* 28 février 2023.

lieu, elle fausse les lois de l'économie « standard », et donc risque de rendre inopérants nos outils et nos organisations d'intervention, pire de rendre « nos intelligences aveugles ». Les chercheurs de l'Accenture Institute ont identifié et décrit les « innovations foudroyantes », véritables ruptures dans l'ordre établi des stratégies[29]. Nouveau type d'innovation, indétectable, il peut potentiellement perturber toutes les positions établies, rendre obsolètes les capacités stratégiques traditionnelles et rendre inopérantes les capacités d'intelligence et d'anticipation.

Ainsi l'innovation est diverse. Son champ d'application est multiple. Elle se transforme et mue. Dans l'ère de l'intensif - attaché aux pays développés et à leur lutte pour le leadership technologique par l'innovation et l'industrie, à la source du pouvoir sur les marchés et les sociétés (les individus), une tension apparaît clairement entre radicalité (innovation radicale, innovation de rupture) et progressivité (innovation incrémentale). Cette tension se calcule en « intensité de l'innovation » et de la capacité de repérage/prévision. L'innovation radicale crée un nouveau marché ou transforme en profondeur un ou plusieurs marchés. Dès lors cette dynamique de rupture crée un « avant » et un « après ». Tel est le cas pour les innovations foudroyantes décrites plus haut. L'innovation incrémentale ne crée pas de rupture, mais améliore l'existant, apporte de la compétitivité sans que de profondes transformations ne soient effectuées - de la compétitivité ou du « mieux vivre », de la sécurité sociale en quelque sorte. Nous voulons noter ici que bien évidemment les pays émergents ou faiblement développés ne sont pas exclus de ces processus. Ils le subissent comme ils peuvent en bénéficier.

Dans notre approche, notons que nous nous intéressons plus avant à l'innovation de procédé et d'organisation, plus encore à l'innovation sociétale. Cette dernière répond à des besoins sociaux à la fois dans ses fins et ses modalités. Ainsi répond-elle aux réalités du développement des « Afriques » et permet-elle d'ajuster les projets de développement en les « encastrant » dans les réalités de la vie sociale.

---

29. Larry Downes, Paul Nunes, Big Bang disruption. Strategy in the age of devastating innovation. Accenture institute, 2014. Voir aussi Philippe Clerc, « Comment détecter les "innovations foudroyantes"? Une nouvelle frontière pour l'intelligence stratégique. ». Conférence donnée le 9 octobre 2019. Académie de l'intelligence économique et Société d'Encouragement de l'Indus- trie Nationale, Paris.

Le guide de l'innovation frugale de Navi Rajdou s'inscrit dans cette approche vers une recherche de la sobriété comme nouveau levier de développement répondant à la demande et surtout aux usages sociaux.

La démarche s'entend parfaitement dans « nos recherches occidentales » d'économie de la fonctionnalité et d'économie circulaire vers la sobriété. Car la « Frugal Innovation » (ou « Frugal Design » ou « Frugal Pattern » ou

« Jugaad Innovation »), l'innovation frugale, donc, est une méthodologie de priorisation par la valeur à travers la création de solutions durables et régénératrices, en façonnant le comportement client, en cocréant de la valeur avec les « consom'acteurs » et en collaborant avec des partenaires innovants.

Une seconde référence est proposée par la Banque européenne d'investissement qui rapporte ceci : « *Pour lutter contre la pandémie de coronavirus, les pays africains recourent aux technologies de multiples façons, sans craindre d'innover, en particulier dans le champ sociétal*[30]*. Le rapport expose certaines des meilleures solutions numériques et évalue les investissements nécessaires à la mise en œuvre des technologies à grande échelle.* » Ainsi, « *le laboratoire d'accélération du PNUD au Kenya a compilé une carte des systèmes montrant les liens entre les effets de la pandémie de COVID-19 et les mesures prises pour y faire face. Sur le plan méthodologique, le laboratoire s'est appuyé sur les données et les récits des médias sociaux, y compris les analyses de Twitter et les hashtags les plus en vogue.* »

Les innovations qui ont vu le jour par nécessité durant la pandémie sont susceptibles de renforcer plus globalement l'infrastructure socio- économique dans l'avenir. Par exemple, en ce qui concerne l'accès au système judiciaire formel, la crise pourra inspirer le pouvoir judiciaire et d'autres instances gouvernementales, en les aident à repenser leur approche de la technologie au service des parties prenantes techniques et de la société.

Mutations des risques

Le risque ou comme l'écrit Xavier Durand[31] « l'océan de risques » qui pèse sur nos stratégies en menace le déroulement et crée des chocs,

---

30. Banque Européenne d'Investissement, COVID-19 : les solutions numériques de l'Afrique, juin 2020

31. Xavier Durand, Oser le risque. Le management dans un monde incertain, Ed. Hermann, 2021.

des bifurcations et des ruptures. Ainsi, est-il « l'effet de l'incertitude sur l'atteinte des objectifs » nous indiquent les normalisateurs[32] qui précisent :

« L'incertitude est l'état, même partiel, de manque d'information qui entrave la compréhension ou la connaissance d'un événement, de ses conséquences ou de sa vraisemblance. ». Le risque est défini donc à la fois comme évènement et/ou comme résultat d'un processus : référence à des « événements » potentiels et à des « conséquences » également potentielles ou référence à une combinaison des deux. L'intelligence des risques s'impose ici comme réductrice d'aléas et d'incertitude vis-à-vis du processus et de son impact. Elle ouvre de ce fait la voie au « génie de l'anticipation[33] » mis en œuvre pour « prendre le risque convenablement en compte » et le réduire à la source. Mais la démarche serait insuffisante sans une « sociologie compréhensive[34] » du risque enchâssé dans nos sociétés.

Nous sommes en effet entrés dans une société du risque[35] différente de la société industrielle classique. Les risques y sont engendrés par la société elle-même. Les promesses de bien-être collectif et individuel faites aux hommes ne sont pas tenues. La misère n'a pas été vaincue, les inégalités se sont remises à croître et le progrès a produit toutes sortes de maux, menaces, dangers comme autant de risques : pollution, catastrophes industrielles ou nucléaires, risques alimentaires, menaces sur l'environnement, atteintes à la santé, à la sécurité des individus. Ici Ulrich Beck distingue « les risques sociétaux majeurs, susceptibles de conduire à des effondrements ou des impasses collectives ou déstabilisations durables, qui doivent faire l'objet d'une prévention spécifique. » Une telle société crée un manque de repères pour les individus au regard de leur existence qui devient plus incertaine et traversées de peurs.

Plus récemment, le risque augmenté prolifère au cœur de « polycrises », ces « crises disparates qui interagissent de telle sorte que l'impact global

32. ISO 37101 : 2016 Développement durable au sein des communautés territoriales — Exigences et lignes directrices pour son utilisation.

33. Éclairante formule de Philippe Durance, « Penser la rupture », in Dir. Philippe Durance, La prospective stratégique en action, Odile Jacob, 2014

34. Bertrand Badie, Quand le Sud réinvente le monde, Essai sur la puissance de la faiblesse, La Découverte, 2018, p.13.

35. Ulrich Beck, La société du risque. Sur la voie d'une autre modernité, Aubier, Paris, 2001

dépasse de loin la somme de chaque partie[36]» sont susceptibles de créer ces situations hors de contrôle. Il s'agit bien ici d'une rupture. Or, aujourd'hui encore, le risque tel que nous l'entendons correspond à la conscience que nous avons de pouvoir agir sur le monde avec « la possibilité de conjurer certaines menaces et de braver le danger pour en tirer profit[37]». Au cœur de l'approche des risques, le débat tarde à être tranché entre ceux qui estiment que les meilleures décisions sont prises sur la base des chiffres et de l'analyse des données antérieures (risques maîtrisés et analyse des données antérieures, passées) et ceux qui considèrent que « le futur est toujours imprévisible et qu'il faut l'inventer ». D'où le concept de « conquête de nouveaux risques » sur lequel nous reviendrons, car il est essentiel en innovation. Poursuivons nos définitions.

Rupture : comprendre.

Les évolutions profondes de l'environnement géopolitique, économique et social et les crises systémiques qu'elles entrainent convoquent « les mots de la rupture » tels qu'« aléa, bifurcation, bouleversement, catastrophe, chaos, discontinuité, surprise », mais aussi chocs et violence, au cœur des analyses de situations contemporaines en nous poussant sur la voie de l'anticipation. « En 5 ans, nous sommes passés de l'ère des transitions à l'ère des ruptures. Certaines d'entre elles sont sûres, d'autres sont incertaines, d'autres encore sont imprévisibles[38].»

Dans son texte éclairant, Philippe Durance[39] souligne le caractère flou de la rupture dans les réflexions et insiste sur la nécessité d'engager ce que nous avons appelé « une sociologie compréhensive » de la rupture. Il tente en premier lieu la définition : « évènement brusque et imprévu (et non pas imprévisible), susceptible de bouleverser toutes les prévisions, aussi « scientifiques » soient-elles, et de les réduire à de simples spéculations. Et de mentionner « l'échec de prévision » des économistes face à la crise

---

36. Voir le dernier « The Global Risks Report 2023 » du World Economic Forum.

37. Xavier Durand, ibid.

38. Yannick Blanc, « comment apprivoiser les cygnes noirs » en introduction du Forum des Futurs 2023 de Futuribles International tenu en février 2023 sous le sceau des ruptures.

39. Philippe Durance, ibid.

financière mondiale de 2008[40]. L'approche sociologique a été tentée bien sûr, mais elle se confronte à « des difficultés pour donner du sens à des situations d'imprévisibilité, de rupture ». L'approche des dynamiques sociales prenant en compte formes d'imprévisibilité et changements brusques reste à construire. En effet, il est intéressant de noter la tension entre les tenants de la continuité et de « la prévision assurée[41] » et les tenants de la discontinuité qui relancent les réflexions sur la rupture. Philippe Durance constate alors que la prospective n'est pas mieux placée pour comprendre et anticiper. Il en conclut que la méthode se fait attendre. Ici, anticiper les pandémies - nous avons vécu le COVID-19 -, anticiper de nouveaux conflits de haute intensité suite à la guerre russo-ukrainienne, anticiper les catastrophes naturelles, les dislocations sociales, les « innovations foudroyantes » du champ digital constitue autant de « chocs futurs », de ruptures qui nous imposent de revisiter, voire repenser nos capacités d'anticipation, plus précisément nos capacités d'intelligence des situations et du futur – et donc nos grilles et nos outils.

II - Repenser nos approches

En effet, la tentative d'appréhension de cet état « de surprise permanente » révèle que bon nombre de nos outils, organisations et méthodes de détection et d'analyse s'avèrent inopérants. Il s'agit là d'une autre rupture vis-à-vis du passé : celle opérant au cœur de nos réflexions, ainsi que de nos « agirs stratégiques et prospectifs ».

Cette rupture constitue un redoutable défi en particulier pour la « discipline d'intelligence économique et stratégique » dont les porteurs, praticiens et chercheurs, doivent d'urgence « innover » face à des situations augmentées

---

40. Lire dans le numéro de la revue française de socioéconomie intitulée « Futurs économiques » second semestre 2018, l'article de Jean-Sébastien Vaire , « Les machines à produire des futurs économiques. Entre prédiction et prévision ». p. 105.

41. Le grand prospectiviste Jacques Lesournes considérait « que l'avenir était une suite de présents à peine déformés ». Mais aussi : « …face à l'incertain, formatés par les dispositifs institutionnels, idéologiques et cognitifs de « l'ancien monde », les acteurs ont du mal à se projeter dans le nouveau. » écrivent Jean-Eric Aubert, Jacques Theys, Christine Afriat de la Société française de prospective dans la note « Le monde d'après la COVID. Traces, Scénarii, Questions ». https://www.societefrancaisede- prospective.fr/wp-content/uploads/2021/03/SFDP-le-Monde-apr%C3%A8s-la-Covid-Traces- sc%C3%A9narios-questions.pdf.

et accélérées « d'incertitude de toutes les données »[42] créant comme « un brouillard ». À la fin Clausewitz nous indique que face à cette insuffisance de lumières et d'information, il convient de faire appel au « talent ou tout simplement de se confier au hasard ! ». La méthode se fait toujours attendre…

Pour une contribution à la nécessaire réflexion vers la construction d'une réponse mieux outillée à ce que nous appellerons volontiers une intelligence des ruptures, nous proposons de présenter des grilles de lectures significatives, « éclairantes », mises au point par des stratégistes confrontés à l'inconnu et aux surprises stratégiques et mobilisant la démarche d'intelligence économique et stratégique. Nous les avons identifiées dans le champ des stratégies d'innovation.

Leur objet est de comprendre et de « voir avant », pour se prémunir, échapper au pire, pour « survivre » en inventant des grilles de lectures et d'alertes composées à partir de ces briques de savoir évoquées dont l'enseignement premier est qu'elles sont pluridisciplinaires (sciences économiques, psychologie sociale, sociologie, anthropologie, sciences de l'ingénieur…).

Nous interrogerons en conclusion leur capacité à répondre aux réalités du monde de « l'innovation intensive » qui naît et se développe sous nos yeux, créateur à chaque instant d'inconnu et d'événements imprévisibles.

III - L'intelligence économique et stratégique au cœur de la dynamique d'innovation

Le diagnostic du monde VUCA

Les analystes en intelligence économique utilisent une méthode (doctrine) conçue au sortir de la guerre froide par les stratèges militaires qui permet de caractériser la réalité mouvante du monde des environnements économiques, sociaux, géopolitiques et géoéconomiques jusqu'à l'imprévisible. Le monde VUCA - pour volatil, uncertain, complex, ambiguous – nourrit une méthode de qualification des risques et s'applique parfaitement aux nouvelles dynamiques de l'innovation.

---

42. Carl von Clausewitz, Op. cité.

Volatil, l'environnement entraine des risques liés aux fluctuations des prix, à l'interruption de chaînes d'approvisionnement (suite pandémie), à l'apparition de nouveaux acteurs innovants dits « barbares », car ne respectant pas les règles du jeu et sans stratégie véritable. Incertain, l'environnement produit un risque créé par le manque de visibilité sur les menaces que constituent des acteurs sur lesquels une entreprise s'appuie (dépendance sur segment de sa chaine de valeur) ou bien des acteurs qui innovent hors de règles et schéma traditionnels – tiers-lieux, fab lab, hackathons. Complexe, l'environnement entraine des risques associés à la conduite d'activité dans de nombreux pays aux exigences réglementaires et culturelles spécifiques. Ambigu (« brouillard »), l'environnement produit du risque pour l'entreprise sur des marchés immatures ou émergents porteurs de nombreux facteurs inconnus.

Management de l'intelligence stratégique au service du management de l'innovation

Plus précisément et plus récemment, en 2015 (Comité européen de normalisation, CEN), puis en 2021 (ISO), praticiens et experts de la normalisation ont proposé respectivement des spécifications techniques et une norme sur le management de l'intelligence stratégique au service du management de l'innovation.

a) Management de l'intelligence stratégique (CEN)

Les rédacteurs du document « spécifications techniques » ont défini le système d'intelligence stratégique comme le processus et les structures qui permettent de produire l'intelligence stratégique nécessaire au décideur au cœur d'un projet d'innovation. L'intelligence stratégique est définie comme le résultat de l'analyse d'informations stratégiques dont l'objet est d'éclairer et organiser la stratégie en vue d'une meilleure anticipation, influence, d'un meilleur positionnement de l'entité porteur de projet.

L'intelligence stratégique a pour objet en particulier, la planification prospective en réponse aux changements de l'environnement, la réduction des risques, mais aussi l'innovation. La veille y est décrite comme démarche intégrée de surveillance active des environnements, afin d'anticiper les changements et les risques et identifier les opportunités.

b) Outils et méthode de l'intelligence stratégique

Les recommandations de l'ISO fondent une démarche moins ambitieuse que celle du CEN sur le diagnostic du « monde VUCA».

« Les organismes évoluent dans un environnement volatile, incertain, complexe et ambigu, caractérisé par l'accroissement des flux de connaissances, l'intensification de la concurrence mondiale et le rythme effréné des changements. Il est donc nécessaire d'anticiper le changement, d'influencer l'environnement et de prendre des décisions rapides et éclairées en matière d'innovation. Le croisement de la connaissance mondiale et des informations sur l'environnement exige que les leaders en charge de la réflexion stratégique exploitent ces connaissances pour définir leur stratégie en matière d'organisation et d'innovation. Cela aide les organismes à répondre aux changements de leur environnement, par exemple les changements sociaux, technologiques, de marché, de réglementation, de politique. »

L'intelligence stratégique est définie comme le résultat d'un processus structuré visant à collecter des données, informations et connaissances, à les traiter et à les communiquer aux décideurs; ce processus peut être appliqué en continu ou sur des projets spécifiques amenés à être lancés.

La méthode des signes d'alerte précoces

Le professeur Humbert Lesca a cherché à donner corps à l'anticipation à travers des méthodologies de veille stratégique et d'intelligence économique. Il installe sa réflexion dans le paradigme de la pensée stratégique et considère qu'anticiper consiste à « détecter les signes annonciateurs d'un possible changement dans l'environnement, de façon à pouvoir agir très vite avant la réalisation complète du changement... et avant les autres entreprises, notamment les concurrents». À cette attitude correspond la « veille active » destinée à « capter des signes que personne n'a voulu émettre délibérément», mais qu'il est possible de détecter/capter si l'on sait s'organiser pour ce faire. L'action d'anticipation se décompose en trois étapes :

- Prendre conscience qu'il existe plusieurs situations possibles parmi lesquelles l'une d'entre elles est susceptible d'advenir.
- Préparer la situation qui permettra d'être en mesure d'agir immédiatement dès qu'un des scénarii envisagés advient et imaginer la sortie de crise si le scénario attendu n'advient pas.

- Se mettre « à l'affût de signes d'alerte précoce » ou signaux faibles annonciateurs d'une situation identifiée par avance ou non préparée.

La méthode des « Strategic Early Warnings »

Dans une démarche d'intelligence compétitive et stratégique et un mode de pensée similaire à celui de Lesca, publié en 2002, le stratégiste américain, Ben Gilad s'interroge : « comment utiliser l'intelligence compétitive pour anticiper les évolutions de marché, maîtriser les risques et créer des stratégies de puissance ? »

Il part du constat suivant : les attaques-surprises d'entreprises sur leurs concurrents qui ont été couronnées de succès ne l'ont pas été à cause de la mise en place de leurres puissants rendant les signaux faibles indétectables. Elles l'ont été à cause des erreurs d'appréciation, des crispations stratégiques, des représentations erronées ou des certitudes et des croyances obsolètes qui ont conduit le stratège à ignorer les risques.

Dès lors en croisant psychologie sociale, intelligence organisationnelle, intelligence compétitive, il propose aux décideurs et aux stratèges d'entreprises de se prémunir contre ce qu'il appelle les « surprises stratégiques » par l'anticipation. Il distingue trois catégories de risques stratégiques : les risques opérationnels, les risques de dépréciation d'actifs, les risques dus à des évènements extérieurs.

Conjugués, ces risques créent un risque majeur pour l'entreprise: la « dissonance de l'organisation par rapport à la réalité de son secteur d'activité (positionnement/spécialisation/innovation/avantages compétitifs) et donc les attentes du marché. Quasi indétectable, ce risque majeur engendre une surprise stratégique et une rupture qui risquent d'être mortelles. Les grandes lignes opérationnelles de sa méthode du Système concurrentiel d'alertes précoces sont les suivantes :

- Identifier les risques futurs: cibler les facteurs de changement (évènement, variables qui déforment la réalité des secteurs ;

- Surveiller les risques et déployer une démarche d'intelligence compétitive: à la recherche des scénarios en train de se construire chez les concurrents.

- Gérer l'action, ciblée sur le risque en développement en intervenant sur la culture des managers face aux changements-surprises).

L'approche de l'assureur AXA : anticiper l'émergence des risques

La démarche propose un pilotage stratégique qui exige une veille qualitative renforcée afin de détecter les signaux faibles et repérer des risques jusqu'alors inconnus. Elle s'appuie sur la publication de travaux innovants sur ces risques. Il s'agit de détecter le plus tôt possible toute apparition d'un nouveau risque, tout changement dans les caractéristiques d'un risque.

Les experts d'AXA vont utiliser des outils automatiques d'analyse (intelligence augmentée) : il s'agit de travailler sur l'évolution d'occurrence de mots-clés associés à ces risques sur internet, de capturer des pics d'actualités liés à une publication scientifique ayant potentiellement un impact sur l'environnement ou la santé. Comment dès lors rendre opérationnelle l'anticipation de risques émergents? La réponse est intéressante, qui s'appuie sur l'innovation organisationnelle à travers une gouvernance revisitée (réseaux de capteurs pour remonter les premiers éléments de connaissance et les meilleures actions de prévention et d'innovation).

Ces formalisations de la démarche de management de l'intelligence stratégique semblent pourtant déjà dépassées, car l'ensemble de ces démarches et de ces modes opératoires suggèrent, somme toute, que le risque est prévisible. L'incertitude ici, et ce qui la caractérise - le manque d'information - peut être compensé par un dispositif d'intelligence de situation réajustée, aussi par un processus d'intelligence augmentée d'intelligence artificielle (AI). Cela est-il opérationnel et efficient quand la « puissance de l'imprévisible » déploie ses effets ?

IV - Comprendre les rupture et imprévisibilité : contribution

Nous retenons du regard aiguisé de Philippe Durance que « Penser la rupture » est un chemin neuf à découvrir et à concevoir et que l'approche des dynamiques sociales en la matière reste encore à construire. Tentons quelques pistes. Reprenons des situations exemplaires.

Dans la définition des nouvelles dynamiques d'innovation, en introduction, nous avons décrit les « innovations foudroyantes », véritables ruptures dans l'ordre établi des stratégies formalisées par les chercheurs de l'Institut Accenture[43]. Nouveau type d'innovation, il peut potentiellement perturber

43. Larry Downes, Paul Nunes, préc.cité.

toutes les positions établies, rendre obsolètes les capacités stratégiques traditionnelles et rendre aveugles les capacités d'intelligence et d'anticipation. Il n'est plus question de surprise stratégique ! Ces nouveaux types d'innovations (produits ou de services) et les stratégies qui les entraînent sont indétectables. Ils peuvent « anéantir votre position sur le marché » et créer un potentiel de situation entraînant la « mort subite » de tout leader sur un marché.

L'innovation ouverte, en réseau, sort de l'entreprise. Elle se déploie dans des lieux informels - fab labs, living lab. Elle peut surgir d'évènements particuliers (hackathons), selon des dispositifs d'échanges difficilement lisibles et prévisibles, car produits généralement sur le cloud (plateformes).

Ces innovations, ni prévues ni intentionnelles, créent des « effets foudroyants » au-delà de la surprise. Elles imposent de repenser la notion de stratégie et donc des capacités d'intelligence pour les piloter.

À cet égard, les ouvertures outillées que proposent les chercheurs sont surprenantes. Exemples : savoir déceler ce qui se cache derrière des expériences apparemment aléatoires, scruter l'horizon, embaucher des « voyants » autrement dénommés « diseurs de vérités ». Cela nous renvoie à des savoir-faire et des savoir-être anciens : la divination ou l'art d'interpréter les signes, voire « la rationalité divinatoire » ou savoir interpréter les signes avant-coureurs d'une réalité en devenir. Cette « mentalité indicielle[44] considère essentiellement les évènements et les phénomènes comme des indices d'une réalité en devenir. ». En 1994, le stratégiste américain, Richard A. D'Aveni, rédige un ouvrage - « Hypercompetition » - dans lequel un chapitre est dédié à « la divination stratégique » ou la capacité d'imaginer pour le rendre possible ce qui n'existe pas encore (produit, usage, besoin des clients…).

Autre chemin. Pour penser « l'agir stratégique » en situation de chaos, de bouleversement créé par la rupture, se dessinent les travaux récents de Soufyane Frimousse[45]. Il s'inspire des analyses de Nassim Taleb[46] sur

---

44. Sun Tzu, L'art de la guerre, commentaire Alain Thote, Nouveau Monde éditions, 2010.

45. Guide de l'antifragilité ou "comment évoluer dans et par le chaos en devenant antifragile"? (Editions ems, management & société. 2022).

46. Nassim M. TALEB, « Le cygne noir ou la puissance de l'imprévisible », Les Belles Lettres, 2012.

les cygnes noirs pour tenter une démarche nouvelle. « La puissance de l'imprévisible » est la norme du nouvel univers qui est le nôtre et peut tout emporter sur son passage, les positions les mieux établies. Selon l'auteur, les « Cygnes noirs » sont des évènements hautement improbables à l'impact gigantesque et que nous rationalisons a posteriori pour tenter de comprendre. Il met en avant des « failles de l'esprit humain », les biais cognitifs, les mensonges à soi-même, les « tâches aveugles » sur l'œil qui empêchent de mesurer/ apprécier le risque à sa juste valeur. Nous retrouvons ici la démarche d'intelligence économique dont l'un des objets principaux est de lutter contre ces « défauts d'intelligence » des situations, ces biais cognitifs.

Nassim Taleb identifie à cet égard le « triplet de l'opacité » qui obère la compréhension des situations et donc la perception des risques. En premier lieu, l'illusion de comprendre, lorsque chacun croit savoir ce qui se passe dans le monde complexe. Ensuite, la déformation rétrospective qui ne permet d'évaluer les situations qu'après qu'elles se soient développées. Enfin, interviennent la surestimation des informations factuelles et les personnes d'autorités qui simplifient à outrance. Ce triplet aboutit à des erreurs radicales et des décisions absurdes. Soufiane Frimousse conclut qu'en situation de rupture, il convient de ne pas s'échapper et de "se nourrir du désordre et de l'incertitude ce qui permettra de se relever..."

Une dernière perspective nous conduit sur la piste de l'approche socio-économique pour comprendre les ruptures et cela précisément dans les dynamiques d'innovation. Jean-Eric Aubert[47] dans son ouvrage percutant sur les cultures et les systèmes d'innovation dans le monde replace « l'esprit des peuples », les cultures et leurs influences sur la performance économique.

Dans cette démarche d'intelligence des systèmes d'innovation, il préfigure, à travailler, une démarche indiciaire (repérage dans des détails de comportements, de politiques publiques...) qui permettra d'ouvrir le champ à une intelligence des ruptures dans les innovations sociétales comme technologiques. Quand les circonstances dominent, il convient d'utiliser le potentiel de situation, en particulier sociétal, pour avancer.

---

47. Jean-Eric AUBERT, Cultures et systèmes d'innovation., Presses des Mines, Paris, 2017.

Conclusion

Cette approche de la rupture dans un contexte d'innovation intensive donne du sens aux travaux qui interpellent l'impact de l'innovation sur la vie sociale, prenant en compte les perceptions des populations et les revendications collectives. L'approche replace au cœur de l'outillage nécessaire les capacités et les méthodes de l'intelligence économique à condition que soit effectué un travail d'innovation croisant le paradigme de l'enquête jusque dans sa dimension prospective. L'intelligence du présent doit nous inciter à projeter nos stratégies vers le futur.

III
QUELLES APPROCHES POUR UNE INNOVATION DURABLE ET INCLUSIVE EN AFRIQUE ?

1- APPROCHE FORMATION

PRODUIRE DU SAVOIR ET DES CONNAISSANCES SUR LE CONTINENT AFRICAIN

Soufyane Frimousse

De nombreuses organisations et institutions enracinées en Afrique se sont engagées dans un véritable processus de transformation inclusif. Pérenniser et renforcer cette dynamique réclame notamment d'engager une métamorphose du système d'éducation et de formation des Africains. Il s'agit, entre autres, de passer de l'extraversion à la contextualisation.

L'extraversion façonne depuis l'extérieur les appareils productifs, les systèmes éducatifs et de formation, les rapports sociaux de production, les sphères intellectuelles. Cette extraversion en Afrique a été rendue possible bien plus pour les desseins des agents de l'ultralibéralisme économique et financier qu'elle sert que par une quelconque capacité à comprendre les situations africaines. Ceux qui mettent en œuvre des programmes d'éducation et de formation calqués sur les modèles dominants expriment très peu de tolérance à l'égard de l'esprit critique et de l'expression d'opinions contraires aux leurs, à quelque niveau que ce soit.

A l'inverse, l'introversion/ contextualisation s'appuie sur des dimensions territoriales locales réelles et subjectives (sens, symboles...) pour engendrer son modèle de développement. Pour les épistémologies populaires africaines (Frimousse, 2020), la réalité va au-delà de ce que l'on voit. Elle est plus vaste que la logique. Elles créent des passerelles entre ce qu'on appelle le naturel et le surnaturel, le physique et la métaphysique, le rationnel et l'irrationnel, l'objectif et le subjectif, le scientifique et le superstitieux, le visible et l'invisible, le réel et l'irréel, l'explicable et l'inexplicable. Le réel n'est pas seulement ce qui peut être observé ou ce qui fait appel au sens cognitif. Il englobe également l'invisible, l'émotionnel, le sentimental ou l'inexplicable. Il incombe donc aux universités, aux universitaires et aux chercheurs africains la responsabilité de combattre les prétentions de l'extraversion qui tendent à nier ces dimensions. En Afrique, les différentes modalités d'extraversion se renforcent les unes les autres, pour créer un système dual, au sein duquel les élites, d'un côté, et la population, de l'autre, vivent chacune leur propre histoire (Nubukpo, 2019).

L'Afrique devra s'employer à former une nouvelle génération de dirigeants afin que les succès présentés à travers les 39 chapitres s'inscrivent dans un paradigme managérial, politique et économique garant d'impacts positifs sur la société (personnes, planète). C'est à travers une formation reposant sur la contextualisation que ces dirigeants seront le plus à même de répondre aux défis mondiaux.

Rappelons que l'Afrique est le continent le plus jeune de la planète avec 200 millions d'habitants âgés de 15 à 24 ans. Ces jeunes africains deviendront pour certains les leaders et la force motrice du développement économique, social et culturel du continent. Un système éducatif performant et accessible au plus grand nombre est donc essentiel. D'après l'UNESCO, l'Afrique doit former 2,5 millions de scientifiques, de techniciens et d'informaticiens pour atteindre les objectifs du millénaire pour le développement. Dans des pays comme la Namibie, le Zimbabwe, la Tanzanie, les universités forment en moyenne chaque année un ingénieur qualifié pour 6000 habitants. La Chine en forme 1 pour 200 habitants. La recherche publique africaine consacre moins de 1% du PIB continental à l'investissement dans la recherche et le développement.

Malgré des avancées (ex. : abolition des frais de scolarité dans le primaire dans certains pays, recours aux plateformes éducatives…), le système d'éducation et de formation en Afrique demeure généralement obsolète et inopérant. En fait, l'Afrique doit se demander si son actuel système d'éducation et de formation contribue à la transformation ou s'il ne sert qu'au maintien et à la reproduction du système. Le plus souvent, les formations sont centrées sur une logique de reproduction, car les écoles et les universités sont généralement des milieux conservateurs et élitistes, qui forment des managers, des théoriciens, des décideurs qui vont tendre à reproduire les mêmes modèles avec les mêmes modes de pensée. De trop nombreux diplômés ne sont pas prêts, aujourd'hui, à évoluer pour faire face au monde de demain, car les instances traditionnelles d'éducation et de formation ne sont pas disposées à leur offrir la formation à ce monde à venir.

Le savoir instrumental et immédiatement rentable a éradiqué le savoir constructeur de sens et de synthèses créatrices. Les savoirs « boîtes à outils », axés sur le développement de réflexes de résolution de problèmes, ont pris la place des vrais savoirs, nourris d'intelligence et de capacité d'innovation. Ce modèle éducatif et de formation repose sur les capacités mécaniques décisionnelles impliquant de moins en moins la réflexion. Or l'intelligence humaine suppose la capacité d'effectuer des combinaisons conceptuelles originales, mais aussi et surtout une idée de finalité, et de sens. Il ne saurait donc y avoir d'intelligence que là où il y a conscience.

Il ne faut pas confondre penser avec calculer et réfléchir avec analyser. À force de techniciser et de rendre strictement utilitaires à peu près tous les enseignements, la culture et les humanités ont été supprimées des bancs des écoles et des universités.

Les disciplines consacrées à l'humain sont source de pensée et de comportements plus relativistes, en opposition à l'intensification de la production et à la consommation effrénée dans notre société. L'enseignement actuel est devenu une sorte de justification du cynisme de l'économie ultra- libérale. La plupart des enseignements n'amènent pas à chercher, à comprendre et à se poser des questions, mais à ingurgiter des réponses toutes faites. Reproduire des automatismes et modéliser une pensée opératoire, même sophistiquée, n'est sûrement pas enseigner ni former…

Or, l'Afrique a besoin de citoyens qui pensent et non pas uniquement des citoyens qui produisent et consomment. N'oublions pas que le rôle premier de l'institution d'éducation et de formation est de donner à chacun les moyens de se révéler et de devenir ce qu'il sera. Afin d'éduquer et de former chaque être humain à devenir un citoyen prêt à jouer pleinement son rôle, il est nécessaire, au préalable, de tout mettre en œuvre pour favoriser l'émergence en lui de capacités de discernement, d'une part, d'aptitudes à interroger les modèles et les pratiques en place, d'autre part. La finalité étant de participer au progrès de la société en l'impactant positivement. La principale vocation de la fonction éducative et de formation est de transmettre de façon totale à tous ses membres, l'ensemble des savoirs, valeurs, culture… d'une génération à la suivante. La création de repères facilite en effet la prise de conscience d'éventuels maux survenus en vue de les corriger et les dépasser. Ceci est loin de l'objectif actuel qui est de former pour les besoins du marché donc de sortir des employables, machines à profits privés sans règles et sans limites. Vouloir être en adéquation avec les attentes du marché du travail est louable à condition d'interroger et d'évaluer la nature de ces attentes et ces besoins ! Prenons garde des décisions prises à courte vue et de leurs répercussions sur la planète ! Avec un système de formation et d'éducation orienté vers la satisfaction des besoins du marché et un citoyen de plus en plus dépourvu de capacité de pensée propre, peut-on réellement et sérieusement envisager l'avènement de l'organisation apprenante inventive sociétalement responsable en Afrique ?!

Pour Aktouf (2019), les espaces éducatifs et de formation formatent et produisent uniquement des diplômés destinés au marché de l'employabilité au service du grand capital détruisant au passage la création artistique et plus généralement la pensée. L'innovation, l'économie de la connaissance et la transformation que réclament et glorifient toujours davantage la littérature managériale et les entreprises ne peuvent sûrement pas venir d'employables dupliqués ! Par contre, ils seront certainement provoqués par des citoyens correctement formés et cultivés ! Cette dynamique peut être enclenchée par un système public et/ou un système privé complémentaire et non concurrent, car l'éducation et la formation ne doivent être livrées aux lois de l'argent et de sa fructification. Dans cette optique, l'enseignement et la formation en sciences de gestion revêtent un rôle crucial.

En effet, William Wright (1956), dans son livre The Organization Man, a bien décrit comment les écoles de management et les procédures de sélection dans les entreprises étaient très souvent des procédures de fabrication du conformisme à grande échelle. Il insistait sur l'impasse d'une telle fabrication du conformisme qui ne pouvait engendrer que des sociétés bloquées et figées. Il dénonçait le passage du conformisme de conservatisme des écoles de management à celui spécifique de chaque organisation pour donner à la fin ce nouveau produit si apprécié : l'homme bien arrondi, bien assimilé, conforme… l'homme de l'organisation ! Cet auteur est plus que jamais d'actualité. Dans cette optique, l'éducation et la formation en management doivent à l'avenir s'intégrer dans un projet social plus large. Car le management appelle à des actions, à une transformation, à une logique prescriptive. Cette dimension du management doit être au service d'objectifs collectifs. Cela exige une sensibilité humaine, une tendance à la déviance positive, une culture générale et un pragmatisme. Il s'agit de s'actualiser et de s'adapter à un monde qui est en constante mutation.

Il est urgent de redonner à l'éducation et à la formation, du primaire à l'universitaire, leurs rôles premiers de socialisation communautaire de l'enfant futur citoyen et d'aiguiser l'esprit critique. Il faut refuser de défendre un univers humain et une nature, réduits à leur seule contribution à la croissance économique. N'oublions pas que l'analphabétisme n'est pas qu'absence d'instruction…il est tout aussi bien l'absence de sens et de valeurs autres que matériels.

Bien évidemment, une vision systémique et non fragmentée est indispensable pour fournir un terreau et un écosystème assez fertile aux actuelles et aux futurs succès. En effet, un système d'éducation et de formation doit être pensé en lien avec celui de la santé, du logement, de l'alimentation, des transports, de la démographie… tout cela est lié. Cela s'appelle un projet de société !

Bibliographie

Aktouf O. 2019. « Loi du profit, éducation et lois du marché néolibéral : absurdes tautologies et mortifères dogmes-syllogismes. ». L'observatoire. Espaces et sociétés.

Frimousse S. 2020. « Pour une épistémologie frontalière en Sciences de Gestion » in S. Frimousse et J.M. Peretti, Produire du savoir et de l'action. Le vade-mecum du dirigeant-chercheur. EMS. Éditions. Collection ASMP.

Nubukpo K. 2019. L'urgence africaine. Changeons le modèle de croissance. Odile Jacob.

Wright W. 1956. The organisation man. Simon and Schuster.

L'APPORT DE L'INTELLIGENCE ARTIFICIELLE POUR L'INNOVATION - PRÉDIRE LE SUCCÈS OU L'ÉCHEC D'UN PRODUIT

Marie Saade et Imad Saleh

Introduction

Depuis trente ans, les entreprises privées ou publiques vivent des transformations majeures dans leur gestion et dans leur production. Des compétences nouvelles ont émergé et sont intégrées dans leurs activités, de nouveaux métiers apparaissent en lien étroit avec les informations. Grâce aux nouvelles technologies, les informations circulent rapidement et plus simplement. Elles sont devenues le patrimoine et la richesse immatériels des entreprises et des organisations. Le bon usage de ces informations joue un rôle stratégique pour le succès ou l'échec d'une entreprise. Elles deviennent le pétrole du 21ème siècle.

Les entreprises et les gouvernements donnent de plus en plus d'importance à l'innovation pour le développement de l'économie. Maroun Jneid a constaté que « *Nombreux gouvernements, institutions et entreprises sont conscients de l'importance de l'innovation pour la compétitivité de leur économie et projet de développement : ils promeuvent l'innovation à travers différentes formes de soutien* » (Jneid 2014).

Les outils technologiques permettent aux entreprises d'explorer de nouveaux marchés ou de nouvelles perspectives pour leur développement dans un monde concurrentiel. Actuellement, les entreprises innovantes basent leurs stratégies sur les technologies de l'information et de la communication pour rester compétitives et maintenir leur présence dans un marché très concurrentiel. (Monino 2013, Henry 2019).

Les entreprises doivent avoir un comportement dynamique, proactif et de remise en question en permanence pour maintenir leur compétitivité et leur présence sur le marché. La concurrence est un des facteurs clés qui oblige les entreprises à être en innovation perpétuelle (Delpeuch 2016).

Il existe un lien étroit entre les notions « concurrentiel » et celle de l'« innovation ». De petits actes innovants sont les moyens pour les entreprises de rester compétitives et pour maintenir leur avantage concurrentiel. Actuellement les entreprises mettent des moyens humains et financiers pour créer des produits innovants. Elles ont créé des centres de recherches destinés à l'innovation et l'invention.

L'innovation « *c'est avant tout une accumulation de petites idées et d'avancées plutôt que l'avènement d'une idée révolutionnaire. Souvent, il a été constaté que l'innovation n'est pas une idée « nouvelle » au sens propre du terme. C'est souvent une idée qui n'a pas été portée ou menée à son terme au préalable. Pour mener à bien une innovation, la volonté ne suffit pas. Cela reste un savoureux mélange d'investissement croisé entre les compétences, les connaissances, la mobilisation des actifs physiques, mais également de la réputation de la marque adossée à l'innovation* » (Henry 2019).

Organisation de Coopération et de développement économiques (OCDE) a défini l'innovation

« la mise en œuvre d'un produit, que ce soit une bien ou un service, d'un processus nouveau ou sensiblement amélioré, d'une nouvelle méthode de commercialisation ou d'une nouvelle méthode organisationnelle dans les pratiques de l'entreprise, l'organisation du lieu de travail ou les relations extérieures. » (OCDE 2006 ; Henry et al., 2017).

Diffère entre Invention et innovation

Inventer c'est créer « un nouveau produit ou dispositif, un nouveau procédé ou méthode d'obtention d'un résultat inconnu jusque-là » ; innover diffère d'inventer au sens où « tous les éléments constitutifs sont non seulement connus, mais de plus le résultat à obtenir est totalement prévisible » (idem). Exemple : « le fait d'ajouter un chronocontacteur à une cafetière qui mettra cette dernière en fonctionnement à l'heure que vous aurez déterminée à l'avance tout en vous servant de réveil matin n'est en aucun cas une invention, mais une innovation. » (Quenderff 1986, Henry 2019).

Drucker en 1985 a proposé une liste des actions à prendre en compte et d'autres à éviter pour développer l'innovation (Jneid 2014), parmi elles :

1. Vérifier et analyser l'objectif de l'innovation de manière permanente.
2. Comprendre le degré d'acceptation de l'innovation dans la société.
3. Commencer l'innovation sur un petit niveau pour qu'elle puisse se développer avec le temps.

Les trois actions à éviter sont :

1. Ne pas poursuivre l'innovation seulement parce qu'elle est révolutionnaire.
2. Ne pas faire trop de choses en même temps.
3. Ne pas développer une innovation sur le long terme.

L'innovation demeure un facteur essentiel pour réussir l'entrepreneuriat et pour améliorer les avantages compétitifs d'une façon durable

Modèles d'innovation

Gallouj et Savona ont proposé six modèles d'innovation (Gallouj et Savona 2009) :

- **l'innovation radicale :** proposer un changement technologique notable à un produit,
- **l'innovation d'amélioration :** apporter une amélioration sur un produit,
- **l'innovation incrémentale :** ajouter ou remplacer des caractéristiques à un produit,
- **l'innovation ad hoc :** Interagir avec un client pour trouver une solution la plus d'adaptée pour un problème particulier,
- **l'innovation de la recombinatoire :** refaire une nouvelle proposition de combinaison de caractéristiques techniques d'un produit,
- **l'innovation de formalisation :** mettre en ordre les caractéristiques des services ou d'un produit.

Lee et al. (2012) ont décrit les étapes majeures de l'évolution de l'innovation (Jneid en 2014 a fait une synthèse dans sa thèse) :

Innovation 1.0 : innovation fermée

L'innovation fermée est basée sur les synergies internes de l'entreprise, où plusieurs entrées déclenchent le processus d'innovation et conduisent à une seule sortie.

Innovation 2.0 : innovation collaborative

Le progrès des TIC permet facilement aux organisations de rechercher une collaboration avec d'autres possédant des compétences de classe mondiale. C'est une nouvelle forme de partenariat, de partage de connaissances et savoir-faire et également de technologies/brevets. La collaboration devient un outil pour promouvoir les entreprises. Les relations inter- organisationnelles aident à développer des chaînes de valeur qui se dotent d'un avantage concurrentiel durable.

Innovation 3.0 : innovation ouverte

En 2003, Chesbrough a proposé le mot « innovation ouverte » qui prend en considération les aspects intérieurs et extérieurs de l'entreprise dans des efforts de collaboration innovante. Il s'agit d'ajouter des compétences externes de l'entreprise et de les intégrer dans ses propres compétences internes. Cette approche est basée sur le développement des TIC et réseaux qui permettent de collaborer sans contrainte de temps et d'espace (Chesbrough 2003).

2. Intelligence artificielle (IA)

Discipline scientifique inventée en 1955 par deux mathématiciens, John MacCathy et Marvin Lee Minsky. Marvin a défini « *L'IA est la science de programmer les ordinateurs pour qu'ils réalisent des tâches qui nécessitent de l'intelligence lorsqu'elles sont réalisées par des êtres humains* ».

Méthodes

« *L'Intelligence Artificielle (IA, ou AI en anglais pour Artificial Intelligence) consiste à mettre en œuvre un certain nombre de techniques visant à permettre aux machines d'imiter une forme d'intelligence réelle, notamment s'adapter, apprendre, communiquer et interagir d'une manière riche et variée avec leur environnement. Le but n'est pas de remplacer les personnes par des machines, mais d'ajouter aux capacités humaines une possibilité inégalée. La capacité de l'Intelligence Artificielle est d'analyser des quantités phénoménales de données et de déceler des tendances qui seraient autrement impossibles à détecter* » (idem)

Elle couvre plusieurs domaines : la machine Learning, traitement automatique de langue, le traitement de paroles, la robotique, traduction automatique, etc.

La figure 1 donne un aperçu sur les types d'intelligence artificielle (IA)

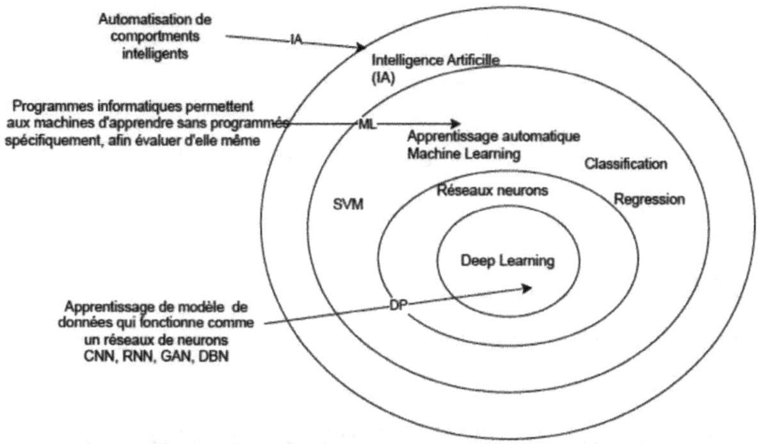

Figure 1 : Retravailler à partir du site https://www.informatiquenews.fr/lintelligence-artificielle-ia-dans-le-monde-numerique-90281 et https://fr.wikipedia.org/wiki/Intelligence_artificielle

La figure 2 (tirée du site de Lilian Buzer) donne un aperçu sur le fonctionnement des réseaux neurones, explication : nous avons quatre valeurs en entrée et au centre 5 neurones et à la sortie une valeur unique.

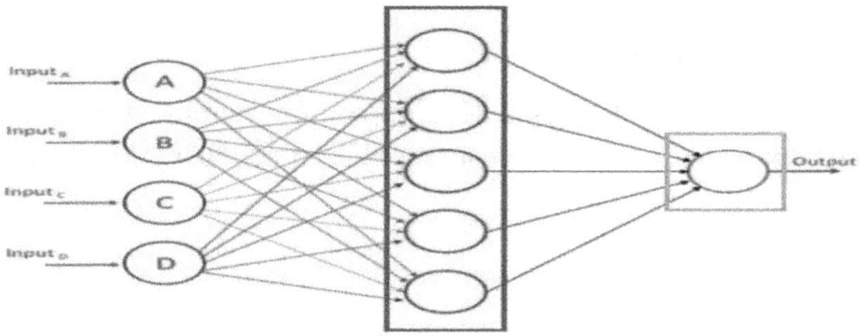

Les processus de fonctionnement des réseaux des neurones (figure 3)

Collecte	Préparation	Apprentissage	Résultat et Action
- Logs - Capteurs - Données des utilisateurs - Données extermes - Métriques	- Nettoyage de données - Normalisation - Hminisation des dates - Enrichissement	- Algorithmes non supervisés - Algorithimes supersvisés - Teste	-Alerte -Décision -Auto remédiation -Freebak -Représentation visuelle des données

Figure 3 : Retravailler à partir de la présentation d'Emmanuel ESTEVES[48]

Il existe deux catégories de l'IA :

« **IA faible :**

- Purement réactive : pas de mémoire, pas d'expérience, perception du monde à un instant donné.
- Mémoire limitée : mémoire, expérience du passé, suivi de l'évolution de la représentation du monde.

IA forte :

- Représentation de l'esprit : Comprend la représentation du monde et a conscience des objets s'y trouvent.
- Conscience propre : construis sa propre représentation du monde. Conscience de soi[49]».

3. Notre proposition

La majorité des entreprises développent constamment de nouveaux produits innovants, mais ils sont susceptibles d'échouer et ceci peut avoir

48. Présentation d'Emmanuel ESTEVES, intitulée l'intelligence artificielle dans le monde numérique (Mardi 5 mai 2020)

49. https://www.mailabs.fr/lintelligence-artificielle-faible-et-forte-en-entreprise/#lintelligencefortecompar%C3%A9%C3%A0lintelligencefaible

des conséquences sur la survie de l'entreprise (Jneid & Tannous, 2012). Il est important que les chefs d'entreprises aient à leur disposition des moyens pour évaluer le cycle de vie d'un produit, en identifier la rupture potentielle pour pouvoir déterminer sa phase de déclin (Sun, et al., 2008), en analysant la situation actuelle du marché mondial tout en prolongeant le cycle de vie du produit en l'améliorant. (Gopalakrishnan & Santoro, 2004, Schramm-Klein, et al., 2011, Saade 2021).

Par la suite dans cet article, nous nous interrogeons :

- Comment les entreprises peuvent-elles mesurer et estimer les risques de manière quantitative et précoce avant d'investir dans un produit donné ?
- Comment prédire le taux de succès d'un produit existant ou nouveau de manière systématique afin de faciliter le processus de prise de décisions dans les entreprises ?
- Comment l'IA peut-elle aider les entreprises à rester compétitives ?

La suite de l'article est basée sur la thèse de Marie Saade, soutenue en 2021 à l'université Paris 8 sous le titre « L'intelligence artificielle dans la gestion de l'innovation des produits dans les organisations : Analyse et conception d'une plateforme d'aide à la décision ». Elle propose de nouvelles méthodologies basées sur deux types de réseaux de neurones (le réseau de neurones large et profond et le réseau de neurones récurrents) pour construire des modèles prédictifs et des modèles d'aide à la décision. Les technologies de l'IA aident les entreprises à améliorer la prise de décision pour ce qui est du développement de produit/service innovant tout en mesurant et prédisant le succès d'un nouveau produit pour le secteur : l'industrie des produits technologiques (dans notre cas).

La prédiction du succès d'un produit est une tâche difficile à cause de la disponibilité des données et de l'importance accordée à la précision de la prédiction :

- **Collecte et fusion de données :** La collecte de données et l'extraction de connaissances pertinentes sont des tâches complexes à cause de l'imprécision, l'hétérogénéité, l'ambiguïté des données (différents types et structures de données, différentes sources de données, etc.) et les limites de leur disponibilité (Hariri, et al., 2019, Ray, et al., 2018).

- **Performance des systèmes d'aide à la décision** : La performance du réseau pour ce qui est de la prédiction est souvent surreprésentée par un taux de précision élevé, étant donné que le taux de précision pourrait varier dépendamment des données disponibles.

État de l'art

Le tableau 1 présente l'état de l'art sur les méthodologies des recherches pour les prédications du succès ou l'échec d'un produit innovant.

Méthodologies	Indicateurs	Références
Détection les nouvelles technologies : un réseau de neurones multicouche	Nombre de brevets délivrés, Nombre de citations de brevets.	(Lee, Kwon, Kim, & Kwon, 2017)
La méthode de la « feuille de route technologique »	Brevets et Publications	(Wang B., Liu, Zhou, & Wen, 2018)
Distribution de probabilités à l'aide d'un modèle de réseau neuronal.	Revenus	(Zhao & Zhao, 2017)

Le tableau 1 : État de l'art

Méthodologie proposée

Cette méthodologie se base sur trois dimensions :
- les brevets,
- les publications,
- Les revenus.

Le but de cette approche est de prédire le taux de croissance du nombre de brevets délivrés ainsi que le taux de croissance des publications qui seront utilisés au cours de la phase finale de la prédiction des gammes de revenus. Pour appliquer cette approche, il faut traiter :

- la collecte de données (Rechercher les mots-clés relatifs à chaque technologie),
- l'intégration des bases de données (extraire des mots-clés de brevets,
- des publications et les montants de revenu par année et par technologie),
- la manipulation de données (calculer le nombre des brevets et publications par année)
- la création de jeux de données (grouper les données sur les brevets par technologie pour max années. max représente le nombre maximal d'années par technologie pour lesquelles les données historiques sont disponibles dans les jeux de données destinés à l'entrainement,la mise en œuvre des réseaux de neurones. Nous avons mis en œuvre deux réseaux : réseau de neurones 1 avec des données sur les brevets et les publications, et Réseau de Neurones 2 avec des données sur les revenus. L'objectif a testé les deux réseaux de neurones : le réseau de neurones large et profond multidimensionnel et le réseau de neurones récurrents multidimensionnel. Le réseau de neurones prédit les données de manière récursive pour les p années à venir.
- la visualisation /analyse des résultats et la prise de décision. L'analyse quantitative des données basée sur : les brevets, les publications,
- les revenus est utilisée pour évaluer l'impact de ces dimensions sur le succès des produits technologiques.

Structures des modèles de réseaux de neurones

Ces réseaux de neurones sont mis en œuvre à l'aide de la bibliothèque du logiciel TensorFlow[50] (TensorFlow 2013, 2019) sous Python. Comme nous l'avons précédemment mentionné, les deux types de réseaux de neurones ont la structure suivante :

Réseau de Neurones 1

Le réseau de Neurones 1 est mis en œuvre à l'aide de deux modèles différents utilisés à des fins comparatives, pour estimer le nombre de brevets délivrés d'une part et le nombre de publications d'autre part.

---

50. Tensorflow est une interface de programmation applicative créée par Google est utilisée pour l'apprentissage automatique.

Le réseau de neurones profond à une dimension (ODWDNN, One-dimensional Wide and Deep Neural Network)

Ce réseau de neurones a la structure du modèle linéaire du « Deep Neural Network (DNN) Linear Combined Regressor » où les données de sorties prédites représentent une variable numérique continue. Le réseau est conçu avec la même architecture et configuration que le réseau de neurones large et profond de l'article de Saade, Jneid et Saleh (Saade, Jneid, & Saleh, 2019, 2020). En effet, le réseau comporte h couches cachées et chaque couche comporte un nombre spécifique de nœuds n. Le réseau est construit en se basant sur l'algorithme d'optimisation Adam[51], conçu pour entrainer les réseaux de neurones profonds, qui peut être plus performant que les autres méthodes d'optimisation stochastique (Kingma & Ba, 2015). Le nombre de brevets/publications sera également prédit pour la technologie donnée pour chaque année de manière séparée de sorte que chaque donnée de sortie prédite soit une donnée d'entrée pour la prochaine prédiction, et ce, jusqu'à ce que le nombre d'années futures p soit atteint.

Le réseau de neurones récurrents à une dimension (One-dimensional RNN, ODRNN)

Le réseau est conçu avec la même architecture et configuration que le réseau de neurones récurrents (Saade, Jneid, & Saleh, 2019). En effet, le réseau comporte h couches cachées récurrentes et chaque couche comporte un nombre spécifique de nœuds n. Le réseau est construit en se basant sur les **caractéristiques suivantes :**

- **Cellules LSTM :** il s'agit de cellules composées de fonctions d'activation qui peuvent être plus performantes que les couches récurrentes traditionnelles.
- **Une architecture neuronale du type Seq2Seq :** où le RNN encode une séquence de données en un vecteur de taille fixe et les décode en une représentation vectorielle de taille fixe en une séquence cible

51. « L'algorithme d'optimisation Adam est utilisé pour la formation de modèles d'apprentissage profond. Il s'agit d'une extension de la descente de gradient stochastique. Dans cet algorithme d'optimisation, les moyennes courantes des gradients et des seconds moments des gradients sont utilisées. Il est utilisé pour calculer les taux d'apprentissage adaptatifs pour chaque paramètre ». tirée https://datafranca.org/wiki/Optimisation_Adam

(Sutskever, Vinyals, & Le, 2014). La taille des séquences de données varie selon les données disponibles sur chaque technologie.

- **Structure du type « many-to-many » :** où les données d'entrée et les données de sortie constituent des séquences de données de mêmes longueurs ou de différentes longueurs.
- **Algorithme d'optimisation Adam :** peut être plus performant que les autres méthodes d'optimisation (Kingma & Ba, 2015).

De plus, la couche de sortie représente une séquence de nombre de brevets/publications prédits au cours d'une seule étape de l'année1 à l'année p.

Réseau de Neurones 2

Le deuxième réseau de neurones est mis en œuvre à l'aide de deux modèles différents utilisés à des fins comparatives. Il s'agit de réseaux qui ont la structure d'un modèle de réseaux de neurones classifieur multidimensionnel. Les données sur les brevets et sur les publications représentent des dimensions d'entrée. Les gammes de revenus quant à elles représentent les classes de sortie. Ce classifieur va émettre une distribution de probabilité pour chacune des classes définies.

Réseau de neurones large et profond multidimensionnel (Multi-dimensional Wide and Deep Neural Network, MDWDNN)

Le réseau de neurones large et profond multidimensionnel a la structure du « Réseau neuronal profond Classificateur et linéaire ». L'algorithme d'optimisation Adam est également appliqué dans le réseau de neurones profond multidimensionnel. Ce réseau de neurones est composé des couches suivantes :

- **Couche d'entrée :** la couche d'entrée représente le nombre de brevets et de publications pour une technologie pour chaque année disponible.
- **Couches cachées :** ce réseau de neurones est composé de h couches cachées et chaque couche contient no nœuds.
- **Couche de sortie :** cette couche représente les gammes de revenus à prédire. Sachant que chaque donnée de sortie prédite sert de donnée d'entrée pour la prochaine prédiction jusqu'à ce que le nombre d'années futures p soit atteint. Le réseau de neurones large et profond multidimensionnel prédit la catégorie de revenu pour chaque année

séparément. Également il vérifie le nombre d'années à chaque étape jusqu'à ce que le nombre d'années p soit atteint ce qui veut dire jusqu'à ce que y devienne égal à p.

Réseau de neurones récurrents multidimensionnel (Multi-dimensional Recurrent Neural Network, MDRNN)

Le réseau de neurones récurrents multidimensionnel traite les séquences de séries temporelles des données d'entrées multidimensionnelles et prédit la probabilité de distribution pour chaque classe de ces séquences. De plus, il est basé sur un modèle encodeur-décodeur[52] qui utilise des cellules LSTM[53] (Long Short-Term Memory en français LMCT), il est structuré en tant que modèle « Many-to-One » employé pour classifier les données. Dans ce modèle, les données d'entrée représentent des séquences de données et les données de sortie représentent une catégorie. L'algorithme d'optimisation Adam est également appliqué dans le réseau de neurones récurrents multidimensionnel en tant que méthode d'optimisation.

Ce réseau de neurones est composé des couches suivantes :

- **Couches d'entrée :** le réseau de neurones récurrents multidimensionnel comporte un nombre spécifique nb de couches d'entrée ou de dimensions d'entrée. Les couches traitent des séquences de séries temporelles de différentes longueurs.
- **Couches cachées :** étant donné que le réseau de neurones récurrents multidimensionnel vise à établir autant d'autoconnexions qu'il existe de dimensions dans les données (Graves, et al., 2007), le réseau de neurones récurrents multidimensionnel comporte h couches cachées récurrentes avec un nombre spécifique no de nœuds, chaque nœud dans chaque couche cachée contient nb d'autoconnexions.

---

52. « C'est un modèle de Deep Learning composé de deux réseaux de neurones. Ces deux réseaux de neurones ont habituellement la même structure » : premier sera utilisée normalement, mais le deuxième fonctionnera de manière inversée ». https://inside- machinelearning.com/encodeur-decodeur/

53. « Un réseau de neurones récurrent (RNR) à longue mémoire court terme (LMCT) com- porte plusieurs mécanismes internes (une cellule mémoire, une porte d'entrée, une porte de sortie et une porte d'oubli) permettant de tenir compte à la fois des dépendances courtes et longues dans les séquences de données. Ces mécanismes de portes sont aussi conçus pour atténuer le problème de la disparition du gradient » https://datafranca.org/wiki/R%C3%A9seau_r%C3%A9current_%C3%A0_longue_m%C3%A9moire_court_terme

- **Couche de sortie :** la couche de sortie représente une séquence de groupes qui sera prédite au cours d'une seule étape de l'année Year 1 à l'année Year p.

Expérimentation

Les données sur les brevets, sur les publications et sur les revenus de 9 tendances technologiques (3D Printing, Artificial intelligence and Advanced Machine Learning, Autonomous Vehicles, Camera Sensors, GPS, LED Lighting, Media Tablets, Rechargeable Lithium Battery et Virtual Reality) sont collectées afin d'entrainer et de tester les réseaux de neurones. Les données relatives à la technologie candidate sont appliquées aux réseaux de neurones afin de prédire ses futurs brevets, publications et gammes de revenus pour les 4 prochaines années.

Collecte des données

Lister les technologies Les technologies choisies sont listées à partir de plusieurs sources en ligne telles que : IEEE (IEEE, 2016) (IEEE, 2015), Gartner (Cearley, Burke, & Samantha Searle, 2017), Elsevier (Peter Edelstein, 2017), Scientific American (Meyerson, 2015), MIT Technology Review (MIT Technology Review, 2018), etc. Les mots-clés relatifs, tels que le terme « Additive manufacturing » relatif à la technologie du « 3D printing », sont donc extraits de manière manuelle à partir de plusieurs références comme le thésaurus (Thesaurus, 2013), « TechTerms » (Tech Terms, 2018), etc., et sont ensuite insérés dans la base de données intégrée.

Source de données sur les brevets

Les données sur les demandes de brevets délivrés publiées avant le 31 décembre 2019 ont été extraites du site du « United States Patent and Trademark Office » (USPTO, 2019, 2020) et importées dans la table intitulée « Patents » de la base de données intégrée. Les brevets sont regroupés par catégories.

Source de données sur les publications

Les données sur les publications telles que le titre et l'année sont extraites automatiquement à l'aide de l'interface de programmation applicative (API) Springer qui comporte plusieurs ressources bibliométriques. Un script a été développé à l'aide de Python afin de chercher les mots-clés relatifs à chaque technologie dans le titre des publications parues avant janvier 2020. Le nombre total de publications par technologie par an a donc été calculé et inséré dans la base de données intégrée.

Source de données sur les revenus

Les revenus relatifs à chaque technologie pour plusieurs années ont été extraits manuellement à partir de différentes sources en ligne telles que le portail international de statistiques « Statista 2021 » et « Smart Insights », qui procurent des informations sur les revenus. (Statista,…)

Création de jeux de données destinés à l'entrainement, aux tests et à la prédiction

Les données ont été divisées manuellement entre les jeux de données destinés à l'entrainement et les jeux de données destinés aux tests. En vue de comparer les valeurs prédites aux valeurs véritables et visualiser la précision des réseaux de neurones, le jeu de donnée destiné à la validation est également utilisé comme jeu de donnée destiné à la prédiction où la « Virtual Reality » représente la technologie candidate dont les valeurs futures vont être prédites.

Les données de sortie prédites par le réseau de neurones large et profond à une dimension et le réseau de neurones récurrents à une dimension sont respectivement intégrées comme données d'entrée dans le réseau de neurones large et profond multidimensionnel et le réseau de neurones récurrents multidimensionnel avec les données historiques sur les brevets, sur les publications et sur les revenus.

Pour ce qui est de la dimension des données de sortie, étant donné que le réseau de neurones 2 (réseau de neurones large et profond multidimensionnel et le réseau de neurones récurrents multidimensionnel) constitue un modèle de classifieur qui prédit les gammes de revenus d'une tendance technologique, les données sur les revenus ont été regroupées en 3 classes à partir des données disponibles (tableau 2) :

Tableau 2 : Classes des revenus

Classe	Gammes de revenus (en USD)				
1	0 <= Revenu <= 10 milliards				
2	10 Milliards	<=	Revenu	<=	50 Milliards
3	Revenu > 50 milliards				

Mise en œuvre des réseaux de neurones

La configuration et les paramètres d'entrainement des réseaux de neurones ont été ajustés et réglés progressivement. Ils ont par ailleurs été déterminés de manière expérimentale conformément aux résultats les plus précis et à la proposition de Chevalier (Chevalier, 2018). En vue de garantir une comparaison juste, 1000 étapes d'entrainement ont été appliquées aux deux types de réseau de neurones.

Réseau de Neurones 1

La précision des résultats des modèles du réseau de neurones large et profond à une dimension et du réseau de neurones récurrents à une dimension a été calculée à partir des mêmes étapes et formules employées, «*prédire le succès d'une technologie à partir des données sur les brevets à l'aide d'un réseau de neurones large et profond et d'un réseau de neurones récurrents*» (Saade, Jneid, Saleh, 2019).

Réseau de Neurones 2

La précision des résultats des classifieurs du réseau de neurones profond multidimensionnel et du réseau de neurones récurrents multidimensionnel est générée à partir de la fonction intégrée Softmax qui assure la distribution de la probabilité pour les classes de données de sorties (Tang, et al., 2015), ce qui veut dire que la fonction Softmax[54] normalise les valeurs de sortie prédites en probabilités.

54. « La fonction mathématique softmax peut être utilisée en machine learning pour convertir un score en probabilité dans un contexte de classification multiclasse» https://www.actuia.com/faq/a-quoi-sert-softmax/

Résultats

Les paragraphes suivants représentent les résultats obtenus pour la technologie candidate de la « Virtual Reality » à l'aide des deux types de réseaux de neurones, illustrant ainsi la qualité des prédictions.

Réseau de Neurones 1

Le réseau de neurones récurrents à une dimension est plus performant et précis que le réseau de neurones profond. En effet, sa performance est meilleure que celle du réseau de neurones profond à une dimension étant donné que sa pression moyenne de prédiction est de 77,52 % contre 67,49 % pour le réseau de neurones profond à une dimension (voir Tableau 3).

ODWDNN		**ODRNN**	
Patents prediction accuracy	Publications Prediction accuracy	Patents prediction accuracy	Publications Prediction accuracy
51.40%	83.58%	84.86%	70.18%
Average prediction accuracy : 67.49%		**Average prediction accuracy: 77.52%**	

Tableau 3 : Précision des prédictions des réseaux neuronaux 1.

Réseau de Neurones 2

Le réseau de neurones récurrents multidimensionnel (MDRNN) (précision de la prédiction 84,98%) est plus performant et précis que le réseau de neurones large et profond multidimensionnel (MDWDNN) (précision de la prédiction 74,85%), étant donné que le MDRNN a pu déterminer la classe de revenu réelle pour la quatrième année de 39,94%, contre 0% pour le MDWDNN (voir Tableau 4).

	MDWDNN			MDRNN		
Future years	Actual Class	Predicted Class	**Actual Class Prediction Accuracy**	Actual Class	Predicted Class	**Actual Class Prediction Accuracy**
Year 1	1	1	99.50%	1	1	100%
Year 2	1	1	99.92%	1	1	99.99%
Year 3	1	1	99.99%	1	1	99.99%
Year 4	2	1	0%	2	1	39.94%
	Average prediction accuracy : 74.85%			Average prediction accuracy : 84.98%		

Tableau 4 : Précision des prédictions des réseaux neuronaux 2.

Conclusion/Discussion

Dans cette étude, nous avons proposé une nouvelle approche quantitative en intelligence artificielle qui se base sur l'analyse des dimensions des brevets, des publications et des revenus à l'aide de modèles de réseaux de neurones capables d'évaluer et de surveiller le développement d'un produit axé sur la technologie candidate. Ces dimensions sont considérées comme des indicateurs de performance clé qui permettent de mesurer la puissance d'une technologie.

Cette étude met l'accent sur deux étapes principales : La première étape consiste à prédire le taux de croissance des brevets et le taux de croissance des publications à l'aide du même modèle de réseau de neurones prédictif. La deuxième étape quant à elle consiste à intégrer les résultats dans un modèle de réseau de neurones multidimensionnel classifieur afin de prédire le volume du revenu qui peut refléter le succès du produit technologique.

Cette méthodologie est appliquée à l'aide de différents types de modèles de réseaux de neurones utilisés à des fins comparatives : le réseau de neurones large et profond et le réseau de neurones récurrents.

Cette méthode a été testée sur 9 tendances technologiques afin d'entrainer les réseaux de neurones avant d'être appliquée sur une technologie candidate « Virtual Reality » au cours de la phase des tests et des prédictions. Les résultats indiquent que les modèles de réseaux de neurones récurrents sont plus précis et performants que les réseaux de neurones larges et profonds pour les deux étapes. Les réseaux de neurones récurrents constituent donc un modèle valable qui peut améliorer le développement des innovations numériques.

Le domaine de l'innovation a évolué en profitant de l'évolution du Web, des concepts et des technologies de l'IA, qui ont proposé des perspectives de recherche en innovation. Les approches actuelles d'innovation se concentrent plus sur les processus et leurs activités correspondantes, tandis que, en pratique, la gestion des flux d'information, l'évaluation, la valorisation et la présentation de l'information avec une valeur ajoutée sont un défi que rencontrent les paradigmes d'innovation.

Bibliographie

Cearley, D. W., Burke, B. & Samantha Searle, M. J. (2017, October 3). Top 10 Strategic Technology Trends for 2018. Retrieved from Gartner: https://www.gartner.com/doc/3811368?srcId=1-7251599992&cm_sp=swg-_-gi-_-dynamic.

Chesbrough, H. (2003). Open Innovation: The New Imperative for Creating and Profiting From Technology. Harvard Business Review Press.

Chevalier, G. (2018, March). *seq2seq-signal-prediction*. Retrieved from GitHub: https://github.com/guillaume-chevalier/seq2seq-signal-prediction

Delpeuch, T. (2016). L'innovation institutionnelle : une entreprise politique à base d'emprunts extérieurs: L'exemple de la diffusion des nouveaux instruments d'intelligence dans les forces de police. Quaderni, 91(3), 61-78. En Ligne, consulté le 09/10/2019, https://www.cairn.info/revue-quaderni-2016-3-page-61.htm.

Gallouj, F., & Savona, M. (2009). Innovation in services: a review of the debate and a research agenda. *Journal of Evolutionary Economics, 19, 149–172.*

Gopalakrishnan, S., & Santoro, M. D. (2004). Distinguishing between knowledge transfer and technology transfer activities: the role of key organisational factors. *IEEE Transactions on Engineering Management, 51, 57-69. doi:10.1109/TEM.2003.822461*

Graves, A., Fernández, S., & Schmidhuber, J. (2007). *Multidimensional Recurrent Neural Networks.* Berlin, Heidelberg: Springer.

Henry, C., Sidhom, S., & Saleh, I. (2017). La mise en place d'un statut de prépublication dans le processus de dépôt de brevet : la gestion des informations sensibles, impacts et propositions de solutions. En Ligne, consulté le 09/10/2019, https://hal.inria.fr/hal-01714154/document

Henry, C. (2019). L'information brevets dans l'amélioration de la compétitivité, de la performance et de l'innovation des entreprises : contributions à la prise de décision par la modélisation d'outil de veille technologique sur les bases de données brevets, Thèse soutenue le 2/12/2019, Université Paris 8.

Jean Philippe Quenderff. (1986). Comment exploiter vos idées, avant propos.

Jneid, M. (2014). Étude et conception: vers une nouvelle approche d'innovation pour améliorer la compétitivité et la performance entrepreneuriale: application aux entreprises libanaises nouvelles, Thèse, Université Paris 8.

Jneid, M., & Saleh, I. (2015). Improving start-up competitiveness and innovation performance : the case of Lebanon. Budapest, Hungary : The International Society for Professional Innovation Management (ISPIM) Conference Proceedings.

Jneid, M. & Tannous, A. (2012). Strategic management and information evaluation challenges facing Entrepreneurs of SMEs in ICT. (pp. 400-407). uploads/2008/09/ecime10-cfp-1. pdf

Kingma, D. P. & Ba, J. (2015). Adam : A Method for Stochastic Optimization. CoRR, abs/1412.6980.

Lee, C., Kwon, O., Kim, M. & Kwon, D. (2017). Early identification of emerging technologies : A machine learning approach using multiple patent indicators. *Technological Forecasting & Social Change,* 127, 291-303. Retrieved from https ://doi.org/10.1016/j.techfore.2017.10.002 Lee, S., Olson, D. & Trimi, S. (2012). Co-innovation : convergenomics,

collaboration, and co-creation for organisational values. Management Decision, 50(5), 817–831.

Manuel d'Oslo. (2005). Éditions OCDE. En Ligne, consulté le 09/06/2019, https ://doi.org/10.1787/978.926.4013124-fr

Meyerson, B. (2015, March). Top 10 Emerging Technologies of 2015. Retrieved from Scientific American : https ://www.scientificamerican.com/article/top-10-emerging-technologies-of – 20151/

Monino, J.-L. (2013). L'information au coeur de l'intelligence économique stratégique. Marché et Organisations, 18(2), 25.

MIT *Technology Review. (2018). 10 Breakthrough Technologies 2015.* Retrieved from MIT Technology Review : https ://www.technologyreview.com/lists/technologies/2015/

OECD. (2006). La Mesure des Activités Scientifiques Et Technologiques: *Manuel D'Oslo: Principes Directeurs Pour Le Recueil Et L'Interprétation des Données Sur L'Innovation (3ᴱ Edition).* OECD Organisation for Economic Co-operation and Development.

OECD. (2009). *Innovation and Growth: Chasing a Moving Frontier.* Paris : OECD.

Peter Edelstein, M. (2017, January 10). *Top trends in health information & communications technology for 2017. Retrieved from elsevier : https://www.elsevier.com/connect/top-trends-in- health-information-and-communications-technology-for-2017*

Saade M., Jneid M., Saleh I. (2019) Predicting technology success based on patent data, using a wide and deep neural network and a recurrent neural network. IBIMA 33rd Conference proceedings, 2019, Granada, Spain.

Saade M., Jneid M., Saleh I. (2020) Enhancing Decision-Making in New Product Development: Forecasting technologies revenues using a Multidimensional Neural Network.EMCIS 202017th European Mediterranean & Middle Eastern Conference on Information Systems, 2020, Dubai, United Arab Emirates.

Saade M., (2021) « L'intelligence artificielle dans la gestion de l'innovation des produits dans les organisations : Analyse et conception d'une plateforme d'aide à la décision ». Thèse soutenue à l'université Paris 8, 2021.

Schramm-Klein, H., & Wagner, G. (2011). Extending the Product Life Cycle within an International Marketing Strategy–Relaunching the German AUDI A4 as the Spanish SEAT.

Statista. (2021). About us – the company behind the successful product. Retrieved from https://www.statista.com/aboutus/

Statista. (2021, June). *Amount of data created, consumed, and stored 2010-2025.* Retrieved from Statista: https://www.statista.com/statistics/871513/worldwide-data-created/

Sutskever, I., Vinyals, O., & Le, Q. (2014). Sequence to sequence learning with neural networks. In *Advances in neural information processing systems* (pp. 3104-3112). Google.

Tang, D., Qin, B., & Liu, T. (2015). Document modeling with gated recurrent neural network for sentiment classification. (pp. 1422-1432). Proceedings of the 2015 conference on Empirical methods in natural language processing.

Tech Terms. (2018). *The Tech Terms Computer Dictionary.* Retrieved from Tech Terms: https://techterms.com

Tensoflow. (2019). *Basic classification : Classify images of clothing.* Retrieved from TensorFlow: https://www.tensorflow.org/tutorials/keras/classification

Thesaurus. (2013). *thesaurus.* Retrieved from thesaurus: http://www.thesaurus.com

USPTO. (2019). *Patent Process Flow.* Retrieved from uspto: https://www.uspto.gov/patents- getting-started/patent-basics/types-patent-applications/utility-patent/patent-process-flow

USPTO. (2019). *USPTO's Prioritized Patent Examination Program.* Retrieved from uspto: https://www.uspto.gov/patents/initiatives/usptos-prioritized-patent-examination-program

Wang, B., Liu, Y., Zhou, Y., & Wen, Z. (2018). Emerging nanogenerator technology in China: A review and forecast using integrating bibliometrics, patent analysis and technology roadmapping methods. *Nano energy*, 46, 322-330. doi:10.1016/j.nanoen.2018.02.020

Zhao, Y., & Zhao, H. (2017). Evaluating Toll Revenue Uncertainty Using Neural Network Models. *Transportation Research Procedia*, 25, 2949–2956. doi:10.1016/j.trpro.2017.05.192.

COMMENT LE MANAGEMENT PAR L'INTELLIGENCE ÉCONOMIQUE AMÉLIORE-T-IL LA COMPÉTITIVITÉ DES GRANDES ENTREPRISES AU MAROC ?

El Haddani Mouna et Baulant Camille

Introduction

Dès le début de l'analyse de l'information, la plupart des grands courants de la pensée managériale mettaient l'accent sur son rôle clé dans la compétitivité des organisations. En particulier, la théorie de la prise de décision qui a conforté l'idée que l'efficacité décisionnelle reposait sur la faculté de disposer de l'information utile, au moment opportun, et dans un univers organisationnel. Par la suite, l'École de la contingence (AGUILAR, 1967) a montré que l'organisation pouvait être assimilée à un système organique qui ne peut survivre qu'en scrutant son environnement socio-économique et en s'y adaptant. Avec le rôle croissant des innovations dans la réussite de l'entreprise, la théorie de la firme basée sur les ressources (PENROSE, 1959; PORTER et MILLAR, 1991; CYERT et MARCH, 1963), qui est reconnue aujourd'hui comme l'une des théories les plus mobilisées dans le domaine du management stratégique (FOSS et ISHIKAWA, 2007), a révélé que le potentiel de ressources stratégiques intangibles et créatrices de valeur existait à l'intérieur même de chaque firme. Dans cette théorie, qui a de nombreux prolongements actuels, c'est la détention exclusive d'une information non publique et précise qui est à l'origine de la création d'un «*avantage concurrentiel durable*» dans l'entreprise et non transposable à une autre. Par la suite, la théorie entrepreneuriale a montré que la traque des informations concernant l'opportunité entrepreneuriale, la connaissance du marché potentiel ou des ressources à employer, était la fonction principale de l'entrepreneur (STEVENSON et JARILLO, 1990).

Avec l'avènement d'une nouvelle économie globale, basée sur l'immatériel et sur des réseaux ouverts, les théories de la firme portent aujourd'hui une attention particulière sur le changement radical qui affecte la nature même des informations réellement utiles. Les théories managériales essayent alors de distinguer l'information blanche et l'information grise. La première est ouverte, publique (JAKOBIAK, 1998; REVELLI, 1998, MOINET 2011).

Chacun peut facilement la voir et la recueillir notamment sur le web[55]. C'est une information utile, mais pas suffisante. Alors que l'information grise, difficilement accessible ou même difficilement identifiable, est souvent diffusée dans un cadre restreint. Dans un univers de plus en plus mouvant et incertain, la collecte d'informations grises, non connues par l'ensemble des acteurs, est la seule à livrer un message privilégié, même s'il ne s'agit que de bribes, d'éléments, de « signaux faibles » ou de nouvelles émergences des voies d'évolution en autorisant la création d'une asymétrie informationnelle à l'avantage de l'entreprise qui les détient (MINTZBERG, 1989; LESCA, 1994 ; DOU, 1995). Les informations grises sont souvent de nature informelle, provenant du relationnel au sens large, recueilli du terrain en mobilisant des réseaux interpersonnels au sein desquels les échanges d'informations verbales ou documentaires peuvent être entretenus.

EL HADDANI et BAULANT (2016) ont étudié comment la progression quantitative et qualitative de l'information grise pouvait modifier le type de compétitivité dominant au sein des entreprises. Ces analyses ont démontré qu'au cours des vingt dernières années, nous avons assisté à une diversification des sources de l'information grise, notamment avec l'exploitation du Web et sous l'influence des pratiques relationnelles liées au Web social. En effet, en plus du terrain qui constitue une source classique de l'information grise, l'usage de la toile mondiale, terrain virtuel, a imposé l'émergence de nouveaux cadres dans lesquels, évolue l'information grise. Dès lors, il s'avère que le modèle classique, invoquant la prédominance de l'information blanche, est radicalement bouleversé aujourd'hui. Au vu de

55. Dès son émergence dans les années 1990, le Word Wide Web, communément appelé le Web est identifié comme source d'information déterminante pour la veille (CRONIN, OVERFELT, FOUCHEREAUX, MANZVANZVIKET, CHA, SONA, 1994; GRAEF, 1997; REVELLI 1998; BOURNOISet ROMANI, 2000; JANISSEK-MUNIZ et LESCA; CHEN, 2002). Cette constatation est largement confirmée par plusieurs études dont une enquête initiée par l'éditeur de logiciels AMI Software et réalisée, en 2013, en partenariat avec l'ADBS et Veille Magazine qui annonce que le Web est devenu un bouquet de sources incontournable de l'intelligence économique : 94% des professionnels intègrent le Web dans leur panel de surveillance.

Ce qui précède, nous nous trouvons face à une problématique de collecte et d'exploitation des informations grises dont la diversité est telle qu'il est impossible d'envisager un système de collecte et de traitement homogène. Or depuis leur mise en œuvre, au début des années 2000, les outils de veille couvrent tout ou du moins une partie du processus de collecte, d'analyse et de diffusion de l'information grise d'origine Web. Mais qu'en est-il du traitement de l'information d'origine terrain ?

Le but de notre analyse est de montrer de présenter dans quelle mesure la complémentarité des canaux d'information dans une démarche d'intelligence économique rend ce mode d'action une source d'innovations créatives hautement performantes, grâce à une nouvelle stratégie de l'organisation et une nouvelle culture dans l'organisation.

La complémentarité des canaux d'informations pour une dynamique complète d'intelligence économique

Si l'information recueillie du Web, bénéfice de l'automate de collecte massive, du classement, de traitement et de diffusion qu'offrent les outils de veille, qu'en est-il de l'information récoltée par l'humain ou d'origine terrain ?

Mobiliser des sources humaines pour remonter des informations est une approche qui du point de vue des auteurs, demeure difficile à appréhender en raison des échanges complexes qui s'établissent à l'occasion de la sélection, de la production et de la mise en circulation (JAKOBIAK, 1998; DOU, 1995; MARCON et MOINET, 2006;). Lorsque JAKOBIAK (2006 :101)

compare la collecte de l'information terrain avec les autres catégories de collecte d'informations dans l'organisation systématique de la veille, il remarque que celle relative au terrain « est de loin la plus difficile à définir d'abord, à organiser ensuite ». MOINET (2011 :29), de son côté, reconnait que le recueil et le traitement de ce genre d'information exigent « un véritable professionnalisme et une culture des réseaux ».

En somme, les chercheurs et les professionnels de l'intelligence économique évoquent la qualité et la fiabilité des sources informationnelles, l'absence de formalisation dans les opérations de collecte et l'ardente nécessité de mise en place d'une méthodologie rigoureuse pour le traitement des informations d'origine homme du terrain. La veille terrain demande par conséquent une certaine organisation et des compétences particulières notamment en matière d'apprentissage collectif, de gestion et d'animation des réseaux humains. Se pose alors la question stratégique des mécanismes psychologiques à prendre en compte afin d'accroître l'efficacité desdits réseaux, et la définition précise des règles d'éthique et de déontologie à respecter.

2. Terrain de la recherche : le cas de l'entreprise Alpha[56]

L'entreprise Alpha est une grande entreprise du secteur industriel. Elle est dans le top 5 de son marché et gère des activités opérationnelles liées à son secteur d'activité, mais aussi des fonctions supports. À cette structure s'ajoutent aussi d'autres structures qui sont chargées des ressources humaines, de la qualité, des affaires juridiques et de la sécurité de l'Information, et de la veille. Entreprise de proximité, Alpha est présent sur tout le territoire national et a de nombreuses implantations géographiques et accords de distribution en partenariat avec d'autres entreprises privées. Ainsi, l'entreprise est organisée autour de différentes Directions générales et Directions régionales, et dispose de filiales à l'échelle nationale et à l'étranger. Pour faire face à tous ces enjeux, l'entreprise décide de construire et mettre en place un dispositif d'intelligence économique. Plus précisément, l'implantation de ce dispositif doit s'inscrire dans le cadre général du développement du groupe et doit répondre à deux soucis majeurs : pouvoir conserver sa place de leader et pouvoir saisir des opportunités de développement à l'international.

2.1 Organisation de la veille web de l'entreprise ALPHA.

Début d'année 2010, Alpha a décidé d'entreprendre un projet de refonte et de restructuration de la veille, et de créer un département rattaché à la direction de la stratégie, dans le but de pouvoir assurer le pilotage et le suivi du dispositif d'intelligence économique, de construire un système d'alerte précoce des menaces et opportunités, et d'intégrer pleinement la démarche d'intelligence économique dans des schémas décisionnels récurrents ou des obligations réglementaires. Compte tenu de cette construction complexe qu'est la dynamique d'intelligence économique, l'approche

56. Pour des raisons évidentes de confidentialité, l'entreprise ici analysée a été rendue anonyme sous le terme d'entreprise Alpha.

épistémologique la plus adaptée à notre travail s'est avérée être l'approche par la complexité : une approche à la fois systémique (SIMON, 1996) et évolutionniste (MORIN, 1981) qui est particulièrement adaptée en sciences de gestion. Considérant les interactions décelées entre la veille terrain et la veille Web, nous nous plaçons dans le cadre d'une recherche longitudinale (plusieurs mois d'intervention), dont la démarche est ici sous-tendue par une intervention qui a préexisté à l'analyse de la remontée des informations; c'est pourquoi que le cadre épistémologique général de cette recherche-intervention, reprend le mode de production des connaissances gestionnaires de type constructiviste. Cette démarche s'organise autour d'un processus d'interactivité cognitive entre les acteurs du terrain de recherche et le chercheur. Nous nous sommes éloignés des voies traditionnelles de la recherche en gestion et avons frayé le chemin à une approche à la fois descriptive, explicative et prescriptive qui nous a largement associé aux porteurs des actions sur le terrain de notre recherche, afin de construire ensemble une intervention qui s'attache à être pertinente et efficace.

Pour réaliser ce projet de mise en place d'une dynamique d'intelligence économique, nous avons choisi d'effectuer, comme le conseillent bon nombre de professionnels de l'intelligence économique, un diagnostic de l'existant afin que nous puissions identifier et proposer des axes d'amélioration. La démarche d'intelligence économique de l'entreprise Alpha a été initiée par une surveillance de base en déployant un dispositif de veille Web avant d'élargir la solution à la veille terrain.

Le dispositif de veille Web couvre différentes thématiques (veille concurrentielle, veille socio-économique, veille technologique, veille image sur Internet, veille internationale…) et il implique plusieurs entités des différents pôles. L'organisation de la veille proposée repose sur une solution mixte avec, d'un côté, plusieurs entités décentralisées, chargées d'une surveillance particulière (veille technologique, veille image, veille concurrentielle…). Et, d'un autre côté, l'organisation de la veille comprend un département veille qui est rattaché au top management et qui est chargée de l'animation, du pilotage du dispositif de veille, de la mise en perspective de l'ensemble des travaux des différentes veilles et de la mise en commun des sources d'information et des outils. L'ampleur du projet a nécessité la mise en place d'un outil susceptible d'être déployé à grande échelle et couvrant l'intégralité des fonctionnalités spécifiques de la veille (collecte, capitalisation, analyse et diffusion).

2.2 Résultats de la refonte de la veille Web

Après 11 mois, les 4000 collaborateurs de l'entreprise ont accès à la plateforme de veille dont 53% sont des visiteurs permanents du portail de la veille stratégique, qui rappelons-le est un tableau de bord dynamique et interactif à base d'onglets, qui permet aux utilisateurs de chercher et de recevoir des informations et une actualité personnalisée. Axé sur les thèmes de veille retenus : concurrence, technologies, secteur d'activité, environnement socio-économique, image d'Alpha sur Internet, veille internationale, ce portail est mis à jour quotidiennement par les différentes entités opérationnelles et supervisé par la cellule veille stratégique, pour répondre aux besoins internes en matière d'information économique et technique fiable et de qualité. Les thématiques sues indiquées sont alimentées par un bouquet de plus de 360 sources électroniques : sites Web nationaux, régionaux et internationaux (sites de sociétés, sites d'actualités généralistes, études de marché, sites d'actualités économiques et financières, sites d'organismes réglementaires, syndicats professionnels, d'organes contestataires…), blogs, fils RSS, newsgroups, pages d'actualités, forums.

En plus du portail, des lettres de veille, des rapports, des études et synthèses sur le secteur d'activité et l'environnement de l'entreprise sont également publiés selon des fréquences bien déterminées.

D'un point de vue opérationnel, maintenant que nous avons mis les principales veilles sur les sources électroniques, il est nécessaire et utile d'élargir la solution en intégrant une veille à partir des sources humaines via une collecte, une analyse et une mise à disposition organisées et efficientes de la richesse des informations dont disposaient ses collaborateurs.

3. Nécessité de mettre aussi en place la veille terrain

Le sujet de l'amélioration du traitement de la remontée des informations du terrain est ressorti de nombreuses fois durant les entretiens de diagnostic des pratiques de veille. Lors de ces rencontres, il a été possible de constater qu'il existait un volume très important d'informations sur différents domaines qui était connu des collaborateurs de terrain de l'entreprise, notamment les commerciaux. En règle générale, les collaborateurs de l'entreprise informent leur hiérarchie, mais, le plus souvent, les informations ne remontent pas jusqu'aux professionnels qui sont à même de prendre les décisions ou les mesures adaptées pour les exploiter au mieux. Il existe ainsi toute une série d'informations à forte valeur ajoutée, qui est en possession des collaborateurs dans les différents services et régions, mais qui ne sont pas exploitées pour développer la réactivité de l'entreprise à tous les niveaux. Il y a donc là un capital inexploité qui, traité de bonne manière, permettrait certainement un gain de performance de l'entreprise Alpha dans de nombreux domaines.

3.1 Diagnostic des pratiques de veille terrain de l'entreprise Alpha

Nous avons opté pour des entretiens semi-directifs à usage exploratoire qui privilégient la liberté de parole dans un cadre relativement strict. Dans cette optique, nous avons conçu un guide d'entretien (annexe), qui a vocation de présenter les questions à poser lors des différents entretiens à réaliser en région auprès de 66 personnes identifiées (six directeurs régionaux et un échantillon de dix de leurs collaborateurs), et auprès de 12 personnes en central (le directeur marketing et quatre de ses collaborateurs, et le directeur des ventes et six responsables commerciaux). Ce guide contient une partie commune et des parties spécifiques par catégorie d'interlocuteur rencontré.

D'un point de vue analytique, ce document (en annexe) a pour but de : premièrement, prendre en compte la perception et les attentes des répondants par rapport au projet, et deuxièmement contribuer à créer une vision commune autour du projet et des actions à mettre en œuvre, et troisièmement s'assurer de l'appui des interviewés au projet. Les entretiens se sont déroulés sur une période de temps qui n'a pas dépassé quatre semaines bien que les directions régionales sont territorialement éloignées et la durée moyenne de l'entretien est de 90 min.

3.2 Principaux constats relevés lors des entretiens

Lors des différentes réunions, nous avons présenté notre premier diagnostic du dispositif existant des remontées d'informations. Ce diagnostic faisait notamment ressortir l'existence de plusieurs canaux de remontées du terrain, non automatisés et présentant. Des limites telles que : le retard dans l'exploitation des données, la multiplicité des supports de remontée (mail, téléphone, papier), l'absence de mécanismes de traitement fiable, absence de suivi, etc. Au-delà de ces points auxquels l'ensemble des interviewés ont adhéré, ces derniers ont mis en avant trois principaux constats.

1) Il y a un véritable gisement d'informations pour Alpha sur le terrain, mais la surcharge du travail ne laisse pas le temps aux employés de scruter le terrain. L'ensemble des collaborateurs sur le terrain sont confrontés chaque jour dans le cadre de leur activité à des situations qui pourraient faire l'objet de remontées d'informations utiles aux parties prenantes sur le plan local ou national. Il existe des fiches de remontées, mais peu de collaborateurs jouent le jeu. Certains d'entre eux ont évoqué la surcharge du travail causée par la réduction des effectifs.

2) Les collaborateurs ne voient pas l'intérêt de remonter une information Le dispositif existant est inefficace et les retours réalisés auprès des contributeurs sont rares; ils ne sont pas réguliers et ils ne sont pas toujours utiles, selon les témoignages des interviewés.

3) La plupart des salariés (managers ou collaborateurs) sont conscients de l'intérêt de la remontée d'informations d'origine terrain, mais ne voient pas l'intérêt de mobiliser une ressource, sachant qu'ils sont en sous-effectif, pour remonter une information pour laquelle le retour n'est pas automatique.

À l'issue des rencontres, les interviewés ont remonté aussi des attentes générales par rapport au dispositif.

Les différentes directions régionales rencontrées ont manifesté un intérêt réel et des attentes importantes quant au dispositif de remontées d'informations. De manière précise, les Directions régionales attendent du dispositif les résultats suivants. Le dispositif doit permettre de faire remonter rapidement certaines informations. Le dispositif doit être en mesure d'assurer un acheminement rapide des remontées d'informations nécessitant une prise en compte et un traitement urgent. Certaines remontées ne peuvent pas attendre la consolidation mensuelle pour être traitées. Certaines Directions régionales ont insisté sur le fait qu'il s'agissait d'un critère de succès du dispositif. D'autres Directions régionales ont insisté sur le fait que le dispositif doit se focaliser sur le traitement des remontées d'informations et non sur la consolidation à des fins de suivi et de reporting uniquement.

Le dispositif doit permettre de donner une réponse rapidement une fois l'information remontée. Une fois les informations remontées, celles-ci doivent faire l'objet d'un traitement rapide de manière à proposer des actions dans les meilleurs délais. Les actions proposées et réalisées doivent être pertinentes et efficaces. Toutes les actions proposées pour traiter les remontées d'informations doivent être évaluées de manière à mesurer leur efficacité. Certaines Directions régionales souhaitent que le dispositif utilise des indicateurs tenant compte de la pertinence et de la qualité des réponses apportées par les fonctions centrales.

3.3 Processus et organisation de la veille terrain

Pour définir le processus et l'organisation de la veille terrain, nous abordons une présentation problématisée des différents acteurs du terrain décrits ci-dessus, dans la figure 3, et nous monterons, leur complémentarité pour remonter, vérifier, enrichir, analyser et utiliser l'information traquée. Le dispositif de veille terrain s'appuie sur une plateforme logicielle et une organisation reposant sur six acteurs :

Le contributeur enregistre sur la plateforme de veille, l'information dont il a pris connaissance. Idéalement il la remonte le jour même où il en prend connaissance. Il définit la rubrique correspondante selon l'axe concerné ainsi que le niveau d'urgence souhaité pour son traitement. Le traitement de l'information ne doit pas se faire de manière uniforme. Cela dépendra du degré de sa sensibilité pour agir beaucoup plus vite et être lié directement au décideur. Une remontée est qualifiée d'urgente si elle doit être communiquée dans un délai maximum de 24h et si elle nécessite la mise en place d'un plan d'action en urgence.

La validation des remontées vérifiées et éventuellement enrichies génère une alerte chez l'expert. Ce dernier analyse ces informations et identifie celles nécessitant la mise en place d'un plan d'action. La consolidation de

l'ensemble des remontées traitées par axe d'analyse se fait automatiquement au niveau de la plateforme. L'animateur central transmet ce consolidé au décideur pour acter une décision. Suite au retour de celui-ci, le responsable d'action exécute les plans d'action et les trace au niveau de la plateforme pour que les acteurs du dispositif en soient informés. Le traqueur du terrain peut visualiser les retours associés à sa contribution dès leur clôture par le responsable de l'action. À partir des résultats des analyses des synthèses des informations remontées et du suivi de l'évolution des résultats des indicateurs et de la mise en œuvre des actions d'amélioration, l'animateur central établit le tableau de bord général des remontées. Ce tableau de bord est préparé en deux versions : - une version synthétique faisant apparaître les grandes tendances par axe pour le décideur ; - une version plus détaillée pour l'ensemble des responsables concernés des directions régionales et du service central.

En somme, le dispositif proposé, développe un réseau de savoir visant la construction de la connaissance partagée. Il repose sur Les coopérations intellectuelles de deux familles de profils d'acteurs : ceux qui remontent l'information : Le contributeur et l'animateur régional (la contribution), et ceux qui utilisent l'information (l'action) pour des visées stratégiques : les experts et les responsables d'actions. L'efficacité du dispositif passe par la maitrise du couple contribution-action qui, à son tour, passe par la mobilisation, l'accompagnement, la motivation, l'assistance et la formation des acteurs.

3.4 Les règles du jeu dans le cadre du dispositif de veille terrain d'Alpha

De façon à définir et partager les directives générales précisant les modalités d'exercice de collecte et d'exploitation de l'information terrain, nous avons décidé de rédiger une « charte » qui fixe les principes sur lesquels se fonde l'engagement mutuel du département veille stratégique, des directions centrales et des directions régionales ainsi que les actions qui en découlent dans le cadre du dispositif veille terrain. Cette charte a constitué un cadre de référence pour l'établissement d'une vision commune matérialisée par un dispositif partagé. Présentant le fonctionnement du dispositif de manière attractive pour l'entreprise Alpha et ses collaborateurs, cette charte a créé chez les collaborateurs de l'entreprise le désir d'être « partie prenante » de son fonctionnement, car elle a décrit les buts atteignables par les uns et les autres dans le cadre du dispositif et elle a mis l'accent sur leur valeur ajoutée pour l'entreprise dans son ensemble.

La Charte a été aussi un moyen pour pouvoir communiquer à tous les niveaux de manière rapide et claire sur le dispositif de veille.

Les directions centrales se sont engagées dans deux domaines : la prise en compte des remontées, leur traitement dans les meilleurs délais, et leur intégration des plans d'action qui y sont associés dans les processus métiers.

Les directions régionales se sont engagées pour leur part dans trois domaines : le soutien du projet à travers la communication auprès de l'ensemble des collaborateurs conscients du rôle et de l'importance du dispositif, une implication et un appui marqués du directeur régional pour désigner un animateur régional et mobiliser les acteurs relevant de sa région.

En tant que cellule de veille stratégique, nous avons veillé à la concrétisation des engagements des directions centrales et régionales à travers nos diverses fonctions : l'animation, la motivation, l'administration de la plateforme logicielle, la formation et le déploiement des éléments de pilotage. L'animation a contribué à optimiser le bon fonctionnement du processus de la veille de terrain dans son ensemble et de le pérenniser. Elle a pris la forme de rencontres individuelles et de réunions de suivi régulières avec les opérationnels pour présenter l'état d'avancement du traitement des informations de terrain et pour évaluer les plans d'action mis en place. Pour sensibiliser et créer plus de proximité avec les traqueurs du terrain, nous avons organisé chaque année, depuis la mise en place du processus veille de terrain, une tournée de trois mois qui couvre les six directions régionales. L'objectif était tout d'abord de présenter le bilan annuel national des remontées du terrain, et, ensuite, de prospecter de nouveaux profils, notamment les attachés commerciaux et les techniciens, sources d'informations à haut potentiel, pour élargir la base des contributeurs. Par ailleurs, les tournées au niveau des directions régionales nous ont permis d'apporter des réponses et éclaircissements nécessaires quant aux retours associés aux remontées du terrain. En outre, nous avons visé à travers ces séances de sensibilisation de rapprocher la vision et la stratégie du service central aux contributeurs. Enfin, la tournée nous a servi aussi à présenter l'apport de la remontée en matière de réajustement de nos offres, de ripostes, de normalisation des dysfonctionnements…

Notre fonction d'animation du dispositif nous a permis de dispenser aussi des formations à l'ensemble des différents acteurs (contributeurs, animateurs régionaux, experts et responsables d'action) pour l'utilisation optimale de l'outil de veille. Nous avons formé aussi les animateurs régionaux à l'animation et la mobilisation des contributeurs pour qu'ils soient aptes à développer des réseaux personnels, à partager et à médiatiser l'information. Pour stimuler la remontée d'information d'origine terrain, nous avons développé des mécanismes de reconnaissance et de valorisation.

Dans cette optique, nous avons mis en place des mesures, dont les lettres de félicitations qui sont adressées aux meilleurs contributeurs, meilleurs animateurs régionaux et à leurs responsables. Pour puiser dans le caractère compétiteur des traqueurs du terrain, nous avons lancé, depuis la mise en place du dispositif de veille terrain, un challenge annuel, d'une durée de trois mois visant à remobiliser de différents acteurs (traqueurs du terrain, experts et responsables d'actions) et à renforcer leur stimulation. Les gagnants du challenge et les traqueurs du terrain les plus dynamiques au cours de l'année sont primés lors d'un événement national, un rendez-vous annuel, que nous avons baptisé « Journée de la veille Alpha ». Lors des deux premières versions de cet événement, nous avons primé les meilleurs traqueurs du terrain. Or au fil des mois, nous nous sommes rendu compte que le contributeur n'était pas le seul acteur qui pouvait garantir le dynamisme du dispositif et que la maitrise du processus nécessitait la motivation aussi bien de ceux qui remontaient l'information que de ceux qui la traitaient. De ce fait, nous avons décidé dès la 3ème année d'organisation de cette rencontre d'accorder également des prix aux responsables d'action. En conséquence, nous avons réussi à stimuler la remontée et l'utilisation de l'information. La définition des critères retenus pour primer les meilleurs contributeurs a été délicate. Les critères que nous avons retenus portent sur la pertinence, la régularité des remontées et le respect des règles d'éthique. Les animateurs régionaux sont récompensés sur la base d'un ensemble d'indicateurs : le taux d'accroissement des remontées, le taux d'accroissement du nombre des traqueurs du terrain dans sa région et la qualité de l'information. Les experts et les responsables d'actions sont quant à eux primés sur la base de l'efficacité des plans d'action et de correction mises en place à la suite de la remontée d'information et sur les délais qu'ils ont mis à les mettre en œuvre.

Une année après le déploiement de notre dispositif de veille terrain, les remontées du terrain sont devenues surabondantes puisqu'elles couvraient un périmètre transverse et qu'elles n'étaient pas organisées dans une perspective décisionnelle, permettant d'avoir une meilleure connaissance de ses clients, de son environnement ou de sa compétitivité. S'est posée alors la question problématique du pilotage et de suivi de l'activité des remontées du terrain, imposées par l'environnement concurrentiel, les stratégies d'optimisation des coûts ainsi que les objectifs de performance.

L'objectif pratique a ainsi été d'aider les décideurs par le biais d'un reporting fiable et des tableaux de bord précis, à faire les bons choix et à se projeter au minimum, grâce à la fourniture (1) d'une information catégorisée que les utilisateurs pourront agréger ou ventiler facilement selon leurs besoins propres d'analyse, (2) d'une information exhaustive fournissant l'ensemble des données remontées, (3) d'une information historiée, datée, qui puisse servir à effectuer des comparaisons entre plusieurs dates possibles, (4) d'une information nettoyée de toute inconsistance ou erreur pour permettre d'obtenir des résultats d'analyse sûrs, et (5) d'une gestion de la sécurité permettant de définir quels utilisateurs pourront accéder à quelle information.

Il s'est agi de restituer des données aux utilisateurs, sous forme de graphes, de tableaux croisés dynamiques ou de rapports pour fiabiliser, simplifier et pérenniser un processus déjà existant, ce qui constitue assurément la finalité du décisionnel, mais elle n'en reste pas moins la partie visible de l'iceberg puisqu'il ne répond pas uniquement au besoin déjà existant, mais sa mise en place va créer de nouveaux besoins, de nombreux concepts et technologies.

Conclusion

Le déploiement du dispositif de la veille terrain dans l'entreprise étudiée dans le présent article, a permis de favoriser, à travers un canal unique et large, la rapidité de transmission, d'enrichissement et de prise en compte efficace des informations diversifiées et de qualité pour établir des stratégies, des plans d'action et de correction ainsi que des prises de décisions. L'utilisation de ces informations a permis de revoir et d'ajuster notamment les actions commerciales de l'entreprise et de mieux cerner la stratégie du concurrent sur le terrain... Dans ce cadre, nous avons donc déployé une approche d'intelligence d'entreprise qui va bien au-delà des mécanismes de veille aboutissant à des alertes ou des newsletters habituellement utilisées dans les grandes entreprises du secteur concurrentiel.

La dynamique d'intelligence que nous avons menée regroupe toutes les formes d'intelligence : l'intelligence humaine, l'intelligence organisationnelle, l'intelligence partagée et l'intelligence d'entreprise...

L'interaction dynamique de ces formes d'intelligence a ainsi fait naître un véritable mode de fonctionnement en communauté stratégique de connaissances. Ce nouveau mode de pensée et d'action, a fondu, de manière créative, à la fois la stratégie de l'organisation et la culture de celle-ci, en l'articulant dans un ensemble dynamique avec leurs environnements respectifs. Tel est le sens du passage d'une démarche complète d'intelligence économique à un management « par l'intelligence économique » qui doit absolument se nourrir de la transversalité, du partage de l'information, de l'apprentissage continu et d'un travail en réseau pour pouvoir augmenter durablement la compétitivité des organisations agissant dans un environnement de plus en plus mondialisé, ouvert et complexe.

Références bibliographiques

Aguilar F.J., "Scanning the Business Environment", New York, NY : Macmillan Co, 1967.

Ansoff I., "Managing Strategic Surprise by Response to Weak Signals", California Management Review. Vol. 18, n° 2, 1975.

Chen H., Chau, M., Zeng, D., "CI Spider : a tool for competitive intelligence on the Web". Decision Support System 34. pp. 1-17, 2002.

Dou H., "Veille technologique et compétitivité l'intelligence économique au service du développement industriel", Paris. Dunod, 1995.

Doucet V., Gingali G., "Légitimité de la veille et ses ambiguïtés". Colloque VSST – Veille Stratégique Scientifique et Technologique – Toulouse III. 25-29, 2004.

El Haddani M., Baulant C., "La progression quantitative et qualitative de l'information grise dans le cycle de la compétitivité des entreprises". Colloque international : Recherche et Pratiques en Marketing et Communication Kénitra/Maroc, 16 et 17 décembre 2016.

Jakobiak F., "L'intelligence économique en pratique". Les Éditions d'Organisation. Paris, 1998.

Jakobiak F., "L'intelligence économique : la comprendre, l'implanter, l'utiliser". Les Éditions d'Organisation, Paris, 2006.

Lesca H., " Veille stratégique pour le management stratégique : état de la question et axes de recherche". Économie et Sociétés, Série Sciences de Gestion, SG N°20, vol 5, p 31-50, 1994.

Marcon C., “Réseaux d’intelligence économique. L’éthique au centre des problématiques organisationnelles ”. Revue internationale d’intelligence économique 2009/2 (Vol 1), 2006.

Morin E., “Introduction à la pensée complexe”. ESF éditeur, Paris 1990.

Mintzberg H., “Mintzberg on Management : Inside Our Strange World of Organizations”. Front Cover. Free Press, Business et Economics, 1989.

Moinet N., Intelligence économique, Mythes et réalités, Paris, CNRS Editions, 2011.

Porter M., Millar V., “How information gives you competitive advantage”.

Harvard Business Review, vol. 63, n°4, P149-160, 1985.

Revelli C., “Intelligence stratégique sur Internet”. Dunod. Paris, 2000.
Simon H., “The new science of management decision”. Harper et Row. New York, 1960.

2- APPROCHE START-UP

L'INITIATIVE « TREMPLIN START-UP UEMOA »

Khady Evelyne Denise Ndiaye

Créée le 10 janvier 1994 à Dakar, l'Union économique et Monétaire Ouest Africaine (UEMOA) a pour objectif essentiel, l'édification, en Afrique de l'Ouest, d'un espace économique harmonisé et intégré, au sein duquel est assurée une totale liberté de circulation des personnes, des capitaux, des biens, des services et des facteurs de production, ainsi que la jouissance effective du droit d'exercice et d'établissement pour les professions libérales, de résidence pour les citoyens sur l'ensemble du territoire communautaire.

C'est Huit États côtiers et sahéliens, liés par l'usage d'une monnaie commune, le franc FCFA et bénéficiant de traditions culturelles communes, composent l'UEMOA : le Bénin, le Burkina, la Côte d'Ivoire, la Guinée-Bissau, le Mali, le Niger, le Sénégal et le Togo. L'UEMOA couvre une superficie de 3 112 233 km² et compte 130,8 millions d'habitants. Le taux de croissance du PIB, à prix constant, est de 6,1% en 2021.

Se fondant sur les orientations du Traité, la Commission de l'UEMOA, l'organe de Direction de l'UEMOA, a fait adopter par les instances compétentes de l'Union par Acte additionnel n°5 du 8 décembre 1999, une Politique Industrielle Commune (PIC). La PIC est opérationnalisée à travers le Programme Régional de Développement Industriel et de l'Artisanat. Ce programme dont l'objectif général est la mise en place d'un environnement favorable à l'initiative privée et à la compétitivité des entreprises vise à i) élaborer et mettre en œuvre des mesures d'amélioration du climat des affaires et de promotion des investissements et de l'initiative privée, ii) mettre en place des mesures de renforcement de la compétitivité des entreprises et iii) mettre en place des dispositifs régionaux de promotion de la qualité.

La Commission de l'UEMOA intervient à travers la mise en œuvre de projets dont l'objectif global est de répondre aux besoins du secteur privé afin d'améliorer le climat des affaires, accroître l'accès au financement, parvenir à une meilleure éducation, à de meilleurs emplois et compétences, et promouvoir le commerce, la concurrence et l'innovation.

Dans cette perspective et sur proposition de la Commission de l'UEMOA, le Conseil des Ministres Statutaire de l'Union a adopté en septembre 2019, l'Initiative Régionale pour l'amélioration du Climat des Affaires (IRCA) qui a pour objectifs spécifiques de promouvoir l'entrepreneuriat, accroître la compétitivité des entreprises et stimuler les investissements privés.

Afin de soutenir la promotion d'un entrepreneuriat moderne et innovant et l'émergence de "Champions nationaux et régionaux" dans le secteur privé communautaire, la Commission de l'UEMOA a lancé en partenariat avec la Chambre Consulaire Régionale de l'UEMOA et les Chambres consulaires nationales, l'Initiative « Tremplin Start-Up UEMOA».

Cette Initiative est destinée à mettre en place une activité pérenne en matière d'appui à la promotion d'un nouveau type d'entrepreneuriat. Elle vise à contribuer à encourager l'innovation en entreprise, à travers l'accompagnement de start-up innovantes, et cela en vue de la diversification et de la densification du tissu économique de l'espace communautaire.

On entend par start-up, une jeune entreprise généralement innovante qui a un fort potentiel de développement et qui nécessite des investissements importants et adaptés pour financer sa croissance ou son développement.

L'objectif général est de soutenir la promotion d'un entrepreneuriat moderne et innovant et l'émergence de « Champions nationaux et régionaux » dans le secteur privé communautaire.

Les objectifs spécifiques de l'activité sont les suivants :

- insuffler une dynamique de compétition sous régionale pour la promotion de l'entreprise ;
- stimuler les structures de promotion de l'entreprise pour l'accompagnement des start-up dans les secteurs innovants, stratégiques et à fort potentiel de développement ;
- promouvoir dans les États membres des start-up innovantes et compétitives.

Les principaux résultats attendus de la mise en œuvre de l'activité sont :

- une dynamique de compétition sous régionale pour la promotion de l'entreprise est insufflée ;
- les structures de promotion de l'entreprise pour l'accompagnement des start-up dans les secteurs innovants, stratégiques et à fort potentiel de développement sont stimulées ;
- des start-up innovantes et compétitives sont promues dans les États membres.

Le Concours est ouvert à toute start-up formellement créée dans l'un des États membres de l'Union et qui remplit les conditions suivantes :

- Créer après le 1er janvier 2017 ;
- Exercer ses activités économiques dans un ou plusieurs État membre de l'UEMOA ;
- Être (le promoteur principal) citoyen ou résident d'un État membre de l'UEMOA ;
- Œuvrer dans le secteur du thème retenu.

Ne sont pas éligibles, les start-up non formellement créés, en activité ou non, les projets de création de start-up, les start-up non créées dans l'espace UEMOA même si elles exercent leurs activités économiques dans l'espace UEMOA.

L'édition 2020 a porté sur l'économie verte et l'édition 2021 sur l'économie numérique au service de l'agro-industrie. Les années 2022 et 2023 sont consacrées à la mise en œuvre d'un programme de renforcement des capacités des lauréats afin de leur permettre d'accroître leurs capacités de gestion et d'améliorer leurs performances au regard du développement économique dans l'espace communautaire.

L'intelligence économique, levier de la compétitivité, fait partie des thématiques clés à leur inculquer. Elle joue un rôle crucial pour les start-up, car elle leur permet de se positionner stratégiquement sur le marché, de repérer les opportunités, de prendre des décisions éclairées, de se protéger contre les risques, d'accéder aux ressources nécessaires à leur développement, à se différencier de la concurrence et à établir des partenariats stratégiques. En intégrant cette approche dans leur stratégie, les start-up peuvent augmenter leurs chances de succès sur le marché compétitif d'aujourd'hui, renforcer leur position sur le marché et maximiser leurs chances de croissance et de succès dans la zone UEMOA.

LE CENTRE D'ENTREPRENEURIAT DE LA CHAMBRE DE COMMERCE INTERNATIONALE :
UN LEVIER POUR LA PROMOTION DE L'EMPLOI ET DE L'INCLUSION

Mohamed Ourdedine*

Le Centre pour l'entrepreneuriat de la Chambre de commerce internationale (CoE) met à la disposition des entrepreneurs, les outils, les ressources et les solutions nécessaires pour donner vie à leurs idées et à leurs projets. Ce projet mondial vise d'une part, la promotion de l'emploi et de l'employabilité des entrepreneurs et des jeunes et la lutte contre la pauvreté, les inégalités et l'exclusion d'autre part.

Qu'est-ce que la CCI ?

Créée en 1919 par les « marchands de la paix », la Chambre de commerce internationale est le représentant institutionnel de plus de 45 millions d'entreprises dans plus de 100 pays. La mission principale de la CCI est de faire en sorte que les affaires fonctionnent pour tous, chaque jour, partout dans le monde.

Grâce à un mélange subtil de plaidoyers, de solutions et de production de normes, elle assure la promotion du commerce international, la conduite responsable des affaires, une approche globale de la réglementation, et offrant des services de règlement des différends aux standards internationaux.

La CCI compte parmi ses membres un grand nombre de grandes entreprises mondiales, de PME, d'associations professionnelles et de chambres de commerce locales.

La CCI représente les intérêts des entreprises aux plus hauts niveaux de la prise de décision intergouvernementale, que ce soit à l'OMC, aux Nations unies ou au G20, et ce, en veillant à ce que la voix des entreprises soit entendue.

* *Secrétaire général de la CCI Maroc.*

Cette capacité à rapprocher les secteurs public et privé fait d'ICC une institution unique, répondant aux besoins de toutes les parties prenantes du commerce international.

Par ailleurs, la CCI joue un rôle essentiel dans la généralisation de l'action en faveur des objectifs de développement durable et formule depuis longtemps les règles volontaires qui régissent la conduite des affaires, qu'il s'agisse des règles Incoterms® ou des RUU 600 (Règles et usances uniformes relatives au crédit documentaire) largement utilisées en finance internationale.

Enfin, la CCI assure à travers ses structures spécifiques, des formations juridique et commerciale de haut niveau et publie des outils pratiques pour le commerce international, la banque et l'arbitrage.

Qu'est-ce que le CoE de la CCI ?

Pour contribuer à la création d'emplois et permettre aux PME et starts-up de s'intégrer effectivement au commerce mondial, ICC a lancé le Centre pour l'entrepreneuriat (CoE).

Les Hubs de CoE à travers le monde auront comme objectifs de développer les compétences des jeunes et d'impulser et de consolider l'esprit d'entrepreneuriat dans les pays concernés.

Ils serviront également de plateformes de partage des expériences locales et régionales réussies en matière d'entrepreneuriat.

Enfin, ils serviront à travers la connectivité numérique de mettre en relation, les entrepreneurs de ces pays et les experts du réseau mondial de l'ONU et de la Chambre de commerce internationale pour un encadrement et un tutorat à distance appropriés.

Il convient de souligner que le principal partenaire du CoE - avec les comités nationaux et les chambres de commerce -, est la Commission économique et sociale des Nations unies.

Les missions prioritaires dévolues à ces centres peuvent se résumer comme suit :

1. **Promouvoir l'esprit d'entrepreneuriat** en particulier chez les jeunes.
2. Favoriser la **digitalisation** des **PME** en assurant leur (1) **connectivité,** leur (2) **accès aux marchés** et leur (3) **transformation digitale.**

3. Accompagner les **start-up** à travers des formations, du monitoring et des **services de support.**
4. Soutenir **l'entrepreneuriat inclusif** en appuyant la création des entreprises à impact économique et social pour toute la communauté.

De 2020 à nos jours, plusieurs centres ont été déployés dans les différentes régions du monde :

Le premier **Centre** a été créé à **Istanbul**, en Turquie, pour soutenir les entrepreneurs de l'Asie centrale et la région du Caucase.

Le **CoE d'ICC-ESCWA** a ouvert ses portes à Beyrouth, au Liban, afin d'apporter son soutien à la région du monde arabe.

Le **CoE d'ICC-CEA** a lancé un partenariat continental pour l'Afrique avec des centres en **Afrique de l'Est** (Nairobi, Kenya), en **Afrique de l'Ouest** (Accra, Ghana et Lagos, Nigeria) et en Afrique du Nord (Casablanca, Maroc).

Le premier **CoE pour la région Asie-Pacifique** a été lancé à **Jakarta**, en Indonésie.

Le CoE s'est étendu en **Amérique latine** avec l'ouverture du premier centre pour la région Sud à **Buenos Aires**, en Argentine et du second à **Bogota**, en Colombie.

Un CoE d'ICC dédié à l'**Ukraine** a été lancé pour renforcer la résilience des PME ukrainiennes et soutenir les réfugiés.

Un CoE d'ICC à **Séville**, en Espagne, a été lancé pour soutenir et mobiliser la prochaine génération d'entrepreneurs en Europe du Sud.

Le dernier Centre lancé par ICC est situé à **Tbilissi**. Celui-ci s'efforcera d'inspirer, d'innover et de soutenir l'environnement commercial des entrepreneurs et des PME en Géorgie et dans toute la région de l'Asie centrale et du Caucase.

Quid du hub de Casablanca ?

Bien que principalement axé sur le Maroc, le centre de Casablanca, lancé effectivement le 1er décembre 2022, contribuera également à soutenir les programmes du CoE qui seront développés en **Afrique du Nord.**

Il travaillera avec l'équipe du Centre de l'Entrepreneuriat à Paris ainsi que la Commission économique des Nations Unies pour l'Afrique et la Commission économique et sociale des Nations Unies pour l'Asie occidentale.

Outre les quatre missions prioritaires dévolues à tous les centres de ce programme mondial, le hub de Casablanca pourra, après accord du siège, se concentrer éventuellement sur certains domaines / activités (jeunes, femmes entrepreneurs, etc.) jugés prioritaires.

En termes de pilotage, le centre de Casablanca sera placé sous la responsabilité d'un Steering Committee qui supervisera le développement et la mise en œuvre de la stratégie du centre et qui orientera également le travail du coordinateur exécutif. Ce coordinateur exécutif, est dans une première étape, un membre de l'équipe actuelle de la CCI Maroc et sera l'interlocuteur exclusif vis-à-vis de l'extérieur.

L'un des projets phares du Hub est le programme eCAP (The eCommerce Acceleration programme).

Destiné aux PME ayant un produit ou un service adapté à la vente en ligne, ce programme est conçu pour leur donner les moyens de leur transition vers la vente en ligne, soit en créant des sites de commerce électronique transactionnel ou en vendant sur des places de existantes, en leur offrant une formation, un accompagnement, une expertise technique, ainsi que des opportunités de mise en réseau.

BANK OF AFRICA, L'INTELLIGENCE ÉCONOMIQUE AU SERVICE DE LA CRÉATION DE VALEUR INTERNE ET EXTERNE

Omar Ezziyati

Créé en 1959 par les pouvoirs publics, le Groupe BMCE Bank of Africa a, dès sa naissance, eu, dans son ADN, cette volonté d'accompagner les différents opérateurs économiques et financiers du Royaume, et plus particulièrement dans la conquête des marchés étrangers[57].

Parmi les différents outils mis en place figurait une entité dédiée à la collecte, à l'analyse et au traitement d'informations et de données, utiles à tout acteur souhaitant initier des opérations de commerce extérieur (Figure 1).

Extrait du Dahir n° 1-59-391 du 16 novembre 1959 fixant les responsabilités de la Banque dans le cadre de sa Mission d'intérêt public

D'après l'article relatif à la mission d'intérêt public de la banque, cette dernière se doit de réunir « une documentation sur les législations marocaines et étrangères en matière de commerce extérieur ». En effet, cela correspond aux études, enquêtes et renseignements relatifs aux différents domaines. Une prospection et une veille constante sont préconisées afin d'informer et de conseiller sur de « nouvelles raisons d'activité et d'initiative ». Enfin, les documentations et conseils resteront à disposition des différents acteurs économiques, notamment les exportateurs, importateurs et services d'exécution afin d'assurer un support des activités.

À l'image des nombreuses institutions publiques post - indépendance, la montée en charge et en compétences a du se faire rapidement, tout en

57. Dahir n° 1-59-391 du 16 novembre 1959 fixant les responsabilités de la Banque dans le cadre de sa Mission d'intérêt public

déployant un modèle propre à l'environnement local. De ces premières années, datent aussi les nombreuses relations tissées par cette entité avec ses homologues du secteur public – Haut-Commissariat au Plan[58], Ministères…

Ces années et ces synergies ont alors permis d'asseoir une expertise dans le traitement de l'information, renforcée par la privatisation du Groupe en 1995, avec la volonté d'offrir des services à plus forte valeur ajoutée également à la clientèle interne à la banque. L'évolution vers un Centre d'Intelligence Economique – CIE[59] -, en 2007, s'est appuyée sur ce modèle, propre au Groupe et correspondant à ses valeurs.

Participatif et centré sur l'information principalement blanche[60], ce dernier permet, classiquement, l'identification des opportunités et des menaces pour l'entreprise et, surtout, facilite, après automatisation, l'appropriation de la collecte par les différentes entités de la banque. Un des mots d'ordre est que les spécialistes de la veille ne pourront jamais être aussi performants, en termes de qualification de l'information, que les métiers à qui cette information est adressée.

S'agissant de l'élément humain, il occupe une place centrale dans notre dispositif. Pour C. Bourret & A. David (2014), « Dans une entreprise ou toute autre organisation, l'intelligence économique doit être l'affaire de tous. Ainsi, nous considérons notre capacité à mobiliser tout le personnel dans le cadre d'un management participatif comme un facteur clé de succès de notre démarche. Dans ce schéma, la conduite de changement est un élément fondamental comme le considèrent N. Moinet et P. Darantière (2007).

Par ailleurs, notre vision du concept d'Intelligence est alignée à celle de P. Achard & J.P. Bernat (1998) qui le considère comme la capacité à analyser des problèmes complexes et la capacité à synthétiser et à créer

---

58. Haut-Commissariat au Plan : Une structure ministérielle érigée en septembre 2003 en une administration de mission, sous l'autorité d'un haut-commissaire au plan nommé, avec rang de Ministre, par Sa Majesté le Roi. Principal producteur de l'information statistique, économique, démographique et sociale et chargé de l'établissement des comptes de la nation. Élabore des études dans les domaines de la conjoncture, du cadrage macroéconomique et de la prospective.

59. CIE : acronyme que nous utiliserons dans cet article pour désigner Centre d'Intelligence Economique

60. L'information « blanche » : publique ou réservée, elle est issue de publications, entretiens avec des experts de centres techniques, des fournisseurs, des clients, des partenaires... Elle est donc libre d'accès et d'exploitation. Source : https://portail-ie.fr/resource/glossary/49/information.

des schémas nouveaux. Les auteurs résument ainsi leur définition : « la capacité d'analyse et de synthèse orientée vers l'action ».

Dans le même temps, le principe que l'information peut regrouper un éventail très large de concepts, y compris la data, est au cœur de notre démarche. Déjà, cela souligne l'évolutivité permanente de notre modèle et renforce la performance des process à caractère itératifs et *stratégiques ayant pour ultime objectif de mener à une prise de décision, à un moment opportun* de l'IE Goria et al. (2005).

Cette décentralisation, massive, du processus de veille informative s'est ainsi traduite par un recentrage du CIE sur les tâches et les fonctions à bien plus forte valeur, et particulièrement les démarches d'analyse, d'animation des réseaux et d'influence, plus propices au développement d'outils d'aide à la décision. La synthèse des principales fonctions de l'IE réalisée par Dhaoui(2008) illustre parfaitement le périmètre fonctionnel du CIE.

Fonction	Description
La fonction de lecture pertinente de l'environnement de l'entreprise et de management stratégique de l'information	L'IE permet à l'entreprise de disposer d'un dispositif efficace et en permanent fonctionnement de lecture pertinente de l'environnement concurrentiel, de décryptage des règles de la compétition, de perception et de compréhension des stratégies dissimulées des concurrents
La fonction de production des connaissances stratégiques à haute valeur ajoutée	Cette fonction concerne la production et l'organisation des connaissances stratégiques exploitables dans le processus décisionnel stratégique.

La fonction d'anticipation des menaces qui pèsent sur l'entreprise et des opportunités de développement d'affaires	Les entreprises sont confrontées à des mutations de leur environnement que certains qualifient de mouvements incessants, protéiformes et instables. De telles mutations qu'elles soient d'ordre économique, culturel, technologique, réglementaire ou social, ont des conséquences profondes sur la pérennité de l'entreprise.
La fonction de maîtrise du moment de la décision	En IE, le temps et l'information en temps réel sont considérés comme deux variables décisives dans la saisie des opportunités, dans la décision et dans 'action stratégique parce que l'entreprise joue le rôle d'acteur et non pas seulement de témoin de l'évolution de l'environnement ou de spectateur au regard d'un environnement qui ne cesse de se transformer.
La fonction de gestion du risque informationnel	Dans un environnement incertain, la capacité de l'entreprise à maitriser et protéger l'information stratégique en temps réel et à tout moment, constitue un véritable avantage concurrentiel.
La fonction de sécurisation du patrimoine immatériel de l'entreprise	L'IE intervient pour la sécurité de l'entreprise contre les menaces, la protection de tout le patrimoine immatériel de l'entreprise et la préservation des actions d'influence, qui traduisent la dimension sécuritaire de l'IE.
La fonction de coordination des stratégies en interne et en externe	La coordination des stratégies représente l'une des principales fonctions de l'IE. Ainsi la dimension « réseau » est fondamentale afin d'assurer une meilleure pratique de l'IE.
La fonction de mise en pratique des actions d'influence et de contre influence	Cette fonction permet de mettre en pratique et en toute légalité, des cations d'influence et de contre influence sur l'environnement de l'entreprise.

Tableau 1 : Fonctions de l'intelligence économique (Source : Dhaoui (2008)

En effet, et afin de pouvoir renforcer la crédibilité et la légitimité de l'entité sur le chemin critique de la décision, il convenait, impérativement et rapidement, d'avoir de premières victoires (Figure 2).

Schéma illustrant l'évolution de la gestion et de l'usage de l'Information au sein du BBOA[61]

> *Depuis 1962, l'usage de l'information chez BANK OF AFRICA a évolué. Le département est passé de « étude et documentaire » (DED) à Centre d'Intelligence Economique (CIE). Cette transition a été possible grâce à l'évolution du métier. En premier lieu, on remarque le démarrage au niveau des « études statistiques, puis documentations et ensuite veilles informatives », qui avait pour fin d'accompagner les investisseurs par l'information économique, de rassembler des dossiers documentaires, revue de presse .... En second lieu, la progression a donné naissance à un département organisé en « veille stratégique, IE et innovation », qui approfondit le premier volet avec de l'analyse, des études sectorielles, des projets-veille, une stratégie de connaissance client, une dynamique d'entrepreneuriat et Big Data.*

Cette transition a été possible grâce à : (i) un fort engagement au plus haut niveau de la hiérarchie (ii)une implication systématique des parties prenantes et (iii)une logique incrémentale et des itérations courtes.

Deux axes ont été bien approfondis : analytique et technologique. En termes analytiques, le CIE s'engage sur ce qui peut apparaître comme étant le plus facilement appréhendable ; principalement les aspects Risque, International et Marchés. La soixantaine d'études publiées chaque année est partagée pour accompagner la décision d'accompagnement de notre clientèle, la compréhension des enjeux dans les pays dans lesquels nous sommes implantés, l'identification des marchés porteurs pour nos produits et services.

Au niveau technologique, de nombreux outils ont été mis en place pour faciliter l'exploitation des données et informations terrain. Ainsi, un système d'information géographique, proposant de nombreuses couches démographiques, économiques, urbaines..., est utilisé pour identifier des zones d'implantation de nos agences. De même, l'ouverture vers le Big Data s'est accompagnée de la nécessaire maîtrise des outils de modélisation.

---

61. BBOA : Acronyme pour désigner BMCE Bank Of Africa

Ainsi pour les outils de veille stratégique, ils sont utilisés principalement pour l'automatisation de la collecte de données, la génération des cartographies d'acteurs et la systématisation d'une diffusion sélective d'information à travers des newsletters thématiques (figure 2).

Sélection des publications du CIE à travers ses outils de veille

Les différentes publications de l'entité CIE sont possibles grâce à des outils de veilles qui récoltent l'information et l'organisent.

La veille terrain à travers la mobilisation de l'humain occupe également une place centrale dans le dispositif de veille stratégique de la Banque. Ainsi, le CIE a lancé une démarche de veille collaborative impliquant l'ensemble de la force commerciale dans le cadre d'un processus structuré décliné en plusieurs axes : commercial, concurrentiel, environnement social, projets, dynamiques entrepreneuriales. S'agissant des remontées d'information, une démarche multimodale a été entreprise : Remontée standard à caractère permanent; Remontées standard à caractère ponctuel et ciblé; le Challenge et les Notes d'étonnement.

Le second niveau d'intervention concerne l'influence directe de notre environnement extérieur pour offrir de nouvelles opportunités de croissance au Groupe BMCE Bank of Africa. Dans ce sens, la création de l'Observatoire de l'Entrepreneuriat a été un moment critique puisqu'elle a permis le gain de légitimité et de crédibilité auprès des différentes cibles extérieures et la création d'un écosystème aux nombreuses externalités.

Plus concrètement la doctrine de la Banque en matière d'influence est basée sur l'attraction scientifique et centrée sur trois piliers en faisant appel à deux leviers majeurs.

- **Pilier 1 - Entrepreneuriat :** Agir sur l'axe Entrepreneuriat comme enjeu et problématique nationale et véritable impératif stratégique pour la Banque.
- **Pilier 2- Innovation :** Proposer des solutions et des dispositifs innovants avec une exclusivité de la Banque.
- **Pilier 3 - Terrain :** Privilégier des actions de mobilisation terrain pour plus de proximité avec la cible finale.
- **Levier 1 - Digital :** Accompagner le dispositif par une forte mobilisation sur les réseaux sociaux, portails et newsletters.

• **Levier 2- Ecosystème[62] :** Capitaliser sur les différents partenariats de l'Observatoire de l'Entrepreneuriat.

D'un point de vue opérationnel, l'effort a d'abord consisté, dans un premier temps, en la mise en place d'un écosystème créateur de valeurs avec la signature de plus d'une quarantaine de partenaires de référence - universités, écoles, médias, associations professionnelles… -, tous tournés vers l'entrepreneuriat (Titre 4). Dans le même temps, l'ODE a grandement participé au débat public en publiant études et indices de confiance.

Écosystème

L'écosystème entrepreneurial s'articule en 04 sous-groupes constitués de :

- *La banque,*
- *Les associations professionnelles actives notamment l'Alisca, Business Edge, Enactus,*
- *Les universités-écoles-facultés comme le Groupe ISCAE, l'OFPPT, l'Université Cadi Ayaad...*
- *Et les dynamiques entrepreneuriales bancaires comme l'ODE et l'African Entrepreneurship Award.*

Cet élan nous a alors permis de contribuer à renforcer le positionnement du Groupe sur le segment de l'entrepreneuriat et d'offrir des services à très forte valeur pour cette même cible. L'organisation de séminaires de haut niveau pour les TPE a ainsi répondu à un double objectif pour les deux parties : une population de près de deux cents PME ont été accompagnés par des experts pendant 10 jours avec la possibilité de leur placer des produits, tandis que du côté TPE, ils ont vu, pour 60% d'entre eux, leur chiffre d'affaires croître de plus de 40% (Figure 4).

62. Notre perception de l'écosystème : Il s'agit d'un projet à la fois délibéré et co-évolutif qui conduit à un alignement des acteurs créateurs de valeur au travers d'un processus d'innovation collectif. Gouverné de façon démocratique, à la fois compétitif et coopératif, c'est un agencement modulaire de firmes partageant une communauté de destin. Kœnig Gérard, « Le concept d'écosystème d'affaires revisité », M@n@gement, 2012/2 (Vol. 15), p. 209-224. DOI : 10.3917/mana.152.0209. URL : https://www.cairn.info/revue-management-2012-2-page-209.htm

Quelques axes de formation pour la cible des TPE-PME

La cible TPE-PME est formée et accompagnée sur plusieurs domaines, notamment la gestion des ressources humaines, la gestion des opérations, la gestion financière et comptable, la gouvernance, le marketing, la productivité personnelle, la gestion hôtelière…

Ce modèle d'influence a très vite posé les bases de la démarche du Groupe avec la mise en avant d'une offre désintéressée et à très forte valeur pour la cible, et plus globalement, la communauté, et la création d'opportunités business pour la banque. Cette dilution totale du Groupe dans son environnement a fait que le grand public ne perçoit plus du tout le Groupe dans sa dimension bancaire, mais sa dimension de Partenariat Public Privé d'expertise, ce qui contribue à renforcer son image et son positionnement. Ainsi, « *L'entreprise ne se trouve ainsi pas limitée à son seul savoir-faire. Elle développe un discours cohérent, porteur de sens, appuyé par des repères* » B. Racouhot (2012).

Les différents membres du CIE ont ainsi mis à la disposition du grand public toute sa compétence, via les actions d'influence. Les associations de retraités se sont vues offrir un espace d'échange et de partage d'expertise, des programmes de sensibilisation à l'endettement ont été développés auprès de certaines catégories de fonctionnaires… L'Intelligence Economique permet de ce fait de renforcer, voire même créer, de nouveaux marchés pour la banque. Il s'agit d'un véritable outil à la prise de décision d'innovation El Haouad N (2011).

Pour Deschamps et Moinet (2011), « l'utilisation du schéma systémique permet de saisir les dynamiques externes, définir les scénarios d'innovation et évaluer leurs impacts sur les capacités internes de l'entreprise ». Ainsi , les méthodes classiques de l'Intelligence Economique se sont aussi traduites par la déclinaison d'un programme d'innovation interne, véritable réceptacle de l'ensemble de l'approche IE de la banque.

En effet, il représente la fusion interne / externe avec l'organisation classique de campagnes de sourcing de nouvelles idées ou concepts pour identifier les meilleurs projets au sein du Groupe – campagne mail, challenge des collègues… - mais aussi l'intégration totale de l'écosystème de l'Observatoire de l'Entrepreneuriat avec le déploiement de compétitions au sein même des universités et écoles. Ainsi les meilleurs porteurs de projets universitaires ont été coachés avec les équipes internes pour pitcher ensemble devant un jury composé de membres de direction générale de la banque. De fait, des projets externes ont été retenus pour une incubation en interne.

Programme d'Open Innovation Territoriale SMART BANK

Le programme est un challenge déployé au niveau des 12 régions du Royaume. Il est rythmé par 05 grandes étapes où les partenaires internes et externes de la banque participent et s'impliquent :

1. *Le Sourcing des Projets via des problématiques BOA, les propositions des laboratoires universitaires ou des projets individuels des bénéficiaires ;*
2. *La sélection des idées de projet/ projets les plus innovant(s) ;*
3. *Le Proof of Concept qui est une étape qui permet aux bénéficiaires sélectionnés de tester et approfondir leurs idées grâce à un Bootcamp ;*
4. *Restitution à travers un premier jury régional puis un jury national pour les meilleures idées ;*
5. *Une Déclinaison des projets innovants à travers un accompagnement au sein de réseau d'incubateurs, des stages, la création.*

Ce mélange permanent est source d'externalités extrêmement positives puisqu'au-delà d'assurer une présence permanente du Groupe au sein même des universités et écoles, il répond à un besoin sans cesse rappelé de proximité Université – Entreprise, Recherche – Application...

Désormais, c'est ce mode de fonctionnement, permis par l'Intelligence Economique et ses principes, qui est décliné par la banque. Cette dernière apporte toute sa valeur ajoutée à la communauté, en contribuant à créer de la valeur et agrandir ainsi les zones de création de richesses. Exemple concret de cette contribution sociétale est la mise en place d'incubateurs[63] externes au sein même des centres d'enseignement vont ainsi directement contribuer à la création d'entreprises à fort impact – emplois, innovations…

---

63. Un incubateur d'entreprises ou un accélérateur de start-up est une structure d'accompagnement de projets de création d'entreprise. L'incubateur peut apporter un appui en termes d'hébergement, de conseil et de financement, lors des premières étapes de la vie de l'entreprise. Wikipédia

En effet, initié dans le cadre d'une démarche d'influence, la création d'un réseau d'incubateurs/accélérateurs au niveau des régions répond à trois enjeux majeurs :

- **Sociétal :** consiste à contribuer efficacement à développer des solutions concrètes pour l'employabilité des jeunes
- **Économique :** accéléré la dynamique entrepreneuriale par la création de nouvelles entreprises et des start-up
- **Territorial** : à travers la mobilisation des acteurs fortement ancrés dans leur territoire à savoir les universités et acteurs de la société civile et des associations professionnelles

Aujourd'hui, nous comptons deux projets d'incubateurs/accélérateurs développés avec une université et école de commerce. Avec l'université, il s'agit d'un incubateur spécialisé orienté vers 5 métiers : Développement territorial, Digital & Fintech[64] et Entrepreneuriat social. Quant à celui avec l'école de commerce, il s'agit d'un incubateur généraliste. À noter que les deux incubateurs sont ouverts aux porteurs de projet de toute la région, y compris les étudiants.

Faire partie de manière légitime, et sincère, de l'environnement que nous souhaitons influencer offre de toutes nouvelles perspectives à la banque puisqu'elle peut désormais se positionner comme créateur de tendances dans le secteur bancaire, voire plus. Il est de la responsabilité des grandes entreprises de s'investir dans l'enrichissement de son environnement.

Le recours aux services du Centre d'Intelligence Economique est désormais reconnu comme essentiel par tous les acteurs internes et externes. Ainsi, La Banque met ce dispositif d'IE, complet et intégré, au service de sa stratégie, de son développement, mais aussi de tous les acteurs économiques désirant adopter une telle démarche. Dans ce sens, BMCE Bank of Africa assure un transfert de compétences en matière d'IE de l'interne vers l'externe, via tant des formations spécifiques, des séminaires pour la communauté des TPE, PME et même grandes entreprises, que des missions d'accompagnement

---

64. Fintech : La technologie financière, aussi dénommée fintech, est une nouvelle industrie financière qui déploie la technologie pour améliorer les activités financières. Le terme « fintech » est une contraction de « finance » et de « technologie. Wikipédia

auprès de plusieurs organismes publics et privés. Il s'agit in fine d'un modèle où le secteur privé joue le rôle de locomotive en matière d'IE. Encore mieux, l'expérience de cette institution s'avère même une première à l'échelle internationale, au moment où la majorité des entreprises n'osent même pas afficher l'existence d'une telle fonction dans leurs organigrammes ou en faire référence dans leur discours.

Bibliographie

Achard P. (2011), « La dimension humaine de l'intelligence économique: valeurs, organisation, réseaux et influence : compte-rendu de la 8ème Journée franco-suisse en intelligence économique et veille stratégique, 16 juin 2011 », Haute école de gestion de Neuchâtel. Url : http://www.ressi.ch/ num12/article_080

Achard P., & Bernat JP. (2005), « L'intelligence économique : mode d'emploi », Éditions ADBS, 1998, 2ème édition.

BOURRET C. & DAVID A., « L'INTELLIGENCE ÉCONOMIQUE COMME CATALYSEUR DE NOUVELLES DYNAMIQUES DE

COOPÉRATION (2014). Les cahiers de la SFSIC n°9 | janvier 2014. p. 199

El HAOUD N, « L'intelligence économique au service de l'entreprise innovante », Revue internationale d'intelligence économique, 2011/2 (Vol 3), p. 175-187. URL : https://www.cairn.info/revue-internationale-d-intelligence-economique-2011-2-page-175.html

DESCHAMPS C., MOINET N. (2011), « La Boîte à Outils de l'intelligence économique », Dunod, 2011

MOINET N., DARANTIERE P. (2007), « Organiser la veille stratégique dans l'entreprise : conduite du changement, communautés professionnelles et stratégie réseau », Market Management, 2007/4 (Vol. 7), p. 94-109. DOI: 10.3917/mama.044.0094. URL : https://www.cairn.info/revue-market-management-2007-4-page-94.htm.

GORIA S. et al. (2008), « Le processus d'Intelligence Economique : Une étude selon le point de vue de l'infomédiaire et des problématiques de recherche d'information », L'Harmattan. Benchmark Européen de pratiques en Intelligence Economique, Pierre LARRAT, pp.115-138, 2008. <halshs-00311486>

DHAOUI C. (2008), Les critères de réussite d'un système d'intelligence économique pour un meilleur pilotage stratégique : proposition d'un Modèle d'Évaluation de la Réussite d'un Système d'Intelligence Économique

MERSIE

KOENIG G., « Le concept d'écosystème d'affaires revisité », M@n@gement, 2012/2 (Vol. 15), p. 209-224. DOI : 10.3917/mana.152.0209.

URL: https://www.cairn.info/revue-management-2012-2-page-209.htm

RACOUCHOT B., THOME H., « Lobbying et communication d'influence », Fusions & Acquisitions Magazine, septembre-octobre 2010, n° 242-243, 102 p.

RACOUCHOT B., VANDOMME R., « Strategies of influence : the key role of ideas », Journal of the Royal Canadian Military Institute, March-April 2009, volume 69, number 2, 16 p.

RACOUCHOT B., « De la stratégie d'influence à la communication d'influence », in HARBULOT C. (sous la dir. de), Manuel d'intelligence économique, Paris, PUF, coll. « Major », 2012, 432 p.

DAHIR n° 1-59-391 du 16 novembre 1959 fixant les responsabilités de la Banque dans le cadre de sa Mission d'intérêt public

LA CONTRIBUTION DES START-UP À L'AMÉLIORATION DE LA PRODUCTION DU COTON DANS L'ESPACE UEMOA
CAS DE LA CÔTE D'IVOIRE ET DU BURKINA FASO

Mora Dandagui Sero

Contexte

L'Union Economique et Monétaire Ouest-Africaine (UEMOA) est une organisation qui œuvre pour le développement socio-économique de ses États membres. Créée en 1994, l'UEMOA regroupe aujourd'hui huit (8) pays en Afrique de l'Ouest (Bénin, Burkina Faso, Côte d'Ivoire, Guinée-Bissau, Mali, Niger, Sénégal et le Togo). Elle représente une superficie de 3 512 233 km^2 pour une population de 130,8 millions d'habitants.

Riche en ressources humaines et naturelles, la zone UEMOA a un potentiel économique important et sa situation géographique est favorable à la pratique de plusieurs types de cultures tropicales vivrières et industrielles.

Le coton, « l'or blanc », est cultivé depuis plusieurs générations et représente une source de revenus directs et indirects pour près de 15 millions de personnes de cet espace UEMOA.

La culture est assurée par de petits producteurs avec de petites exploitations de superficies moyennes inférieures à 5 ha.

Quelques innovations ont été introduites ces dernières années par des start-up pour soulager les producteurs dans certaines opérations culturales. Il ne s'agit pas des innovations conduites par la recherche et faisant l'objet d'un long processus comprenant l'expérimentation en milieu contrôlé puis en milieu réel, la validation et enfin la vulgarisation, mais juste des solutions novatrices pour alléger la pénibilité du travail des producteurs dans l'accomplissement de ces opérations culturales.

Planification et suivi des activités agricoles par l'utilisation des données météorologiques

Dans le contexte du réchauffement climatique, les producteurs cherchent à anticiper et à prévenir les évolutions de la météo. La start-up toulousaine *Weather* Force a mis au point une application permettant de mieux connaître et d'anticiper les évolutions de la météo. C'est dans ce cadre qu'un projet pilote a été financé par la Banque mondiale au profit des producteurs de coton ivoiriens et burkinabés.

Weather Force travaille avec la Sodexam (service météo ivoirien), et l'Agence nationale de la météorologie burkinabé (ANAM) en lien avec des producteurs de la filière coton.

L'application permet de fournir aux utilisateurs des données indispensables pour leur activité, notamment des indicateurs de températures et de pluviométrie faciles à utiliser. Il s'agit aussi de fournir des éléments sur les impacts de ces indicateurs sur les végétaux.

La Sodexam et l'ANAM fournissent des données à Weather Force, qui ayant accès aux bases des grands centres mondiaux de météo, analyse et transforme les éléments météorologiques et climatiques, couplés à des modèles pour les cultures. Les données sont affinées, simplifiées et traduites *afin de les rendre cohérentes et pour qu'elles soient proches des besoins des utilisateurs finaux potentiels, c'est-à-dire* les quelques centaines de milliers de petits producteurs de coton.

En donnant des informations plus précises aux producteurs, on aide à :

- effectuer des semis sans crainte et permettant d'obtenir de bons taux de levée et peu de resemis ;
- choisir les périodes optimales d'application des intrants pour éviter i) le transport des engrais et des pesticides en cas de fortes pluies tombant après leur application et ii) la brûlure des plantes en cas de poche de sécheresse intervenant après l'application des engrais ;
- assurer la durabilité de la culture du coton par une meilleure maîtrise des apports en eau et en intrants pour améliorer les rendements dans le cadre d'une agriculture plus respectueuse de l'environnement.

Traitements phytosanitaires par les drones

Pour assurer le bon développement de la plante, le cotonnier est protégé des attaques parasitaires par l'application de pesticides en utilisant des appareils de traitement (pulvériseurs), pratique utilisée en culture de coton. Cette activité requiert d'importants efforts physiques, notamment les travaux liés aux traitements phytosanitaires du cotonnier, reconnus comme des activités essentielles, voire indispensables pour l'obtention de meilleures récoltes. Le traitement insecticide réalisé manuellement est très pénible pour les agriculteurs. En effet, il nécessite assez de temps de travail et emploie une main-d'œuvre abondante. À cela s'ajoute le poids de l'appareil de traitement que doivent supporter les agriculteurs, auquel il faut ajouter les difficultés liées à la précision des épandages et la répartition homogène des doses des produits sur la parcelle à traiter.

Cas de la Côte d'Ivoire

En **Côte d'Ivoire**, le projet est en phase expérimentale avec un échantillon de 240 producteurs de coton et 6 drones acquis.

À travers ce projet, il s'agira de contribuer à l'optimisation des applications des produits phytosanitaires et à la réduction de la pénibilité du travail dans la culture de coton par l'utilisation de drones. Au total 240 producteurs de coton des départements de Boundiali, Korhogo (sous-préfecture de Napié) et Mankono bénéficient de cette technologie pour le traitement de leur parcelle. Ledit projet s'effectuera sur 20 mois. Des outils didactiques ont été élaborés et mis à la disposition des acteurs de la filière coton pour contribuer à la pérennisation du projet.

Pour maîtriser et surveiller les cultures, une jeune start-up ivoirienne, Investiv Group, utilise des drones permettant d'identifier et de cibler depuis le ciel, les zones problématiques nécessitant un traitement.

Cette solution durable et bénéfique pour l'environnement permet ainsi d'éviter un traitement des cultures généralisées et permet aux agriculteurs de réguler l'utilisation de leurs produits phytosanitaires. Avec moins de pesticides, les cultures sont plus saines et les sols moins pollués. Avec les drones, on peut pulvériser 2 hectares en moins de 10 minutes, contre une journée habituellement si la pulvérisation est entreprise manuellement. La solution d'Investiv Group est ainsi une solution plus rapide, efficace, rentable et durable.

Cas du Burkina Faso

Au **Burkina Faso**, plusieurs start-up font la promotion de cette technologie. On peut citer entre autres la Société Africaine des Services Financiers (ASF), KONO DIGITAL, FASO DRONE, etc.

L'utilisation des drones épandeurs fait suite à la collaboration entre le département Agri-Innov de la Société Africaine de Services Financiers (Sté ASF-SA), la SOFITEX et l'Union Nationale des Sociétés Coopératives des Producteurs de Coton du Burkina (UNPCB) avec l'autorisation du Programme Coton de l'Institut de l'Environnement et de Recherches Agricoles du Burkina Faso (INERA) pour l'utilisation du modèle de drone DJI AGRAS T16 au cours de la campagne 2020/2021.

Ainsi, des expérimentations ont été conduites sur 15.000 ha dans la zone cotonnière de la SOFITEX avec plus de huit cents (800) producteurs. Les interventions se sont organisées par zones, départements, villages et par Groupement de Producteurs de Coton. Le protocole d'accord tripartite encadre un prix de départ pour la prestation qui est de 3000 F CFA par hectare au comptant et 3210 FCFA par hectare par crédit.

À la fin de la campagne sur l'ensemble des parcelles qui ont bénéficié du traitement par drone, on peut noter que :

- Aucun signe visuel de toxicité n'a été observé sur les cotonniers ;
- Les applications d'insecticides par drone n'entrainent pas d'effets secondaires sur les cotonniers pouvant conduire à l'apparition de phytotoxicité ;
- Le niveau d'infestation du cotonnier est quasi inexistant ;
- Les rendements ont augmenté de 20 à 25% par comptage capsulaire et de 30% par les carrés de rendement, ce qui permet de couvrir les frais de prestation du drone.

L'utilisation des drones représente pour des petits agriculteurs un système d'aide à la décision efficace leur permettant de mieux maîtriser les coûts de production et d'optimiser les rendements agricoles.

La cartographie de la ferme aide l'agriculteur à connaître le statut de sa ferme. Ceci est important après un évènement météorologique (forte pluie, vent violent, etc.) afin de détecter les dommages sur les cultures.

La surveillance de la ferme permet pendant toute la saison de détecter les problèmes de santé des plantes liés aux attaques des bioagresseurs. Le stress hydrique aide l'agriculteur à prendre la bonne décision concernant l'application d'intrants et l'irrigation. Le dépistage aérien est efficace et rentable par rapport à la marche à pied qui est très fastidieuse et impraticable.

Elle permet de réduire la pénibilité et le temps de travail des agriculteurs, ce qui leur permet de gagner du temps supplémentaire et de faire d'autres activités. En outre, la productivité et la production agricole se sont accrues avec la précision dans les opérations et l'utilisation des produits de bonne qualité. La santé des producteurs est améliorée parce qu'ils ne manipulent plus directement les produits chimiques où les mauvaises pratiques sont légion dans nos localités.

Utilisation des drones : une agriculture intelligente et de précision

À travers ces technologies, les start-up sont en train de développer une solution d'agriculture de précision qui va permettre aux producteurs de protéger les cultures, d'augmenter les rendements et de minimiser ou d'optimiser l'utilisation des intrants agricoles.

Cette agriculture comporte ainsi des avantages :

- économiques à travers la gestion d'une parcelle de terre dans un champ avec différents niveaux d'intrants en fonction du rendement potentiel des cultures ;
- environnementaux en protégeant l'environnement de la pollution grâce à l'application précise des engrais et pesticides ;

la réduction des risques liés à la santé humaine (réduction des intoxications);

- réduction de la pénibilité du travail (on marche en moyenne 15 km pour traiter 1 hectare de coton et du semis à la récolte, il faut en moyenne 6 traitements insecticides par hectare, soit une distance de 90 km à parcourir pour traiter un seul hectare. Pour un champ de coton de 5 ha, il faudra marcher 450 km pour le traiter manuellement ! ;
- précision dans les opérations culturales et donc, une meilleure maitrise des coûts avec une optimisation des rendements agricoles ;
- meilleure résilience des agriculteurs au manque de main-d'œuvre agricole à cause de la concurrence liée aux activités d'orpaillage ;
- outil d'aide à la décision.

Les contraintes

La faible communication autour de ces innovations. Il est bien de développer des solutions innovantes, mais il faut aussi communiquer autour de ces solutions pour permettre aux populations concernées d'y adhérer.

La capacité limitée des producteurs à utiliser les drones. En effet, les drones sont équipés de capteurs et enregistrent des données, et non des informations, et les utilisateurs notamment les producteurs veulent des informations qu'ils pourront interpréter et utiliser, et non des données. Dès lors, toutes les données enregistrées par les drones doivent être converties en informations exploitables pour les agriculteurs. Ce sont les agents des start-up ou des agents de terrain formés dans le cadre des projets qui assurent ce service pour les producteurs.

Les obstacles financiers : L'acquisition d'un drone et son utilisation ne sont pas à la portée des petits producteurs. La technologie est pour le moment portée par des projets avec un nombre limité de bénéficiaires.

La réglementation : les préoccupations liées à la sécurité publique dans certains pays pourraient constituer un frein au déploiement de drones en raison des usages civils et militaires non clarifiés.

Les perspectives

En raison des résultats satisfaisants obtenus, « la solution drone » pourrait être étendue à un plus grand nombre de producteurs et aux autres cultures (comme c'est déjà le cas au Burkina Faso avec les parcelles de riz et de bananeraies).

La généralisation de cette technologie à tous les pays de l'espace UEMOA serait un soulagement pour les producteurs et un moyen de booster la production agricole.

Conclusion

L'adoption de ces technologies et des possibilités qu'elles offrent en matière de surveillance des cultures, d'évaluation des superficies cultivées, d'inventaire, de pulvérisation, de précision et d'évaluation des dommages causés aux cultures, est une opportunité pour la productivité agricole dans l'espace UEMOA. Il serait souhaitable d'envisager son expansion à toute la zone avec des mesures en matière de renforcement des capacités des producteurs, de mise en place des infrastructures d'appui, d'harmonisation de la réglementation, ainsi que l'implication des différentes parties prenantes.

Bibliographie :

http://www.afgoesdigital.com/wp-content/uploads/2019/04/Des-Drones%C3%A0-l%E2%80%99-Horizon-Transformer-

L%E2%80%98Agriculture-En-Afrique-fr.pdf http://www.commodafrica.com/13-02-2017-les-startups-africaines-dans-

lagriculture-en-vogue-en-2017 https://africamutandi.com/

cote-divoire-une-start-up-toulousaine-au-service-de-la-filiere-coton/ https://www.leconomistedufaso.bf/2022/04/04/2e-edition-start-up-

uemoa-amazonia-services-prend-le-maillot-jaune/ https://www.francetvinfo.fr/monde/afrique/environnement-africain/cote-

divoire-une-start-up-toulousaine-au-service-de-la-filiere-coton_3937067.html

http://www.coton-afrique.com/La-BAD-lance-un-programme-de-formation-dans-l-industrie-du-textile-en-faveur-des-entrepreneurs-et.html

https://www.agenceecofin.com/industrie/1210-51110-la-bad-lance-un-programme-de-formation-dans-l-industrie-du-textile-en-faveur-des-entrepreneurs-et-des-start-up

https://agridigitale.net/art-les_recettes_d_agritecno_pour_rduire_le_cot_et_la_quantit_des_intrants_agricoles_.html

https://helloplanet.tv/actualites/cote-divoire-quand-les-drones-se-mettent-au-service-de-lagriculture/

https://www.gouv.ci/_actualite-article.php?recordID=8719&d=2 https://www.investivgroup.com/nos-services/

diagnostic-phytosanitaire-par-drone/

https://www.gouv.ci/impact-developpement/accueil/action_detail/aboubacar-karim-met-des-drones-au-service-de-l-agriculture964/1

https://www.aip.ci/cote-divoire-aip-vers-lusage-des-drones-dans-le-traitement-des-champs-de-coton/

https://intercoton.org/nos-projets-en-cours/ http://www.afgoesdigital.com/burkina-faso/ https://www.facebook.com/watch/?v=2007353126063285

RETOUR D'EXPÉRIENCES UTILES AUX START-UP AFRICAINES

Mostafa Taouji

Je souhaite partager avec les start-up et les entreprises en général mon retour d'expériences (REX) sur une vingtaine d'années d'entreprenariat. Retour d'expériences, que j'espère utile aux jeunes et porteurs de projets, qui ne passent pas encore, dans leur grande majorité, à la création effective et au développement de leurs idées en projets puis en innovations créatrices d'emplois.

L'approche REX est aussi un très bon moyen pour les dirigeants à la tête d'entreprise, d'apprendre des mentors, des entrepreneurs ayant vécu des expériences similaires.

I- Constat sur la situation actuelle

Dans les cours que j'ai animés en France et au Maroc, au sein des masters II, des mastères spécialisés et diplômes d'ingénieurs, j'ai constaté que les jeunes étaient très intéressés pour créer leurs start-up ou PME, mais franchissent peu l'étape de création, faute de lisibilité dans les nombreux programmes, et faute de pouvoir bénéficier d'un accompagnement sur le terrain, par les acteurs de l'innovation et des entrepreneurs expérimentés.

- Durant mes 15 années de fondateur et dirigeant d'entreprise, j'ai constaté que les start-up ne font pas appel aux compétences de l'Université ni à celles des Fablabs industriels, pour réussir leurs innovations, et mettre rapidement leurs produits sur le marché. C'est aussi le cas dans les petites et moyennes entreprises (PME-PMI), créatrices de plus de 80% des emplois;
- Ces start-up ne sont pas accompagnées non plus, par des mentors qui ont vécu des expériences similaires. Ce mentorat pourrait leur donner

un avantage compétitif, leur faire bénéficier des retours d'expériences terrain, décisifs pour la réussite de leurs projets innovation, pour les développer, les pérenniser, avec en prime, plus de création d'emplois dans les Régions. C'est aussi le cas dans les PME-PMI;

- Un mentorat efficace pourrait non seulement mettre en selle les porteurs de projets, mais surtout les accompagner avant, pendant et après, et jusqu'à une autonomie complète;
- Les Fablabs sont des plateformes innovantes pour une mise sur le marché rapide des innovations, non utilisées par les start-up et les PME-PMI.

1) Plus de 80% des entreprises sont des PME-PMI, pour la majorité sous-traitante de l'industrie et de grands groupes, des PME-PMI qui ne sont pas appelées à innover !

- Sur les 15 années de pratique sur le terrain du métier de dirigeant d'entreprise, au sein d'un environnement dit « très complexe », comme prestataire direct, j'ai observé sur une dizaine d'années et sur un panel de 250 à 650 sous-traitants de niveau 1, qu'il y a bien obligation d'innover avec agilité dans les prestations et dans le management des projets. Une innovation dictée par la complexité des projets et par l'environnement client, pour une adaptation permanente des équipes et la continuité des prestations 24h/7j des sites clients. Nos principaux clients étaient des leaders mondiaux et nous devons les accompagner dans la compétitivité mondiale et avec grande agilité. Ces PME-PMI pratiquaient peu l'innovation au sens start-up, dont l'ADN est l'innovation d'objets et dont la stratégie est la mise sur le marché rapide de leurs idées, pour se positionner rapidement sur le marché;
- Produire et manager les projets avec excellence et à un coût compétitif, est un modèle d'entreprise bien connu dans l'environnement de la recherche en stratégie d'entreprise. Les prix des prestations sont renégociés à chaque date anniversaire du renouvellement des contrats ou commandes, si et seulement si, les différents audits obligatoires et les évaluations des réalisations durant les deux années du contrat passé ont été passés avec succès. Ce type de stratégie spécifique aux PME sous-traitantes ne laisse pas la place à l'innovation, car ne fait pas partie des priorités: assurer le renouvellement des contrats, le maintien des

emplois, payer les salaires et les charges, puis gagner de nouveaux contrats et commandes toujours dans ce même environnement ;

- Ces clients, des donneurs d'ordre fidélisent ce type d'entreprise sous-traitante, qu'ils ont agréée après maints audits renouvelés périodiquement et qu'ils contrôlent bien pour éviter que ses sous-traitants partent vers d'autres horizons, avec comme conséquence une perte de compétences dans sa chaîne de la valeur. Un sous-traitant qui connaît bien la complexité de l'environnement client, dont le personnel a obtenu toutes les habilitations et formations obligatoires, et qu'il faudra remplacer, avec toutes les difficultés que l'on connaît pour assurer la continuité et la sûreté des installations des sites clients 7j/24h;
- Très peu de PME-PMI sous-traitantes ont une stratégie d'innovation, pourtant utile pour une diversification de leur chiffre d'affaires avec un taux de dépendance qui les menace à tout moment de mettre la clé sous la porte, si perte de ces « gros » contrats clients;
- Ces quelques clients, qui représentent un pourcentage important dans le chiffre d'affaires de la PME, ne demandent pas à celle-ci d'innover, mais bien de produire et de fournir des services dans les délais contractuels, avec toute l'assurance de la continuité des services en toutes situations, le tout avec des prestations certifiées ISO 9001.

2) Des dirigeants de PME-PMI isolés, le nez dans le guidon, pas toujours les yeux sur les tableaux de bord, dont les indicateurs et les alertes aident à piloter et à mener les projets à bon port :

- Les dirigeants des start-up effectuent au quotidien, de nombreuses tâches et occupent plusieurs fonctions, faute de pouvoir embaucher un commercial, ni un responsable assurance qualité pourtant obligatoire pour accéder aux marchés des grandes entreprises. C'est le cas aussi dans les PME-PMI;
- Ces pratiques, on les trouve également dans les start-up où les membres de l'équipe participent à tous les travaux qui se présentent avec une forte adaptabilité, c'est la culture start-up;
- Dans les PME-PMI, le dirigeant est parfois plus dans une position de pompier : assurer un chiffre d'affaires pour payer les salariés et les lourdes charges, gérer les urgences, les non-conformités, les relations

clients, les conflits, alors qu'il est plus attendu comme stratège, un pilote pour mener les projets à bon port, les yeux sur un tableau de bord efficace alimenté par un dispositif de veille adapté au mode de fonctionnement start-up.

3) Des dirigeants qui ne font pas appel aux services des Universités pour mettre en œuvre leurs projets d'innovation :

- Les portes des labos des universités n'étant pas encore ouvertes aux PME-PMI et aux jeunes start-up, les dirigeants ne connaissent pas l'offre de services, les compétences et les plateformes tests qui peuvent les aider à mettre leurs innovations sur le marché.

La start-up ou PME n'a pas les moyens de se payer un labo R&D :

- Pour ce type de dirigeant, l'innovation n'est pas prioritaire, car il doit d'abord satisfaire ses clients et au juste prix avec une organisation certifiée. L'enjeu reste le renouvellement des contrats et le maintien des emplois;
- Elle n'a pas les moyens pour embaucher un chargé de mission Intelligence Économique, un commercial ou même un responsable assurance qualité pour la certification des prestations aux normes ISO et son suivi exigé pour travailler avec les grands donneurs d'ordre.

Pour assurer le renouvellement des contrats annuels avec ces grandes entreprises et la pérennité des emplois, ce type d'entreprise travaillant souvent dans des environnements industriels complexes et de pointe, innovent pour rester compétitifs dans :

- L'organisation et le management des équipes externes (du personnel détaché chez les clients et isolé du reste de l'équipe);
- Les nouveaux services nécessités par les nouveaux besoins réguliers de ces entreprises leaders mondiales;
- Elles accordent un gros budget à la formation permanente de leurs équipes, pour une montée en compétences, vitales pour répondre aux nouveaux besoins de leurs principaux clients, qui représentent une part parfois très importante dans leur chiffre d'affaires;
- Elles partagent leur veille technologique avec leurs plus gros clients, qui demandent dans les audits annuels d'en bénéficier.

Le partenariat avec les universités est pratiquement inexistant :

- Les PME et les universités ne se parlent pas. Les petites structures ne s'adressent pas aux labos pour développer leurs innovations ni utiliser les matériels ni les plateformes tests, car certains pensent que c'est impossible. Ces labos universitaires contractualisent bien avec les grandes entreprises et rarement avec les petites et moyennes structures, qui représentent plus de 80% des emplois;
- L'université doit ouvrir les portes des labos aux start-up et PME, et les accompagner dans le développement de leurs innovations, au service de la création d'emplois;

4) Des dirigeants qui ne connaissent pas l'offre de services des FABLAB industriels :

- Le Fablab offre une plateforme de services uniques qui proposent aux entreprises d'étudier la faisabilité de leurs idées, concevoir le prototype de leur innovation (CAO, DAO), le fabriquer et l'adapter par la suite avec les retours clients;
- Pour les entreprises, c'est accéder à des technologies avancées, comme l'impression 3D pour les objets techniques de l'industrie, comme la découpe laser et l'usinage des pièces autrefois fabriquées par des tourneurs et fraiseurs;
- Les Fablab, c'est transformer son idée en produits concrets et bénéficier de précieux commentaires d'experts dans le domaine. C'est aussi le lieu pour alimenter sa veille technologique (dernières technologies, dernières tendances de l'industrie, outils disponibles sur le marché) et de se former à l'utilisation de ses machines industrielles à commande numérique. Le tout pour prendre des décisions validées par des experts, pour le lancement de leurs produits sur le marché.

5) Des jeunes formés à l'entrepreneuriat, qui rêvent de créer leur propre start-up ou PME, mais qui ne passent pas à l'étape de création :

- Malgré de nombreux programmes entrepreneuriat, les jeunes ne se lancent pas en majorité dans la création de leur entreprise, ils préfèrent encore le statut de salarié ou occuper un poste dans l'administration;

- Le Fablab offre un environnement pour passer de l'idée à la fabrication de son prototype, dans un objectif de la mise sur le marché rapide de son innovation. Une équipe d'ingénieurs Fablab accompagne le porteur du projet de l'étude, avec un premier entretien pour valider la faisabilité de son idée, et par la suite tout au long des processus, la conception du modèle numérique, la fabrication avec des machines industrielles dernier cri;
- Le Fablab offre également les services pour faire évoluer le prototype à partir des retours des expériences utilisateur (clients et prospects). C'est l'assurance de la mise sur le marché rapide de son idée.

II) propositions pour les start-up africaines

1) Les Régions doivent rendre plus visible et plus lisible leur schéma régional d'intelligence économique:

- Ce schéma est la déclinaison opérationnelle de la politique nationale en termes d'Intelligence Économique au niveau de chaque Région, avec des axes stratégiques pour cinq années. Ce schéma régional fait travailler ensemble les acteurs économiques, la formation et la recherche des universités et des écoles d'ingénieurs. Ce schéma régional est piloté par deux comités de pilotage État – Région : un comité qui accompagne les projets sur les aspects défensifs et un second pour les aspects offensifs;
- Avec une meilleure visibilité et lisibilité des dispositifs en Région, un accès possible pour les start-up et les PME-PMI et leur accompagnement pour le montage de leur dossier pour l'obtention des aides financières pour développer leurs projets;
- Avec un dispositif d'accompagnement à chaque étape de la croissance de la start-up (incubation, pépinière d'entreprises, accompagnement pour développements national et international);
- Des FABLABS professionnels pour une mise sur le marché rapide de son innovation.

Un schéma régional d'Intelligence Économique qui réunit, et fait travailler ensemble au sein de pôles de compétitivité (clusters) :

- Les filières et entreprises dites stratégiques, les fédérations et associations professionnelles;

- Les universités pour leurs compétences en R&D;
- Les centres de formation (pour une montée en compétences permanentes au service de l'économie et de l'emploi);

Les start-up dont les modèles d'agilité intéressent les grandes entreprises;

Un accompagnement terrain sur les aspects offensifs et défensifs, par les comités de pilotage État - Région, va booster les projets d'innovation, et mettre le pied à l'étrier des jeunes porteurs de projets qui hésitent à passer à l'action.

Avantages pour la start-up :

- Pouvoir sous-traiter la R&D à un labo de l'université ou à une école d'ingénieurs;
- Ou bien encore, faire appel à un labo privé : un grand groupe a créé avec ses propres équipes R&D et marketing, une entité pour proposer aux PME des prestations pour leur mettre en œuvre leurs projets d'innovations (conception, développement du prototype, accès aux plateformes tests, avec un accompagnement à toutes les étapes);
- Sachant que les start-up ne pourront jamais se payer un vrai labo de R&D ni accéder à des plateformes de conception et de tests en environnement réel.

2) Un accompagnement tout au long de leur croissance avec sur un même lieu :

- Un incubateur, pour accélérer la création de la start-up et optimiser son offre;
- Une pépinière d'entreprise : pour un accompagnement régulier par des experts;
- Un espace Coworking : un espace de travail partagé (bureaux, salle de réunion, une cuisine commune qui est un lieu de convivialité et de partage des pauses repas), un lieu pour ses rendez- vous professionnels, loué à l'heure ou la journée, idéal pour les auto- entrepreneurs et les free-lance;
- Un Fablab technologique orienté industries : un accélérateur de projets pour concevoir, créer son prototype avec l'aide d'experts pour fabriquer les premières séries.

3) La start-up, la PME, doit avoir une stratégie :

- Choisir un secteur d'activité qu'elle maîtrise, et se lancer dans son domaine d'excellence;
- Se lancer dans un secteur ayant une très forte demande;
- Un business model (le modèle économique) est vital pour répondre à la question « comment je vais gagner de l'argent avec mon idée ? », il est différent du business plan destiné aux banquiers;
- Le business model résume toute la stratégie qui sera mise en place pour le bon fonctionnement de l'entreprise. On le rédige avant le lancement de l'entreprise puis on l'améliore et on l'adapte au fur et à mesure avec son dispositif de veille.

4) La start-up, la PME doit réaliser un benchmark de positionnement stratégique, un benchmark de positionnement dans la chaîne de la valeur de son secteur d'activité:

Sur mon secteur d'activité et le marché ciblé :

- Quels sont la chaîne de la valeur et les segments qui vont de l'idée, à la conception, à la production et jusqu'à la logistique, la formation et le S.A.V ?
- Quels sont les 10 leaders de ma chaîne de la valeur ?
- Je fais un benchmark, j'analyse les données clés , j'identifie les niches d'activité possibles et je fais mon positionnement stratégique avec mes forces et mes faiblesses, pour répondre à des besoins en très fortes demandes;

Je mets à jour mon business model avec le résultat de mon benchmark.

5) Pourquoi positionner mes projets dans les axes du schéma régional d'intelligence économique?

- Inscrire son projet dans le schéma de sa Région, c'est l'assurance de faire connaître son offre de services et de bénéficier d'un accompagnement par le comité de pilotage État et Région, sur les aspects offensifs et défensifs;
- Dans le cadre du schéma régional, la start-up pourra se faire accompagner dans son innovation par les chercheurs de l'Université, chercheurs qu'aucune start-up ne peut embaucher, faute de moyens;

- Sécuriser son patrimoine immatériel, y compris les transactions électroniques;
- Le schéma va mettre en réseau la start-up avec le pôle de compétitivité de sa filière, avec la Fédération professionnelle de sa filière industrielle ou technologique, et avec l'association des entreprises de sa spécialité. Plusieurs centaines de PME de l'automobile se sont réunies en association, avec embauche d'un chargé de mission, qui fait de la veille technologique et concurrentielle pour l'ensemble, organisent des formations, monte les dossiers d'aides et organise toutes les actions, comme les visites de salons, la recherche de partenaires, les missions à l'international, le lobbying et la défense des intérêts des adhérents de cette association d'entreprises;
- Identifier de nouveaux marchés, recherche partenaires à l'Étranger;
- Répondre aux appels d'offres avec d'autres entreprises, avec création de GME (groupement momentané d'entreprises) ou GIE;
- Saisir des opportunités y compris avec ses concurrents (savoir travailler en coopétition);
- Le schéma régional sécurise le patrimoine immatériel des start-up et PME.

6) Mettre en place un dispositif d'intelligence économique adapté à l'agilité qu'exige le mode de fonctionnement en start-up :

- Parfois une seule erreur peut mettre fin à la vie d'une start-up. La surveillance des concurrents, des tendances du marché et des technologies propres à sa start-up est une question de survie;
- Très peu de PME et start-up pratiquent l'intelligence économique. Elles font de la veille, surveillent la concurrence et la clientèle, et ne vont pas plus loin;

La démarche d'intelligence économique peut les aider à mettre en action les informations qualitatives.

La start-up sera beaucoup plus agile avec un dispositif de veille et Benchmark, qui met à jour en continue, le Business model :

- Benchmarker les bonnes pratiques et les adapter à sa structure;
- Utiliser les outils de l'Intelligence Économique pour visiter les salons professionnels (veille sur les technologies, innovations dans mon secteur

d'activité, tendances du marché, concurrents, partenaires potentiels, opportunités, marchés);

- Une analyse des données qui inclut les retours d'expériences des utilisateurs, les tendances, les forums produits, les commentaires clients, etc., et qui va permettre aux dirigeants de prendre plus facilement des décisions plus éclairées et garder une longueur d'avance sur la concurrence.

7) Pourquoi adhérer au pôle de compétitivité de son secteur d'activité ?

- Pour bénéficier d'actions collectives, prospecter, innover à plusieurs, accès aux financements, protéger son patrimoine immatériel, accompagnement à l'international;
- La start-up sera bien positionnée dans un environnement favorable à l'innovation et au développement;
- Pour se faire connaître et travailler avec d'autres entreprises, la R&D des universités, la Formation tout au long de la vie;
- Pour bénéficier de l'accompagnement par des organismes de développement technologique et d'innovation.

8) Bénéficier de l'offre recherche et innovation de l'université :

- Une PME ne peut se payer un labo de recherche ni embaucher des experts innovation ;
- Une innovation permanente en partenariat avec les Universités et Écoles d'Ingénieurs ;
- Utiliser leurs plateformes tests, leurs experts R&D aussi experts en veille technologique, veille brevets ;

Un contrat avec l'Université : Un contrat avec universités et grandes écoles pour une veille technologique, réduire l'incertitude, réussir son projet innovation, accéder aux plateformes tests et des matériels parfois très coûteux ;

- Savoir utiliser la veille brevets pour innover et créer de l'activité ;
- Des études de recherche et maîtrise de l'information, et mise en place de dispositifs de veille stratégiques, dans le cadre des projets de fin d'études ;

- Un partenariat Win-Win (gagnant – gagnant) avec la professionnalisation des étudiants ;
- Un terrain pour l'insertion des jeunes diplômés ;
- De la R&D avec les labos des écoles d'ingénieurs et les plateformes tests.

9) Utiliser les FABLABS pour innover et accélérer la mise sur le marché :

Créer rapidement un prototype à présenter à ses clients et aux prospects :

- Les start-up créent puis adaptent leurs produits au fur et à mesure de retours client. Ce modèle lance le produit rapidement pour l'améliorer étape par étape avec un avantage sur des marchés où il s'agit de faire vite pour se positionner. Avec ce modèle la start-up peut démarrer avec des petits moyens, puis investir selon son évolution.

L'offre de services d'un fablab :

- Étude : un rendez-vous au Fablab, un entretien de trois heures, sur la faisabilité technique de votre innovation ou non ?
- Vous pouvez fabriquer vous même ou avec l'appui d'experts techniques dans un ou plusieurs des domaines des compétences du Fablab ;
- Utiliser le parc de machines et les logiciels CAO - DAO avec votre formation à la commande numérique sur des machines de technologies avancées : Impression 3D pour un usage industriel, la découpe laser et l'usinage (Conception du modèle CAO, configuration de la machine usinage puis fabrication automatique par la machine de la pièce avec grande précision);
- Adapter au fur et à mesure votre prototype aux besoins du marché, grâce aux retours des utilisateurs ;
- Lancer la phase industrialisation avec l'envoi les fichiers numériques de votre prototype à l'usine pour la fabrication en grand nombre.

10) Pour développer la commercialisation de vos produits et services :

Les start-up doivent connaître ces leviers :

- Les chambres consulaires pour la recherche de financements, montage de dossiers, recherche de partenariat sur le plan national ou international (chambre de commerce et d'industrie, chambres des Métiers et de l'Artisanat, chambre d'Agriculture ...);

- Les ICC (International Chamber of Commerce) ;
- Les consultants experts du commerce international.

11) Le problème pour accéder aux informations utiles aux développements des projets, une question de compétitivité des PME et start-up. Un handicap par rapport aux concurrents des autres continents :

- Utile aux développements de la start-up et à sa compétitivité;
- L'accès aux informations et données à forte valeur ajoutée est rare: rétention, retard de l'informatisation, dit-on sur le continent, qui handicapent les PME et start-up par rapport à leurs concurrents mieux servis dans leur pays;
- Il est possible de se faire accompagner par un consultant expert dans ce domaine.

12) Il faut se former pour gagner :

- Une stratégie de montée en compétences en continu pour accompagner la montée en compétitivité des start-up;
- Pour une adéquation entre les besoins des clients et les compétences du personnel. Des projets restent bloqués faute d'une main-d'œuvre qualifiée et d'une montée en compétences par la formation continue du personnel.

13) Un mentor pour aider le dirigeant au quotidien :

- Avec un mentorat, les entrepreneurs vont apprendre auprès de professionnels expérimentés qui ont déjà vécu des expériences similaires;
- Pour la phase de démarrage, c'est un excellent moyen d'acquérir des expériences et des idées;
- Les mentors aident les entreprises à prendre de bonnes décisions, en partageant leurs retours d'expériences;
- Pour le problème d'accès à l'information bien connu en Afrique, le mentor peut partager les bonnes pratiques pour acquérir les informations utiles aux projets;

Le Mentor peut les aider à développer leurs compétences et à augmenter leurs chances de réussite.

III) Conclusion :

Les dirigeants des start-up doivent être capables de s'adapter rapidement à l'évolution des tendances, répondre aux besoins réels des clients et prospects et adapter en permanence leurs innovations à partir des retours des utilisateurs.

Pour passer de l'idée à la création de la start-up avec une mise sur le marché rapide de son innovation :

1) Au niveau des Régions d'un même pays :

Une meilleure visibilité et lisibilité dans les politiques publiques d'intelligence économique;

- Faire bénéficier les start-up et les PME-PMI des prestations du schéma régional d'intelligence économique, pour la réussite de l'innovation et pour la création des emplois qui en résulte.

2) Au niveau des universités :

- Faire bénéficier les start-up et les PME-PMI des compétences des chercheurs. Les universités doivent faire connaître leurs offres et accompagnements de terrain, et mettre à disposition les plateformes tests, pour passer de l'idée au produit et à son positionnement sur le marché.

3) Au niveau local (communautés urbaines) :

- Un meilleur accompagnement à chaque étape de la croissance, avec sur un même lieu : un incubateur, une pépinière d'entreprises et un Fablab orienté marchés;
- Des Fablabs pour accélérer la mise sur le marché des innovations et pour gagner en compétitivité. Pour une mise sur le marché rapide, avec l'aide des compétences des FABLAB industriels.

4) au niveau de la start-up ou PME-PMI :

- Avoir une stratégie et répondre en priorité aux besoins en très forte demande;

- Le dirigeant doit repositionner ses projets dans les axes du schéma régional d'intelligence économique, pour bénéficier d'un accompagnement sur le terrain et bénéficier du réseautage avec les acteurs économiques, et les compétences d'innovation de l'université;
- Un dispositif d'intelligence économique adapté à la demande d'agilité du marché : comprendre les changements dans son industrie et garder une longueur d'avance sur les concurrents avec un suivi de leurs stratégies et leurs activités, c'est prendre des décisions plus réfléchies qui augmentent les chances de succès;
- Un business model est vital (modèle économique), il résume la stratégie globale mise en place pour gagner de l'argent avec son idée, et assurer le bon fonctionnement de l'entreprise. Le business model s'améliore et s'adapte au fur et à mesure du développement de la start-up;
- Il faut se former pour gagner : pour la montée en compétences du personnel en continu, c'est une obligation pour adapter en permanence ses innovations aux besoins du marché et rester compétitif;
- Utiliser le mentorat pour apprendre : les mentors sont des professionnels expérimentés qui ont vécu des expériences similaires et peuvent les transmettre aux entrepreneurs, pour relever les défis et développer l'entreprise. Leur accompagnement est très important pour la réussite des start-up et PME-PMI Africaines, le tout pour plus de création d'emplois.

INNOVATION IN POLICY SPACE FOR SUSTAINABLE, INCLUSIVE AND BALANCED GROWTH AND DEVELOPMENT IN AFRICA

Devendranath Chamroo

Africa is a continent of diversity and opportunity with huge resources endowments, myriads of policies, plans, programmes, and substantial international aid and assistance. However economic growth and development have remained elusive for most African countries. Africa's economic global footprint is small and its performance under-par compared to the other continents. The last decade was to be the "time for Africa", the "last frontier" of development. However, the decade has come and gone and the status quo still prevails. The main issue is the divergence in the conception, design, development and implementation of industrial, trade and investment policies.

Africa, a continent of 55 countries, accounts for 20% of the global land area (larger than China, the USA, India, and EU countries put together), 65% of the world's arable land, 10% of the planet's internal renewable fresh water source, largest producer, and reserve holder of precious minerals, and home to 42% of global youth. On the reverse side, 33 out of 46 Least Developed Countries (LDCs) are African states. It should be noted that only three African countries have graduated out of the United Nations LDC list since 1971. Additionally, 10 out of 13 Special Need Countries are African. Collectively Africa contributes only 3% to global GDP, accounts for 3% of global trade, and 5.2% of global foreign direct investment (FDI) inflows. Africa is the world's least industralised region, with the bulk of economic activities being dominated by the primary sector, mostly mining and minerals, and agriculture. Just five countries, namely Algeria, Egypt, Morocco, Nigeria, and South Africa collectively account for over two thirds of value-added manufacturing, and the remaining 50 countries contribute just a third.

Africa offers a very diversified geographical, social, economic, political and cultural panorama and perspective. Despite its rich resource endowments and boundless opportunities, Africa's growth performance remains grossly under-par. Africa's failure is often attributed to poor governance, socio-economic and political instability, restrictive trade and investment policies, inefficient physical infrastructure, weaknesses in its legal, regulatory, and institutional frameworks, volatility in the prices of mineral resources and commodities, and vagaries of nature, among others. Interestingly, over the last two decades, most African countries have taken bold steps to address the above issues through a myriad of Vision Statements, National Development Plans, Sectoral policies, plans and programmes, Reforms, Strategies and Action Plans. Every country has its own industrial, trade and investment policies. The impact of these changes has been mixed as ten of the most reforming countries, before the COVID-19 pandemic, were African countries. However, 25 African countries recorded negative growth rates post-COVID. Their problems have been further compounded by the protracted Russia-Ukraine war, the geopolitical tussles between the USA and China, and rising fuel prices.

The real problem of Africa is not the dearth of appropriate policy response. On the contrary, Africa is over strategised and legislated at the national, regional, and Pan-African levels. Every country. The hierarchy of development policies are depicted in the figure below.

Hierarchy of Development Policies

While the hierarchy of development policies is aligned to the African Union's "Agenda 2063", the main impediments to sustained growth are non-implementation of regional policies and directives, and divergence between regional and national priorities. They "talk regional but act national".

On the domestic front, all countries have their own development agenda and plans, mostly informed by regional and the pan-Africa Agenda. The three key development policies are: (i) Industrial policy (ii) Trade policy, and (iii) Investment policy. These policies are catalysts to sustained economic growth and development, if and only if, they are implemented in a coherent and convergent manner. However, in most African countries the ecosystem for policy making, policy implementation, and policy monitoring and evaluation (M&E) is complex and diverse. Countries have difficulties in prioritising among the three policies, known as the "growth trilemma', as the benefits of each policy are different. Generally, the portfolio of industrialisation, trade and investment are assigned to different ministries and their implementation to different departments, agencies and organisations. Very often, these ministries and agencies do not collaborate, and some even compete (turf fighting) for funds and glory. The whole process lacks the "one nation approach" to policy making and policy implementation.

Literature is abundant to confirm that coordinated policy implementation has a positive cascading effect of economic growth and development. The diagram below provides an overview of the causal relationship between policy design and policy implementation on economic growth. The choice rests with the government of each country and the impact options are snail crawl (less than 5% growth), leapfrog (between 5 and 7.5% growth), and moonshot trajectory (more than 10% growth).

The Growth Trajectory

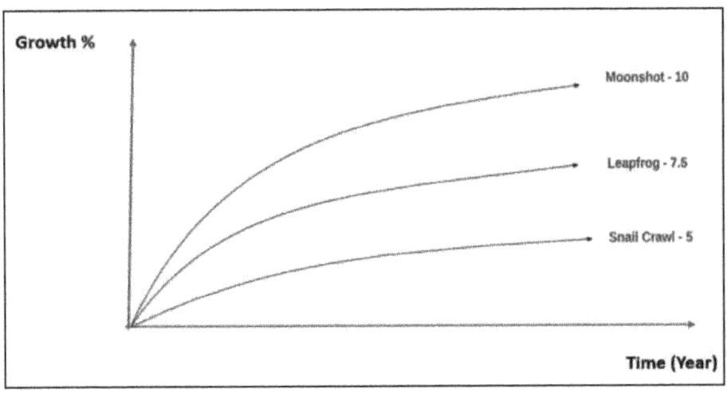

Literature supports that if only one of the three policies mentioned above are implemented, a country will at its best grow along the snail crawl trajectory. However, growth will follow the leapfrog trajectory when any two policies are implemented and monitored in a coordinated way. However, if all the three policies are properly aligned and implemented in a coordinated manner, growth higher than 10 % can be achieved.

Given the competitive context of the global economy, every country, more particularly African countries, has policy space for innovation in policy design, implementation, proper monitoring, and evaluation. Such an approach requires strong political leadership, robust legal, regulatory, administrative and institutional frameworks, strong public-private sector collaborative approach, transparency and accountability, and proper monitoring and evaluation to be followed by appropriate corrective measures. African countries may wish to benchmark against countries that have aligned the three policies to build robust and vibrant economies, namely Germany, Japan, Singapore, South Korea, Ireland, and Mauritius, among others.

Timing is not to reinvent the wheel, but to innovate in the policy space to create the conditions for accelerated, inclusive, sustainable, and balanced economic growth and development in Africa. The magic formula is policy coherence, intuitional alignment and above all a "one nation approach".

QUELLES STRATÉGIES INNOVANTES POUR CONSTRUIRE L'AUTONOMIE STRATÉGIQUE DES PAYS SAHÉLIENS DANS LE CONTEXTE ACTUEL DE BOULEVERSEMENT DE L'ORDRE MONDIAL ?

Moustapha Boulamine

Introduction

Devant la menace existentielle relative à la montée en puissance du terrorisme à laquelle les pays sahéliens, notamment le Burkina, le Mali et le Niger, font face depuis plus d'une décennie et qui a entraîné le déploiement sans précédent des forces armées étrangères dans la zone, les opinions publiques réclament davantage d'autonomie stratégique pour leur pays.

Il vous souviendra qu'en mars 2011, dans le contexte des contestations populaires appelées « Printemps arabe », une coalition militaire emmenée par les USA, la France et le Royaume-Uni lança une offensive militaire en Libye qui a eu pour conséquence la mort du guide libyen Mouammar Kadhafi et la chute de son régime. Cette situation a entraîné par la suite l'effondrement de l'État libyen qui, à son tour, a occasionné, avec la libre circulation des armes de tout genre, l'accroissement exponentiel des menaces terroristes, insurrectionnelles et la criminalité transfrontalière au Sahel, particulièrement au Mali, au Burkina et au Niger.

Ces pays, n'étant pas préparés pour faire face à ces nouvelles menaces, ont appelé la communauté internationale à l'aide. C'est ainsi que la France est intervenue militairement d'abord au Mali avec la mission Serval qui a eu le mérite de stopper la marche des jihadistes sur Bamako. Depuis lors, la France y a maintenu une présence militaire très forte et l'a étendue au Niger et au Burkina. Les Nations Unies aussi ne sont pas en reste, elles ont déployé une mission de maintien de la paix dénommée MINUSMA qui s'est investie à travers des programmes de Réforme du Secteur de la Sécurité (RSS). De plus, d'autres partenaires extérieurs et non des moindres, notamment les USA, ont installé des bases militaires dans la zone, particulièrement au Niger.

Cependant, malgré la présence militaire très forte des partenaires extérieurs occidentaux en général, la crise sécuritaire, qui au départ était localisée sur une portion du territoire malien, s'est aggravée en se métastasant, affectant ainsi leur voisinage immédiat.

Avec la présence militaire de ces partenaires, le Burkina, le Mali et le Niger, ont perdu davantage leur capacité souveraine de prendre des initiatives pour ramener la paix, en témoigne le refus catégorique des autorités françaises lorsqu'il s'est agi pour les autorités en place à l'époque au Mali, de négocier avec certains groupes jihadistes.

C'est pourquoi, de plus en plus, les opinions publiques sahéliennes sont favorables au départ des troupes étrangères et au renforcement de l'autonomie stratégique de leur pays.

L'intérêt de notre thème est double : il est d'abord lié au bouleversement en cours de l'ordre mondial avec la perspective d'un monde multipolaire et plus juste. Il est ensuite dû à l'émergence d'une masse critique de Sahéliens qui pensent que la construction de l'autonomie stratégique de leur pays est une priorité absolue.

Ainsi, notre analyse s'articulera autour de deux points centraux. Dans un premier temps, nous exposerons les opportunités qu'offre le nouvel ordre mondial en construction à l'Afrique et particulièrement aux pays sahéliens pour s'émanciper et sortir des fortes dépendances, sans oublier d'énoncer aussi les menaces et risques qu'il pourrait engendrer. Nous proposerons ensuite une stratégie innovante qui pourrait nous permettre de renforcer l'autonomie stratégique de nos pays dans une seconde partie.

Le nouvel ordre mondial en cours de construction : quelles opportunités et menaces pour le Sahel et particulièrement pour le Burkina, le Mali et le Niger ?

Au sortir de la Deuxième Guerre Mondiale (GM), on assiste à la naissance d'un monde bipolaire avec l'émergence de deux superpuissances, en l'occurrence les USA et l'ex-URSS. L'ordre mondial, qui régule tout le système international, repose principalement sur les accords de Bretton Woods (juillet 1944) qui établissent le système monétaire international et l'institution de l'Organisation des Nations Unies (ONU, octobre 1945) suite à la ratification de la charte par la Chine, les USA, la France, le Royaume-Uni, l'ex-URSS, etc.

Très tôt, les désaccords se multiplient entre les USA et l'ex-URSS. C'est le début d'une nouvelle confrontation mondiale, communément appelée Guerre Froide (GF) qui durera jusqu'en 1989. C'est dans ce contexte qu'on assiste à la naissance de nombreux mouvements de libération des peuples colonisés qui se lancent dans la lutte pour l'indépendance de leurs pays. Ce n'est donc pas un hasard si la plupart des pays africains, particulièrement du Sahel, obtiennent leur indépendance durant les années 1960.

Cependant, la fin de la GF consacre la victoire du camp occidental avec la chute du mur de Berlin et la dislocation de l'ex-URSS. C'est un événement majeur qui marque un tournant décisif dans les relations internationales avec l'avènement d'un monde unipolaire dominé par les USA qui confortent par la même occasion leur hégémonie sur le système monétaire et les relations internationales. Le dollar est imposé comme monnaie internationale et est devenu un instrument de domination. Les USA renforcent également leur puissance militaire en installant des bases militaires partout dans le monde et en élargissant l'OTAN.

Aujourd'hui, on assiste à l'émergence d'un nouveau paradigme monétaire mondial avec la "dédollarisation"et la "désaméricanisation" du système monétaire international par les BRICS emmenés par la Chine et la Russie.

L'avènement de la guerre en Ukraine révèle la perte d'influence du camp occidental dont les directives ne sont plus suivies comme par le passé par bon nombre de pays dans le monde. On assiste alors à un mouvement des plaques tectoniques avec la perspective d'un nouvel ordre mondial multipolaire.

Une analyse SWOT de la situation des pays sahéliens, notamment le Burkina, le Mali et le Niger, permet de montrer les nombreuses opportunités qu'offre le contexte international.

L'ordre mondial multipolaire en cours de construction consacre l'affaiblissement du camp occidental qui, en très grande partie, est à l'origine de la situation actuelle du Burkina, du Mali et du Niger. Les opportunités majeures qu'offre le contexte international actuel peuvent être résumées comme suit :

- L'affaiblissement du camp occidental et particulièrement de la France est une opportunité majeure pour ces pays d'accéder à la souveraineté monétaire. C'est le moment idéal pour ces pays de prendre entièrement le contrôle de leur politique monétaire. Il faut sortir l'ancienne puissance coloniale, la France de tout le processus monétaire ;

- L'affaiblissement du camp occidental et particulièrement de la France est une opportunité majeure pour ces pays de réformer leur système éducatif. Cela devrait se passer par un travail de reconnexion à l'histoire et à la civilisation nègre, la plus ancienne démontrée par Cheikh Anta

Diop. Il est tout aussi important de puiser des éléments positifs dans les autres cultures. À terme, les résultats des réformes du système éducatif devraient se traduire par le renforcement de la compétitivité de notre peuple dans tous les domaines qui est un enjeu majeur à l'ère de la mondialisation ;

- L'affaiblissement du camp occidental est une opportunité majeure pour ces pays de diversifier leur partenariat stratégique à l'international. Cela devrait leur permettre à terme de renforcer leur poids dans le commerce international avec la transformation sur place de leurs matières premières et la vente sur le marché international des produits à forte valeur ajoutée ;
- L'affaiblissement du camp occidental est une opportunité majeure pour la création d'un État fédéral réunissant le Burkina, le Mali et le Niger. Les deux premiers sont déjà dans cette dynamique. Le Burkina, le Mali et la Guinée sont en bonne position pour d'abord définir une vision stratégique commune et ensuite aller à la création de l'État fédéral. Ils devront être rejoints progressivement par les autres pays de l'Afrique de l'Ouest.

Cependant, ces opportunités ne pourront véritablement être saisies que lorsque nous aurons à la tête des États sahéliens des hommes et des femmes intègres, patriotes, visionnaires, progressistes et surtout panafricanistes. C'est pourquoi, la France, l'ancienne puissance colonisatrice, consciente de cet état de fait et dotée d'une capacité d'anticipation a beaucoup œuvré à travers « le système de la Françafrique » à ce que dans la plupart des pays dits du « pré carré » les élites tenants du pouvoir soient très proches de ses réseaux d'influence et soient enclins à défendre plus l'intérêt français que celui de leur propre pays. Ce qui est gravissime, c'est que très souvent, du fait de leur position avantageuse, ces élites ne conçoivent jamais la France comme un adversaire, même lorsque les intérêts de leur pays et ceux de la France se heurtent. On est en droit de se demander si ces élites saisissent bien le sens et la portée des propos suivants qu'on attribue au Général de Gaulle : « La France n'a pas d'amis, mais des intérêts ».

Le bouleversement en cours de l'ordre mondial avec la perspective d'un monde multipolaire ne présente pas que des opportunités pour le Burkina, le Mali et le Niger. Il fait courir à ces pays le risque et les menaces qu'on les transforme en terrain d'affrontement entre des puissances extérieures qui veulent se partager le monde. Ces menaces sont réelles et doivent être prises au sérieux par les tenants de pouvoirs avec toute la rigueur qu'exige leur prise en charge.

Si l'Afrique continue de rester en marge de cette nouvelle confrontation, il y a surtout le risque qu'elle soit l'objet d'un consensus international entre les anciennes et les nouvelles puissances pour continuer à l'exploiter. C'est pourquoi l'Afrique se doit de prendre toute sa responsabilité dans la confrontation actuelle en œuvrant pour l'avènement d'un monde multipolaire plus juste et plus favorable pour son émancipation et son développement.

Comment renforcer l'autonomie stratégique des pays sahéliens particulièrement du Burkina, du Mali et du Niger dans le contexte actuel de bouleversement de l'ordre mondial ?

Conscients des opportunités qu'offre le contexte international, nous pourrions à présent facilement identifier nos principales forces et faiblesses à partir desquelles nous saurions définir nos priorités.

La jeunesse africaine et particulièrement sahélienne est notre plus grande force aujourd'hui dans la lutte pour l'émancipation totale de notre peuple. En effet, avec le développement des Nouvelles Technologies de l'Information et de la Communication (réseaux sociaux) et la mondialisation, les nouvelles générations africaines comprennent mieux le fonctionnement du monde, les enjeux géopolitiques et les rapports de force en jeu et savent bien situer leurs intérêts et sont moins complexées que leurs prédécesseurs. L'émergence d'une masse critique de Sahéliens qui pensent que la construction de l'autonomie stratégique de leur pays est une priorité absolue est un atout majeur.

Notre principale faiblesse vient de la mauvaise gouvernance de nos pays par nos élites qui sont le plus souvent membres des réseaux de la « Françafrique » et dépourvus de toute forme d'intégrité, de patriotisme et de Panafricanisme. Par ailleurs, la méconnaissance de la jeunesse africaine et sahélienne de notre propre histoire, de notre civilisation, mère de l'humanité, est une grande faiblesse.

La principale stratégie consiste d'abord à définir une vision commune aux pays en transition, le Burkina, le Mali et la Guinée et dont les tenants du pouvoir ne sont pas issus des réseaux de la « Françafrique » et sont enclins à défendre les intérêts supérieurs de leurs peuples contre vents et marées. La vision commune définie servira de fondation à la création d'un État fédéral réunissant ces trois pays qui seront rejoints progressivement par les autres pays dits du « pré carré français » qui se seraient entre-temps libérés du joug néocolonial. Les autorités nigériennes actuelles doivent davantage faire preuve de patriotisme, d'intégrité et de panafricanisme en rejoignant le plus vite possible la dynamique sous régionale de construction de l'union sacrée des peuples sahéliens. À moyen et long terme, le Nigeria, le Ghana et les autres pays viendront s'y ajouter pour la création d'un État fédéral ouest-africain.

- Les chantiers majeurs et actions prioritaires à entreprendre de toute urgence, nous semble-t-il, sont les suivants :
- La création d'une armée fédérale constituée des membres des armées des trois États ;
- La création d'une monnaie commune ;
- La refonte ou réforme du système éducatif ;
- Le développement des réseaux ferroviaires, routiers et d'une compagnie aérienne commune ;
- La communication et la sensibilisation des masses populaires sur la défense des intérêts supérieurs de nos États et sur les enjeux géopolitiques mondiaux.

La conclusion la plus importante à retenir c'est que le monde est à un tournant majeur, les plaques tectoniques de la géopolitique mondiale sont en mouvement. L'ordre mondial reposant sur l'hégémonie américaine est fortement contesté par de nouvelles puissances montantes emmenées par la Chine et la Russie. C'est une période trouble et pleine d'incertitude qui s'annonce. Personne ne sait avec certitude qui seront les vainqueurs et les perdants de cette nouvelle confrontation mondiale. Mais tout indique que les vainqueurs seront parmi ceux qui ont accepté de prendre leur responsabilité et de consentir des sacrifices indispensables. L'Afrique et particulièrement le sahel ne doit pas rester les bras croisés, il va falloir prendre position, l'assumer et œuvrer pour l'avènement d'un monde multipolaire plus juste où les intérêts supérieurs des peuples africains sont garantis. C'est une opportunité extraordinaire à saisir particulièrement par les Etats du Burkina, du Mali et du Niger qui sont confrontés en ce moment à des menaces existentielles pour renforcer leur autonomie stratégique et leur développement.

IV
SYNTHÈSE ET CONCLUSIONS

L'AFRIQUE DE L'INNOVATION, ENSEIGNEMENTS POUR L'AVENIR

Driss Guerraoui

Nous voilà, cher-e-s collègues et ami-e-s, arrivé-e-s au terme de la 3ème rencontre du Forum des Associations Africaines d'Intelligence Economique, après deux jours durant d'intenses débats, issus de contributions riches, pertinentes, audacieuses, et ouvertes sur l'avenir, apportant une réelle valeur ajoutée à la problématique de l'innovation en Afrique.

Nous avons, en effet, écouté plus de 28 communications portant sur des sujets que nous avons choisis pour répondre à la question centrale qui nous réunit et unis à Dakhla. Au vu de la richesse des interventions et des débats qu'elles ont nourris, il est très prétentieux de vouloir en faire une synthèse à la mesure de la diversité des thématiques examinées et des expériences nationales présentées.

Aussi, ce que je vais tenter c'est avant tout de partager quelques idées, quelques interrogations et quelques pistes qui se dégagent de notre rencontre et qui pourraient servir de base pour poursuivre notre réflexion et notre action au service d'une meilleure compréhension de la problématique de l'innovation en Afrique.

Pour ce faire, je partirai des questions essentielles suivantes :

- Quelle est la réalité de l'innovation en Afrique et pourquoi les États du continent n'arrivent pas encore à faire un saut qualitatif dans ce domaine ?
- Quels sont les défis que l'Afrique doit relever en matière d'innovation ?
- Quelles doivent être les grandes priorités pour le continent à ce niveau ?
- Quelles formes de partenariats panafricains promouvoir ?

Et quels pourraient être le rôle du Forum des Associations Africaines d'Intelligence Economique et sa contribution à la dynamique de l'innovation en Afrique et à la réalisation de raccourcis technologiques dans ce domaine stratégique pour le développement des pays du continent ?

I- Les réalités

La rencontre a révélé l'existence de plusieurs facteurs qui empêchent les pays du continent africain à disposer d'écosystèmes nationaux forts en matière d'innovation. Il s'agit en particulier des réalités suivantes :

- La crise structurelle de l'école, à travers tous ses étages, du fondamental au supérieur en passant par le primaire et le secondaire, qui persiste dans de nombreux pays et qui rend difficile la production d'une masse critique d'élites scientifiques, la formation de compétences pouvant couvrir les besoins de nombreux secteurs vitaux de l'activité économique et corrélativement de bâtir de véritables centres dédiés à la recherche scientifique et technologique à la mesure des défis que les économies et les sociétés Africaines en cette matière.
- L'absence d'un intérêt réel des États pour la promotion de l'innovation.
- Des moyens très faibles consacrés au financement de la recherche scientifique et technologique se traduisant par des parts dérisoires de la recherche-développement dans le PIB des pays africains.
- Des liens très faibles entre les entreprises et les universités portant sur la promotion de projets communs dont l'objectif est de déboucher sur des innovations majeures utiles pour les deux parties.
- L'absence d'un statut spécifique de l'inventeur.
- L'éclatement et la dispersion des rares institutions dédiées à l'innovation, offrant l'image de semblants de systèmes de recherche scientifique et technique et d'innovation composés de chercheurs et d'inventeurs « isolés » et des recherches et d'innovations déconnectées des réalités de l'économie, de la société et des territoires.
- Quand ils existent, les dispositifs d'encouragement de l'innovation sont l'objet d'une gouvernance inappropriée découlant de procédures complexes et d'inefficience des modalités de suivi, d'évaluation et de contrôle.

- La non structuration de la recherche scientifique et technologique et de l'innovation dans le secteur privé.
- Le cloisonnement de l'innovation entre les secteurs public et privé en raison de l'absence de passerelles entre la recherche publique et la recherche privée.
- Les difficultés à mettre en place des politiques publiques appropriées pour attirer les scientifiques et les inventeurs africains de la diaspora.
- Et, l'existence d'un déficit de coordination des programmes dédiés à l'innovation à l'échelle panafricaine avec toutes les conséquences qui en découlent en termes de convergence des programmes, de cohérence globale des stratégies et de mutualisation des ressources humaines et financières.

Il découle de toutes ces réalités la fuite des cerveaux africains à l'étranger, le déficit d'entreprises innovantes et les faibles classements de l'Afrique au niveau des indicateurs internationaux les plus pertinents dans ce domaine, notamment la part des dépenses publiques allouées à la recherche scientifique et technologique et à l'innovation dans le PIB des Nations Africaines, la part des scientifiques et inventeurs africains dans le Monde, leurs parts dans les publications scientifiques de référence et dans les brevets d'innovation.

La conséquence de toutes ces réalités est l'aggravation de la dépendance technologique du continent et son impact en termes de perte de la souveraineté dans les domaines les plus stratégiques pour les populations, les entreprises et les États comme l'alimentation, la santé, l'énergie, le numérique, la sécurité, l'armement et les services essentiels aux ménages et aux entreprises, mais aussi les technologies de l'espace et l'intelligence artificielle.

Autant de défis que l'Afrique se doit d'affronter pour pouvoir peser sur le jeu futur complexe des relations économiques internationales du XXIème siècle.

II- Les défis

La rencontre a permis, également, d'identifier les défis que l'Afrique est appelée à relever dans le domaine de l'innovation. En effet, en plus des défis liés aux difficultés objectives pour les écosystèmes nationaux d'éducation, de formation, de recherche scientifique et technologique et d'innovation à produire un volume de savants et d'inventeurs en phase avec les besoins croissants des pays du continent, au partenariat Universités-Entreprises-Territoires très peu développé et d'un impact limité sur les rares écosystèmes nationaux d'innovation existants et au financement insuffisant et une gouvernance de la recherche et de l'innovation, quatre autres défis ont été mis en exergue. Il s'agit en particulier des défis suivants :

- La production d'innovations à même d'aider le continent à gérer les risques attenants à l'émergence et au développement des nouvelles générations d'insécurités et de raretés (Les catastrophes naturelles découlant des changements climatiques, le stress hydrique, l'énergie, les médicaments, etc.).
- La valorisation des savoir-faire locaux par la promotion de systèmes d'innovation de proximité par le bas alliant intelligence économique et intelligence sociale des territoires. À cet effet, dans le contexte africain, une attention particulière doit être accordée au monde rural et notamment aux innovations ayant trait au développement des activités non agricoles en milieu rural. À ce niveau, l'objectif est d'offrir aux populations rurales, qui vont demeurer majoritaires dans la totale de la population du continent jusqu'en 2010, les conditions objectives favorables pour vivre et investir dans leurs terroirs. Ce qui contribuera, à la fois, à améliorer le niveau de vie de ces populations et à réguler positivement la pression sur les terres à usage agricole proprement dites ainsi que les flux migratoires.
- La valorisation du capital immatériel des Nations Africaines, dont le continent regorge en abondance et dont l'introduction d'innovations majeures pourrait transformer ses composantes en leviers essentiels de production de richesses nouvelles, d'opportunités d'emploi et de création de valeurs.
- Et la gendarisation de la recherche scientifique et technologique et de l'innovation en vue d'élargir la base sociale des écosystèmes qui lui sont dédiés pour en démocratiser l'accès aux plus grands nombres de femmes chercheurs et inventeurs

III- Les priorités

Si tels sont les principaux défis identifiés, la rencontre a, aussi, permis d'identifier ce que devraient être les priorités de l'Afrique en matière d'innovation. Dans ce cadre, trois niveaux des priorités ont été mis en évidence.

Ce qui est urgent à court terme. Il s'agit des innovations liées aux transitions alimentaire, sanitaire et à la gestion de la raréfaction de l'eau.

Ce qui est possible à moyen terme et souhaitable long terme. Il s'agit des innovations pouvant contribuer à réussir les transitions climatique, énergétique, numérique, la cybersécurité, le développement des infrastructures portuaires, autoroutières, aéroportuaires, et la gestion durable des ressources.

Enfin, au-delà de l'importance de toutes ces priorités, l'Afrique ne pourra pas faire l'économie d'un autre défi qui au cœur de toute la problématique de l'innovation, c'est celui du développement de l'entrepreneuriat en Afrique. Car ce défi est à la base de toute dynamique potentielle d'innovation. En effet, l'observation empirique de cette problématique à travers une évaluation comparative montre qu'il y a un lien de cause à effet entre l'existence d'une économie forte portée par des systèmes productifs qui créent un volume important d'entreprises et la capacité d'un pays à innover et à mettre en place un écosystème national de recherche scientifique, technologique et d'innovation performant.

Aussi, et l'absence d'un observatoire mondial relatif à la démographie des entreprises, les estimations sur les créations annuelles d'entreprises dont nous disposons révèlent que les États-Unis créent environ 2.500.000 entreprises par an pour 350 millions d'habitants, la France entre 750 et 800.000 pour une population d'environ 70 millions et l'Afrique 1.620.000 pour une population totale d'un milliard quarante mille habitants.

Au regard de ces données, l'Afrique de l'innovation passe par la capacité des États, des entreprises et des territoires du Continent à investir dans la promotion de l'entrepreneuriat à la fois public, privé et celui relevant de l'économie sociale et solidaire pour pouvoir susciter une dynamique durable d'innovation.

IV- Quels partenariats panafricains pour l'innovation

La troisième rencontre du FAAIE a proposé quelques pistes pouvant guider et orienter et bâtir une coopération panafricaine pour l'innovation. Ces pistes tournent autour des axes suivants :

- Identifier les domaines prioritaires de l'innovation pouvant permettre à l'Afrique de réaliser à moyen et long termes sa souveraineté économique, technologique, alimentaire, sanitaire, énergétique, numérique, sécuritaire et militaire. À ce niveau, il a été recommandé de prendre appui sur les grands chantiers structurants panafricains en cours d'étude ou de mise en œuvre, comme le projet de Gazoduc Maroc-Nigéria, l'Initiative dite triple SSS portée par le Sénégal, la stratégique alimentaire portée par le Groupe OCP, la stratégie Africaine du médicament pour ne citer que ces exemples ;
- Mettre en place des institutions, des instruments et des mécanismes dédiés appropriés à une mise en œuvre réussie des stratégies de coopération Sud-Sud macro-régionales en matière d'innovation en vue de permettre au continent de réaliser des raccourcis technologiques dans les domaines prioritaires de souveraineté. Dans ce cadre, il convient de rechercher les complémentarités et les convergences en matière de stratégies nationales d'innovation, et ce en vue de mutualiser les ressources humaines, financières et infrastructurelles ;
- Informer les acteurs des écosystèmes Africains d'innovation, les former et les organiser autour de ces priorités et de ces stratégies ;
- Mettre en place une instance panafricaine permanente au niveau de l'Union Africaine permettant d'assurer un pilotage institutionnel unifié des tous les tenants et aboutissants des problématiques et des stratégies de l'innovation en Afrique. Cette instance aurai pour missions d'éclairer la décision, définir les priorités, assurer les complémentarités, réaliser les convergences des politiques nationales d'innovations, veiller à la mutualisation des ressources, assurer le suivi, l'évaluation et le contrôle de l'état d'avancement des projets, alerter sur la fuite des cerveaux, aider à mette en place les politiques d'attrait de la diaspora , mettre en exergue les bonnes pratiques qui favorisent la réalisation de raccourcis technologiques pour le continent, détecter les opportunités et organiser les partenariats entre l'Afrique et le reste du Monde en matière d'innovation;

V- Le rôle du forum des associations africaines d'intelligence économique

Le Forum des Associations Africaines d'Intelligence Economique créé en mai 2018 au Maroc sous l'égide de l'Université Ouverte de Dakhla, en tant qu'organisation non gouvernementale indépendante, a un réel rôle à jouer dans le domaine de l'accompagnement du Continent africain pour la promotion de l'innovation. Il peut et doit le faire de par même ses missions qui visent à atteindre les objectifs suivants :

- Assurer la diffusion, auprès des entreprises, des administrations, des territoires, des Universités et des centres de recherche, la connaissance
- scientifique relative à l'intelligence économique, la veille stratégique et la sécurité économique en Afrique;
- Approfondir la connaissance des dimensions géostratégiques du continent africain;
- Favoriser la création d'associations nationales d'Intelligence Economique dans les pays Africains;
- Mener des études et des recherches en intelligence économique, veille stratégique et sécurité économique;
- Organiser des activités scientifiques, culturelles et tous les autres évènements rentrant dans le cadre des objectifs du forum.

Au regard de ses missions et de la nature des objectifs qu'il vise à atteindre, le Forum doit voir loin et grand. Car, ensemble, les Associations nationales qui le composent peuvent aider à réaliser des raccourcis en matière de recherches scientifiques et technologiques au service du développement de leur Continent.

Par conséquent, le Forum est appelé à définir une nouvelle ambition parce que depuis sa création le Monde connaît des changements profonds et l'Afrique se trouve devant une nouvelle génération de défis. De ce fait, le FAAIE doit travailler autrement en développant de nouvelles solidarités et en innovant en matière d'activités communes à promouvoir.

Dans cette perspective, les débats ont fait émerger des propositions audacieuses, innovantes et ouvertes sur l'avenir parmi lesquelles deux ont bénéficié d'un consensus général des Membres du Conseil d'Administration du Forum :

- La création d'une Université Panafricaine à Dakhla dédiée aux renforcements des capacités des élites Africaines,
- Et l'organisation de séminaires nationaux dédiés à la promotion de

la culture et des pratiques de l'intelligence économique, de la veille stratégique et de la prospective des territoires dans les pays africains membres du réseau du FAAIE.

Pour réussir ce challenge, plusieurs associations nationales ont pris l'engagement d'élaborer un programme d'action au titre de la période 2023-2025 à la mesure de cette nouvelle ambition.

Vaste chantier qui attend le Forum et défis complexes à relever par l'ensemble des associations nationales qui le composent pour les années à venir.

TABLE DES MATIÈRES

III
QUELLES APPROCHES POUR UNE INNOVATION DURABLE ET INCLUSIVE EN AFRIQUE ?

IV
SYNTHÈSE ET CONCLUSIONS

Structures éditoriales du groupe L'Harmattan

L'Harmattan Italie
Via degli Artisti, 15
10124 Torino
harmattan.italia@gmail.com

L'Harmattan Hongrie
Kossuth l. u. 14-16.
1053 Budapest
harmattan@harmattan.hu

L'Harmattan Sénégal
10 VDN en face Mermoz
BP 45034 Dakar-Fann
senharmattan@gmail.com

L'Harmattan Cameroun
TSINGA/FECAFOOT
BP 11486 Yaoundé
inkoukam@gmail.com

L'Harmattan Burkina Faso
Achille Somé – tengnule@hotmail.fr

L'Harmattan Guinée
Almamya, rue KA 028 OKB Agency
BP 3470 Conakry
harmattanguinee@yahoo.fr

L'Harmattan RDC
185, avenue Nyangwe
Commune de Lingwala – Kinshasa
matangilamusadila@yahoo.fr

L'Harmattan Congo
219, avenue Nelson Mandela
BP 2874 Brazzaville
harmattan.congo@yahoo.fr

L'Harmattan Mali
ACI 2000 - Immeuble Mgr Jean Marie Cisse
Bureau 10
BP 145 Bamako-Mali
mali@harmattan.fr

L'Harmattan Togo
Djidjole – Lomé
Maison Amela
face EPP BATOME
ddamela@aol.com

L'Harmattan Côte d'Ivoire
Résidence Karl – Cité des Arts
Abidjan-Cocody
03 BP 1588 Abidjan
espace_harmattan.ci@hotmail.fr

Nos librairies en France

Librairie internationale
16, rue des Écoles
75005 Paris
librairie.internationale@harmattan.fr
01 40 46 79 11
www.librairieharmattan.com

Librairie des savoirs
21, rue des Écoles
75005 Paris
librairie.sh@harmattan.fr
01 46 34 13 71
www.librairieharmattansh.com

Librairie Le Lucernaire
53, rue Notre-Dame-des-Champs
75006 Paris
librairie@lucernaire.fr
01 42 22 67 13

www.ingramcontent.com/pod-product-compliance
Lightning Source LLC
LaVergne TN
LVHW080931071026
849535LV00013B/4167